3 0012 00284570 8

Imogen Edwards-Jones is the co-author of the *Sunday Times* non-fiction bestsellers *Hotel Babylon*, *Air Babylon* and *Fashion Babylon*, as well as the author of the novels *My Canapé Hell*, *Shagpile*, *The Wendy House* and *Tuscany for Beginners*. **Anonymous** works in the music industry.

WITHDRAWN FROM STOCK

D0543983

www.**rbooks**.co.uk

Also by Imogen Edwards-Jones

THE TAMING OF EAGLES
MY CANAPÉ HELL
SHAGPILE
THE WENDY HOUSE
HOTEL BABYLON
TUSCANY FOR BEGINNERS
AIR BABYLON
THE STORK CLUB
FASHION BABYLON
BEACH BABYLON

POP
BABYLON

IMOGEN EDWARDS-JONES
& Anonymous

J 59045
LIMERICK
COUNTY LIBRARY

BANTAM PRESS

LONDON · TORONTO · SYDNEY · AUCKLAND · JOHANNESBURG

TRANSWORLD PUBLISHERS
61–63 Uxbridge Road, London W5 5SA
A Random House Group Company
www.rbooks.co.uk

First published in Great Britain
in 2008 by Bantam Press
an imprint of Transworld Publishers

Copyright © Imogen Edwards-Jones 2008

Imogen Edwards-Jones has asserted her right under the Copyright, Designs
and Patents Act 1988 to be identified as the author of this work.

This book is a fictional account based on the experiences and recollections of the
author's sources. In some cases names of people, sequences or the detail of events have
been changed to protect the privacy of others. The author has stated to the publishers
that, except in such respects not affecting the substantial accuracy of the work, the
contents of this book are true.

A CIP catalogue record for this book
is available from the British Library.

ISBNs 9780593060308 (tpb)
9780593060292 (hb)

This book is sold subject to the condition that it shall not,
by way of trade or otherwise, be lent, resold, hired out,
or otherwise circulated without the publisher's prior
consent in any form of binding or cover other than that
in which it is published and without a similar condition,
including this condition, being imposed on the
subsequent purchaser.

Addresses for Random House Group Ltd companies outside the UK
can be found at: www.randomhouse.co.uk
The Random House Group Ltd Reg. No. 954009

The Random House Group Limited supports The Forest Stewardship
Council (FSC), the leading international forest-certification organization. All our
titles that are printed on Greenpeace-approved FSC-certified paper carry the FSC logo.
Our paper procurement policy can be found at
www.rbooks.co.uk/environment

Typeset in 11.5/16pt Sabon by
Falcon Oast Graphic Art Ltd.
Printed and bound in Great Britain by
Printed in the UK by Clays Ltd, Bungay, Suffolk

2 4 6 8 10 9 7 5 3 1

Mixed Sources
Product group from well-managed
forests and other controlled sources
www.fsc.org Cert no. TT-COC-2139
© 1996 Forest Stewardship Council
FSC

For HE-J

With very grateful thanks to the extremely talented, highly entertaining and delightfully naughty players whom I met within the music industry. I am wholly indebted to them, and to the chief Anonymous, for their humour, generosity, trust, patience, endless explanation, great anecdotage and, most of all, their time. I would also like to thank the fantastic Eugenie Furniss, the handsome Doug Young, the fabulous Laura Sherlock, the dashing Larry Finlay and all at Transworld for their fabulousness. Nothing would get done, written or indeed published without you. Thank you all.

Prologue

All of the following is true. Only the names have been changed to protect the guilty. All the anecdotes, the stories, the situations, the highs, the lows, the drugs, the excesses, the deals and the insanity are as told to me by Anonymous – a collection of some of the finest and most successful managers, song-writers, pop stars and other souls in the music business. Although the incidents are real and the celebrities play them-selves, the band is fictionalized and the stories, narrated by Anonymous, have been condensed into almost a year in the record industry. But everything else is as it should be. The young, the handsome, the talented and the not so talented are all trying to make it, while everyone else takes their cut. It's just another year in the turbulent and exploitative world of pop.

1

Kylie Minogue is sitting on my face. I can smell the sweet soft leather of her golden hot pants as she writhes and moans in vocal antipodean delight. I'm brilliant. She's loving me. I'm so, so good. She should be so lucky! We're going all the way and then some. I'm making her scream. I'm making her yell.

That's not yelling. It's a bell. What's that ringing? What's going on? It's pissing me off. Kylie's so annoyed. She's gone.

Shit. I'm awake. I open my eyes. I suppose I'd better answer the phone.

'Hello?' My head. My throat. I can barely speak.

'You awake?' comes a familiar voice.

'I am now.'

'Good.'

'You ruined the best dream.'

'Who were you shagging this time?'

I can practically hear Paul's eyes rolling down the phone. We've been business partners for ten years, managing a series of increasingly less lucrative bands, so he's used to my early-morning fantasies brought on by wine and many a line.

'Kylie,' I say.

'Poor bitch,' he replies. 'As if she doesn't have enough problems without you getting into her knickers.'

'It was her hot pants actually.'

'Whatever,' he says. 'You in the office?'

'Of course.' I stretch out on the maroon leather sofa.

'Lost your house keys again?'

'No, I've just arrived.'

'Don't lie.'

'I'm not.'

I stretch again and attempt to part company with the leather. But I can't move. My legs are dead. I can't feel my toes. My knees won't work. My thighs are motionless.

'Paul!' Panic rises in my voice.

'What?'

'I can't move.' My hands start to sweat, my mouth is dry. This is serious.

'What do you mean you can't move?'

'My legs are dead. I can't feel anything from the waist down.'

'My God, Kylie's good.' He laughs.

'Shut up. I've had a coke stroke.'

'You wouldn't be able to talk if you had,' he reassures me.

'How do you know?'

'I just know.'

I try to move again, but I can't. 'Shit!' I am really panicking now. 'I can't move at all, Paul!'

'Hold on. I'm in Caffè Nero, I won't be long. Do you want anything?'

'I've had a coke stroke. I don't think a croissant and a skimmed latte are going to help, do you?'

'No. Sorry. I'm coming. Hang on in there. I'm calling an ambulance.'

About three fully clothed, motionless, hungover and hellish minutes later, Paul comes bursting through the door. His round face blushes bright pink with concern as he stares at me lying prostrate on the couch. I can tell he's been running: he's spilt half his latte down his trousers.

'Shit, shit, shit,' he says, his short fingers grabbing at his bleach-blond crop. 'You look terrible.'

'Thanks,' I say, running my sweaty palms down the front of my black denims. 'I feel terrible. I'm not conscious of anything below my legs. Look.' I slap my thigh. 'Nothing.'

'How about this?' asks Paul as he drop-kicks my knee with the point of his Richard James slip-on.

'Aaarrgh, that fucking hurt!' I scream, clutching my knee.

'Good, good, that's good,' he says, bending over and starting to undo my belt buckle.

'What the fuck are you doing? Stop rattling around down there. It's not a bloody jumble sale. Just because I can't feel anything below the waist doesn't mean you—'

'Shut up!' he says, unbuttoning my trousers. 'I've seen them do this on *Casualty*.'

By the third button on my fly, the relief is immediate and palpable. The blood rushes down my legs and thighs, pins and needles flare up in my feet and there are shooting, tingling pains going down my calves. I exhale and stretch. My buttocks squeak against the shiny dark leather.

'You can move!' exclaims Paul, stepping back in delight and admiration.

'Yup,' I cough, slightly. 'I think we can cancel the ambulance.'

'Are you sure?'

'My jeans were just a little too tight,' I mumble.

'Really?' asks Paul. 'I mean, you've had a big night.'

'No, no,' I say, wriggling my fizzing toes, 'I think we can call off the men in green jumpsuits.'

'Shame,' says Paul, reaching for his mobile. 'I was looking forward to that.'

'Yeah, well,' I say, sitting up and running my thumb along the top of my underwear, 'being too fat for your drainpipes is sad, but not exactly a medical emergency.'

'True,' nods Paul, punching away on his mobile while looking me up and down like the lamentable fashion car crash I must be. 'What were you thinking?'

What was I thinking? I have no idea really. There wasn't much time for thinking. I was sitting in the office, playing on-line Scrabble with some stranger in Reykjavik, when my old mate Terry called with an invitation to the Brits. He told me his date had stood him up and asked me if I'd like to join his table. I was the last person on his list and he was desperate. It was a grand a ticket, he told me, so he didn't want it to go to waste. I finished my drink and my game, found an old pair of trousers in the office wardrobe, and joined him.

I was pleased to be asked. Terry and I go way back to the days when lunches were long, lines were even longer and no one thought it wrong to be blown on a regular basis by your secretary. In fact, Terry was famous for it. As head of A&R (artists and repertoire) at one of this country's most successful record companies not only did he have some of the best ears in the business, he also had the best desk. Closed off on three sides, those in the know called it 'the cage'. So when Terry wasn't seeking out and signing up some of the best acts around he was being noshed off in meetings by his PA. The idea was that before anyone could enter the room she'd get inside the cage and suck on his cock while everyone else in the meeting was unaware of what was going on. He'd try to keep a straight face while listening to some young hopeful's tape, and she'd try to keep it up all afternoon. I did once suggest to Terry that this might not go down well with some of the other 'sisters' in the company, but he said I'd got it wrong. She loved doing it, apparently. She got £12K a year for taking coke and giving head all afternoon, he explained, which was better than her mate down at Tesco. And she could leave at four p.m. on Fridays. So it was what's known as a win-win situation, he said, failing to convince me.

Anyway, Terry and I hadn't seen each other for a while. Our

paths hadn't crossed for a good year and a half. He's moved into personal managing of big acts and even bigger celebrities and I'm still looking after indie bands. My nights tend to be spent surrounded by spinning beer bottles and skinny students dressed in black with long faces and plenty of attitude, while he tries not to get papped with his pals leaving The Ivy.

But I was keen to see him, and I've always had a fondness for the Brits. Even in those shambolic old days when the diminutive Sam Fox presented with the towering Mick Fleetwood; they had a certain amount of charm and naivety about them. And the parties are legendary. I remember riding my motorbike with a pretty make-up artist on the back along Westway, looking up at the stars, feeling the wind in my goatee and passing a fat joint across to Terry as he did the same. I also remember a wild night at some Guns N Roses after-show that was packed with booze and birds and mini burgers being handed around on trays. I went to take a leak, and while I was standing at the urinal a hairy rocker came in and positioned this girl up against the wall. He and I had a chat about the show and who'd won what and who performed well as he took her from behind. When he finished, he gave me a high-five, zipped himself up and walked out. And the girl just looked at me, laughed and left, while I was left slack-jawed with surprise.

Last night, however, things were a little different. For a start the goatee's gone, and the jeans were demonstrably a whole lot tighter when I arrived in the back of Terry's blacked-out Mercedes S Class. None of Terry's acts was nominated, but he was still giving it the full camel coat and sovereign ring as he turned, sucking on a Cohiba. Although, obviously, due to the new smoking regulations, he wasn't allowed inside Earls Court, which pissed him off.

'Someone should get a contract out on that Ken Livingstone,' he moaned as he stood chest to chest with a black-clad bouncer waiting for the cigar to extinguish. 'He's got my fags, my cigars, and now he's after my Merc. Twenty-five quid a day to drive to my office. Bloody daylight robbery. What pleasures does a man have left?'

'I know,' I agreed, watching Mika sweep past in an explosion of flash bulbs and checking out most of Girls Aloud as they posed for the press in their cocktail frocks. Attention was focused on Cheryl, the short dark one, since her husband had been caught with his pants down having extra-marital sex, pausing for a vomit before he carried on. She smiled, 'looking brave', while the others were 'supportive'.

'I've got plenty of people who'd be happy to take a pop,' continued Terry, tapping the side of his spongy red nose.

It always makes me laugh when Terry comes over all Don Arden. Both he and I know that as hard as Terry gets is flicking the Vs behind the backs of traffic wardens, and shouting abuse at an answer machine. He is nowhere near the league of Sharon Osbourne's dad. But then the days of hanging a rival manager out of the window for supposedly moving in on your act, or beating the crap out of an Indian accountant for allegedly stealing £75,000 from the company, are over. Arden is long gone, although his daughter still talks about the time when she was pregnant and went to visit her father having taken over the management of his act, Ozzy Osbourne. Arden set his dogs on his daughter, causing her to have a miscarriage. She didn't speak to her father for twenty years and told her children he was dead. Still, some of her father's charm apparently did rub off. It takes a certain kind of woman to place a turd in a Tiffany box and send it off to the head of Sony. But memories are short in this business; if you're hot and happening, no one really cares what you do, or have done. You can be an incoherent drugs casualty and still win five Grammy awards. And Sharon is the woman of the moment. At least she certainly was last night.

'All right, Sharon!' yelled Terry, waving his cigar butt at her as she and the whole Osbourne entourage whipped past us on their way to present the show.

Terry and I followed on behind. Inside, the security was tight. We were checked and tagged with wristbands, like we were going to some open-air festival rather than the music business's premier night out. However, once we got past the men in black, the auditorium was something else. I'd forgotten what a huge event this was. The place was packed. There was table after table of mostly bald men sitting next to ladies in strapless dresses. At ten grand a table there was a lot of corporate schmoozing going on. Hedge fund and City boys had taken over whole sections, with banks like Nomura snapping up five tables at a time. Still, the music biz clung on in there, sealing off the whole of the front section of tables closest to the stage entirely for themselves – proving that money can only get you a certain seat at the table. While the 'haves' quaffed pink champagne and a three-course lamb cutlet dinner followed by cheese, the 'have nots' – fans and competition winners – looked on from the dim and distant seating in the gods.

Not that Terry and I gave a shit about anything other than getting as many bubbles down our necks as quickly as possible and finding a nice, quiet disabled toilet where we could do our coke in peace. The rest of his table were pleasant enough – his secretary, her friend, a couple of hacks Terry owed favours to, and one of his star presenter turns, who pursed her collagen lips and was a little bit pissed off not to be sitting with Leona Lewis or some other nominee. Terry and I chatted to our left and right as you're supposed to do at these events, but gave up on the niceties of dinner relatively early and made use of the disabled facilities. Suitably chemically enhanced, we returned to the table and then set about spotting celebrities, clients, ex-clients and people we hate.

The ceremony went by in a flash and thrash of live music. Take That won, Leona lost, and Mika squealed at his success. Kylie looked sensational in a golden sheath, Amy remained upright enough to steal the show, and Paul McCartney played 'Hey Jude' – for ever. The Arctic Monkeys dressed up like country squires and dissed the Brits school, and Kate Nash got a gong – or was it two?

'What do you think of Bat for Lashes?' asked Terry by way of conversation in one of the many after-show bars.

'They're a little too YouTube for me,' I said, hoping not to reveal my total ignorance.

'Yeah,' agreed Terry, checking out an enormous pair of breasts coming towards us.

The rest of the evening descended into mayhem. We moved on to the vodka and visited the facilities with incontinent regularity. Terry found himself a larger pair of breasts to talk to while I lurched from acquaintance to acquaintance shouting non sequiturs into their ears. Come two a.m. I was wandering the streets looking for my pre-booked cab. Failing to find it, I decided to walk. It was a toss-up between home and the office, but the office was closer.

'So how was it?' asks Paul, leaning back in my chair and putting his slip-ons up on my desk.

'Depressing,' I reply, shaking my legs out in the middle of the office. 'It made me feel irrelevant.'

'Really?'

'I haven't been to the Brits since Take That won first time around. I've never had an act nominated. I could barely afford a table there now. I mean' – I sigh loudly, catching sight of my rotund reflection in the window – 'what are we trying to do here?'

'Make hit records?'

'We're not exactly successful, are we?'

I look up at the rows of framed gold and platinum discs that hang all over one wall of the office. There are twenty-three of them. Not that I count them all that often. The only problem is that most of them are from the nineties. There are a couple in the early noughties, but in recent years our hits have been few and very far between. It's the old stuff that keeps us going.

It's royalties on the back catalogues that pay for my black Range Rover, the West London mews office and my daughter's ever-augmenting school fees. If it weren't for my 1990s ears and Paul's business sense we'd both be stony broke instead of relatively broke, which is what we are at the moment.

'It's not too bad,' says Paul, optimistically.

'Yeah right,' I laugh, somewhat hysterically. 'How many bands do we have in the chart?'

'What, right now?'

'Yes.'

'Singles or albums?'

'Either.'

'Including downloads?'

'Any bloody chart of any bloody description.'

'Um . . .' Paul sits and thinks for a second. 'Debbie knows this better than I do.'

'Debbie's not here at the moment,' I sigh, looking at the door. 'No doubt she'll flop in at eleven with a vocal hangover and be able to tell us what we need to know. But in the meantime . . .'

'Well, we've got Road to Reality in the album chart,' he says. 'They're at number thirty-six or so. Or at least they were last week.'

'And?'

'The Wise Ones are in the singles charts.'

'At number fifty-two, which doesn't count. Anything else?'

Paul pretends to think. I pretend to wait for an answer. But we both know that it is a big fat zero. After nearly twenty years in the business it is hard to believe that it has come to this.

'Leanne is about to start working on her album,' says Paul, clutching at a straw. 'And we both know how big female singer-songwriters are at the moment. Look at Adele and Kate Nash.'

'To name the only two,' I reply.

'And Amy,' adds Paul.

'Three.'

'Lily Allen!' Paul clicks his fingers with delight.

'OK, there are a few,' I admit. 'It's just that I'm not sure I want my future depending on the depressing mumblings of a twentysomething Catholic from Harpenden.'

'Yeah.' Paul nods his head and curls his top lip in agreement. 'But you know, look on the bright side, at least you're not dead.'

'Things are really shit when "health" is your only asset,' I say, walking towards the window.

On the cobbles below I can see Debbie tripping up the street towards the office, dressed in a mini skirt, striped tights and wedge heels, wearing sunglasses, half listening to her iPod while smoking a cigarette and talking on her mobile phone. There is a lot of swearing and exclaiming coming from her vibrant red lips. She suddenly stops in the middle of the road, puts down her large white handbag and pulls out a BlackBerry. Putting her fag in her mouth, she half closes one eye while training the other on the screen. She scrolls up and down with her right index finger while her head is cocked over to one side as she balances her phone on her shoulder. A car comes up the road and stops in front of her. The driver honks his horn for her to move. Despite being so overly occupied, she still manages to give him the finger. Debbie is the epitome of the multi-tasking modern woman.

A few minutes later she crashes through the front door downstairs, still evidently on the telephone.

'Yeah, babe, yeah, I know, he's a tosser, a loser. Listen, I'm at work, I've just arrived, I'll call you back. All right!' she shouts from the bottom of the spiral staircase. 'Anyone want a coffee? I'm just off to get one.'

'No thanks,' Paul shouts back down the stairs.

'All right then,' she shouts back, and before I've managed to open my mouth and say something along the lines of a latte, Debbie's walked straight out of the office again.

I look at my ageing Rolex watch. It's a quarter to eleven so I suppose I should be pleased that Debbie's turned up for work at all. Even if she's left immediately.

The phone goes on my desk and Paul looks at it. Getting up out of my chair, he gestures for me to sit down. 'All yours,' he says as he walks out of the room and over to his office across the landing.

I slump back behind my desk. My legs still feel weird and my stomach is sporting a deep red welt that's going to take the rest of the morning to disappear.

'The One Management,' I say, picking up the phone.

'Mate, hi, it's me,' comes the distinctly nasal voice of Chris, the lead singer of Road to Reality.

'Chris, good morning, how are you?'

'Fine, man, fine, you?'

'Great, thank you. I've got a bit of a hangover, you know. Went to the Brits last night, you know, had a chat with Kylie, that sort of thing.'

I stop myself. There is something kind of tragic about lying and showing off about my close encounter with pop's most famous stunt bum when the person down the other end of the line is neither listening nor actually giving a shit.

'Right, cool,' Chris sniffs down the line. 'Whatever floats your boat.' He coughs and clears his throat of the early-morning bong I know he is prone to. 'The guys and I have been thinking.'

'Don't tax yourselves,' I laugh.

I know what's coming next. My heart starts to race; I can feel my face growing red; my blood pressure is rising. It always starts with them 'thinking'. Bands shouldn't really think. It's the manager's job to think. They should just bloody perform. I squeeze the red stress ball I have on my desk. I hate it when they think.

'Anyway, we were just, er, um, wondering if I can talk to you about us sort of, you know, splitting up.' He coughs again.

'What? The band is splitting up?' A chink of light!

'No, um, splitting from you,' he says.

'Oh?' I say, trying to sound as measured as I can while steam slowly escapes out of my ears and images of mass murder flood into my mind. 'Is that a good idea?'

'Well, um, it's sort of what we've decided.'

Ungrateful bastards. Ungrateful little bastards. I've spent

four years trying to get this bunch of student idiots off the ground. I've travelled backwards and forwards to bloody Bristol, listening to their half-witted whinings in the car, to woo them with beer and the possibility of a record deal. I've watched them play to half-empty halls and bought them more bloody pints in the Fleece in St Thomas's Street than my bank manager would care to remember. I got them a reasonable record deal with EMI too. And this is how they repay me?

I suppose it could be worse. At least Chris has bothered to call. I remember hearing that a famous eighties indie band got rid of their manager by taking photos of their arses with 'You're Fired' drawn on them and left him asleep on the tour bus with the camera. He apparently didn't find out until he had the film developed. Those were the halcyon pre-digital days.

'We've been talking about it all night,' continues Chris.

'Have you now?'

'Yeah, and the thing is, we think we should be doing better than we are, and it's—'

'My fault?'

'Well, yeah.'

'It's my fault that your record is shit, it's my fault that you can't get arrested publicity wise, and it's my fault that the record company don't like you, is it?' I am squeezing the stress ball so much that my knuckles have gone white. I hurl it against the wall and hit a gold record, knocking it clean off the wall. The glass shatters as it hits the deck. Shit.

'Well, you should be pleased you no longer have to manage

17

us then,' announces Chris with about as much energy as a talentless stoner can muster at this hour of the morning before his hit of Frosties and *Home and Away*.

'Fuck you!' I shout.

'Fuck you right back!'

'Fuck you right back again!' I yell at the top of my voice before slamming the phone down so hard I hurt the palm of my hand. 'Shit!' I rub my hands together.

'That looks like it hurt,' says Paul, standing in the doorway to my office with a concerned look on his face.

'Get the lawyers on the phone,' I mutter, still rubbing my hands. 'Those little shits Road to Reality want to leave us.'

'I'll give them a call,' he says, turning to walk back to his office. 'But I am fairly sure they can leave if they want to.'

'I'm sure there'll be something in the contract that means we own their arses for the next ten years. If there isn't, then make something up!'

I can hear Debbie stomping up the stairs. As she appears in my office she is humming along to something on her iPod, her head bobbing up and down. She has one ear permanently wired for sound.

'Oh,' she says, her mouth hanging open slightly, a piece of chewing gum still attached to her molars, 'what's happened here?' She looks around the room, taking in the shattered glass on the floor, and looks back at me.

'Road to Reality have just announced they want to leave the agency,' says Paul.

'Really?' says Debbie, putting down on my desk a skimmed latte that I didn't order. 'That doesn't surprise me.'

'Why's that?' I ask.

'Well, the record's not doing very well and I saw Chris having a drink with that old mate of yours, you know . . .' She looks at me, like I'm supposed to know.

'Who?'

'You know, the one with the rings and the coat, with the dyed blond hair. The old geezer?'

'Terry?' says Paul.

'That's him,' nods Debbie.

'Terry?' I stare at her. 'My mate Terry?'

'Don't shoot the messenger,' she says, moving away towards the door.

'My mate Terry?' I say again, twisting the dagger deeper into my heart.

'That's the one,' she confirms over her shoulder.

'The bastard!' I yell, thumping my desk with my fist. 'The big fat bastard.'

Where's bloody Don Arden when you need him?

Two hours later and Paul's been on to the lawyers and confirmed our worst fears. Our deal, whereby we got 20 per cent of everything they made up to £5m, after which I would politely reduce my rate to 15 per cent of everything, was a sort of latter-day gentlemen's agreement where the deal only stands if both parties are happy and delighted and getting on well with each other. However, since Chris has been having drinks

19

with that turd in the grass Terry, he's now clearly unhappy with all I have done for him and is ready to run for the hills with my record contract under his skinny, malnourished arm. The wanker.

Fortunately, Paul's been to Oddbins and bought a couple of bottles of Sauvignon Blanc, so not only is my hangover feeling a whole lot better, I'm beginning to care a little less about the situation. I have even had a vaguely positive chat with Leanne about her album. She's promised to send me a track later on this afternoon so that Paul and I can listen and give her some sort of feedback.

'I think I much prefer managing girls to boys,' I say, taking a slug of my wine and tucking my white shirt back into my jeans. 'I understand women.'

'So speaks the man who's been divorced twice and only manages to see his daughter one weekend a month,' mumbles Paul.

'I think we should manage more girls,' I suggest, ignoring his facetious yet true comment.

'Absolutely,' nods Paul, not listening to me at all. Instead, he's looking out of the window at the group of handsome Poles who've been digging up the road for the last couple of weeks. In fact, Paul's backside has been practically Velcro-ed to my windowsill ever since the work on the municipal drains began. I can't believe that he finds men at work so appealing; but then he reminds me that if there were five fit girls in uniform outside my window I might be a little distracted as well.

'I think we should go out and get ourselves a girl band to

manage,' I announce, suddenly getting up off my chair and walking over to the wall of golden discs.

'Are you crazy?' asks Paul, finally paying me some attention. 'Take it from me, you don't want to get involved with a girl band.'

'Why not? Girls Aloud are doing well.'

'They're doing OK for a band that haven't sold a record east of Dover,' says Paul. 'Or west of Land's End, for that matter.'

'But they're making money.'

'Someone is,' he says. 'I'm not sure they're as rich as you think. I'm sure part of the reason they work so goddamn hard is because they have to.'

'Maybe.'

'Well, think about it. I heard Granada TV had five per cent of their arses for the first two years of their contracts. Louis Walsh had twenty per cent, and then they get no publishing because they mainly do covers and don't write their own songs, and then what's left is split five ways. No wonder they're on their fifth album in as many years.'

'They must be on a million each after all this time.'

'D'you really think so?' asks Paul.

'Otherwise they'd be getting arsey and ready to split by now.'

'But you don't want to manage them,' says Paul. 'Someone told me the reason Louis Walsh and the girls parted company was because he couldn't bear all the chat on the phone. Five girls call you up every morning to discuss their hair, their make-up, what they should be wearing, who's had the best

JS9045
LIMERICK
COUNTY LIBRARY

press coverage, who's looking fat, or thin, in bloody *Closer* magazine. Cheryl's got a circle of shame in *Heat*, Kimberley's flashing her pants in *Bizarre*, the Ginga's had a row with her boyfriend, the other one's dog's been run over, or got fleas, or pissed on the carpet. Chat, chat, chat. It was enough to make the poor bloke want to change his phone number. He couldn't do anything or talk to anyone else. Westlife were on call-waiting all day.' Paul smiles. 'Imagine how pissed off they were!'

'What's happened to the Ginga?' I ask.

'What d'you mean?'

'I was looking at a photo of them in one of Holly's magazines the other day. Has she been de-ginga'd?'

'Oh they always do that,' says Paul. 'They either make them strawberry blonde and pretend that they were never ginger, or they super-ginga them. Like Chris Evans.' I look at him and slowly shake my head, losing the will to live. 'I'm a gay man,' he smiles. 'I know this shit.'

'But I still think a girl band might be good.'

'And don't you remember what happened to All Saints?'

I shake my head. Paul looks exasperated before going on to tell me some very long and protracted story about how the girls fell out over a coat at some photo shoot or TV show. Apparently Melanie Blatt had a nice coat. Natalie Appleton wanted the coat, Melanie said no, and some sort of fight ensued. Battle lines were drawn, the Appletons versus the other two, and that was that – the end of an extremely lucrative and successful band, and the end of all their careers.

We sit in silence, me staring at the gold record collection, Paul at the handsome men digging up the road.

'Did they really split over a coat?' I ask.

'The writing on the wall was quite large for some time,' he says, still staring out of the window. 'They travelled separately to gigs, and they wouldn't be in the same airport or hotel as each other. And on their last tour they only ever met on stage. The Appletons on one side, the other two on the other.'

'Duran Duran used to do that. Nick Rhodes and Simon Le Bon haven't travelled together for about fifteen years. Christ, the members of Led Zeppelin hated each other so much they had separate managers.' I take another slug of my wine.

'But it's so much more difficult to get it right with girls,' Paul insists. 'I've got a mate who's trying to put a girl band together at the moment and you can't just find some pretty girls who can sing. They need to be averagely pretty, not threateningly pretty. You know, normal, like the Spice Girls.'

'They're not normal,' I say. 'I took Holly to their gig recently and it was like watching five mums having a dance. No wonder they called a halt to the tour. Don't believe any of that rubbish about them splitting up because they hate each other. They do, but they also didn't manage to sell enough tickets outside the UK.'

'Really?' says Paul. He turns to look at me. This is clearly a nugget he's yet to truffle out.

And Paul is the queen of truffling. He always knows anything and everything, before it's even happened. He has his ear to the ground and his bum on a bar stool at some of the most salubrious and insalubrious clubs and pubs in town. He is always out and about, and unlike me – I have the memory of a goldfish with Alzheimer's – he has total recall.

'But they did all those nights at the O$_2$,' he says.

'They bussed the fans in from all over the country,' I reply.

'Didn't they do Manchester?'

'Two nights.'

'Well, they were still the most successful girl group of all time, and for some ropey old birds they scrubbed up OK, and that's the point really, isn't it? If they were too pretty then girls wouldn't buy them. Girls want to shag boy bands and be like the members of girl bands.'

'And girls buy pop records, teenage boys buy heavy metal. We all know that.'

'Exactly,' agrees Paul. 'They can't be too sexy. Let's face it, no one wanted to fuck the Spice Girls.'

'That's true,' I agree, listening to the phone ringing downstairs. 'Debbie! Get that, will you?'

'Hello, The One Management,' I hear Debbie mumbling.

'D'you know,' continues Paul, 'if you're a girl singing country and western, you're not allowed to stand with your legs apart while standing behind the mike?'

'What?'

'They have to stand with their legs together and with their cleavages and upper arms covered.'

'Or my Christian far-right principles might be offended?' I laugh.

'Don't knock it,' says Paul. 'Country and western sells more in the States than anything bloody else.' He smiles. 'Keith Urban's a star, not just Mr Nicole Kidman.'

'I've got Des on the line!' shouts Debbie.

'Put him through,' I shout back.

Des Adams is a singer-songwriter and one of my less high-maintenance acts, mainly because he hasn't had a hit for two years and has been recording in LA for the best part of a year. I don't know what it is about pop stars, but as soon as things go the slightest bit tits-up they all seem to want to abandon their Primrose Hill duplexes and their apparently well-oiled support system and bugger off to LA to discover themselves. I've always thought it weird to go to a place where everyone wants to be discovered by someone else when all you want is to discover yourself. But, you know, rock stars have never been known for their logic. So when Des told me he was off to LA to find himself and do 'some recording, man' I was tempted to say two things. Firstly, I hope what you discover isn't quite as tedious as I suspect it might be. And secondly, there are perfectly good sound recording systems right here in the UK. Anyway, he's been away for nearly twelve months, popping in and out of some studio in Santa Monica, so I should try to inject some enthusiasm into my voice when I talk to him. You never know, he might surprise us all and actually come back with some tapes worth listening to. Hell, James Blunt pissed off to LA and came back with 'You're Beautiful', and I know several cloth-eared twats who passed on that – and the new swimming pool, and the second home in the sun . . .

My phone rings. I pick it up.

'Dessie, how the hell are you?'

'Oh man!' he starts. 'I just had the best time.'

His accent has gone all transatlantic, which is a little irritating since I personally wrote out his biog and know he's from Dorking. But I let this minor annoyance pass in the hope of getting my hands on a hot hit that's going to keep me in hookers and crack cocaine for as long as I live (which clearly wouldn't be long, if that were the case). So I let him tell me how he got to hang out with Robbie Williams (not that tricky to do these days, apparently) and how he played football with him and all his mates.

'D'you know he has a team?' enthuses Des.

'Yes, I did,' I reply, picking old bits of last night's dried-up coke out of my nose.

'It was great,' continues Des. 'A little piece of home.'

I can tell he's on the verge of telling me where he managed to buy his Marmite and his PG Tips, so I interrupt.

'I'm glad Robbie is great and lovely and off the drugs and back on the Red Bull or whatever he's doing.'

'How d'you know about the Red Bull?' asks Des.

'It's always Red Bull and Diet Coke and cigarettes,' I say. 'Anyway, did you manage to get any recording done?'

'Ah.'

'Ah,' I repeat. 'What does that mean, ah yes or ah no?'

'Ah a bit.'

'A bit. That's great news!' Maybe today won't turn out to be so shit after all. Des has come up with 'You're Beautiful' and we can all retire to The Ivy for the rest of the afternoon. 'How many tracks? Don't tell me you've got an album!'

'Well . . .' he says.

I don't like the sound of that 'well'. 'Nearly an album?' I know I sound like I am pleading but I just can't help it.

'Two tracks,' declares Des.

'Two?'

'Two.'

'You've been away for a year in LA playing football with bloody Robbie Williams, pretending you're in bloody *Entourage*, and you've come back with two tracks?'

My blood pressure is rising again. I look across at the stress ball, which is sitting on the floor surrounded by shards of glass.

'Two's not bad,' says Des.

'Not bad? It's shit!' I shout.

'Mahler had a fifty-year gap between symphonies,' announces Des.

'Who?'

'Mahler.'

'Yeah, but Mahler didn't have a two-album deal with fuck-ing Warner's to recoup on, now did he?'

'I'll send you the tracks,' says Des.

'You do that,' I say. 'And let's hope they're good.'

I slam down the phone and knock back the rest of my glass of wine. I look at Paul, who is standing in my doorway again, shaking his head.

'What?'

'I bet Simon Cowell doesn't have these sorts of problems,' he says.

'He signed the Teletubbies,' I spit. 'He's got other problems.'

'Yeah, well,' says Paul, 'at least he's making money.'

'I didn't come into the music business to make money,' I quip. 'I wanted to ride a motorbike, grow my hair long and tell people to fuck off.'

'You've lost your licence and your hair.'

'But I can still fucking swear!' I shout, giving him the finger.

Paul walks back to his office across the landing. He knows better than to disturb me at moments like this. He knows that when the shit hits the fan, I prefer to be on my own. I am half tempted to slam the door shut and play some very loud Sex Pistols. I could thrash around my office for half an hour and feel a whole lot better. Instead I spend the rest of the afternoon polishing off the bottle of Sauvignon and staring at my wall of gold discs, contemplating the future of The One Management.

And it's not looking great. Road to Reality have gone, the Wise Ones are slipping down the chart, Leanne has only just gone through puberty and Des Adams still doesn't have a second album. I know second albums are notoriously hard, but this is taking the piss. I need someone to manage. I recall what the old E17 manager Tom Watkins used to say: 'You can't make chicken soup out of chicken shit.' But at least he had some sort of chicken derivative in the first place. I've got nothing. Not even a coop.

I pour myself another drink.

I also need someone who is manageable. I couldn't cope with

a Pete Doherty type, falling out of cabs with syringes full of his own blood, desperate to do some more 'painting'. Which is how, I heard, he tipped up outside the Bankrobber Art Gallery around the corner from here the other day. I don't care how many supermodels he shags, or how many Biz bits he can garner in the pages of the *Sun*, or how much heroin he can put away in his scrawny arm; he annoys me so much I could hardly bear to be in the same room as him.

Amy's just as difficult, but for different reasons. She is a gorgeous talented girl with a great voice, but I suppose I am too much of an old man to have to worry about where my act is all the time. Will she turn up? Will the rehab work? And can I be sure she'll wake up in the morning? I'd have no fingernails left to bite if I managed her.

What I need is a grown-up singer-songwriter with a nice band who will go on and on, from album to album, causing me no problems and recouping all the time – like Coldplay and Chris Martin. But I don't think I could cope with the sanctimony. Poor Chris Martin. We've got Bono, Peter Gabriel, Sting and St Bob saving the world already; there's no room for Chris and his obscure messages written on the back of his hand.

My mobile goes. My mate Craig's name flashes up on the screen. An A&R legend, Craig is one of the most talented blokes I know. He has signed more bands and discovered more rock stars than Simon Cowell's told civilians they can't sing. But he is also rather dangerous. However, with little to do except contemplate the demise of my business, I take his call.

'Maaaate!' comes this insane yell. 'I'm round the corner. Come and meet me for a drink now! Now! Now! Now! And I won't take no for an answer!'

I think about telling him he needn't be so goddamn enthusiastic and effusive; my company's in a bad way and I'm a pushover, desperate to take my mind off my terrible situation. Instead, I pretend to um and ah and tell him I'll be there in ten.

On the way out I inform Debbie I am off to an important meeting. Not that she appears to care. She barely takes her eyes off *Heat* magazine or her phones out of her ears. It's good to see I hold so much sway in my own piss-poor company.

As I walk into the top-floor members club The Electric on Portobello Road I am forced to stop in my tracks. Standing in the middle of the suits and the low-key successful bohemians is Craig, with a drink in one hand and a mobile in the other. He is the colour of bloody mahogany. He is so slim and so toasted brown he looks like a twiglet. His dark hair has gone white at the tips and his face is cracked and tanned like a crocodile handbag. He looks like he's been on a golfing holiday in Florida for the last fifty years.

'Jesus!' is all I can muster.

'I know, I know,' agrees Craig, 'I look fucking gorgeous. No one can keep their hands off me. This,' he says, moving his hands up and down his svelte body, 'is what a month at the Sandy Lane does to you, mate. Blacker than Chris Rock's bollocks.'

'Actually, Michael Winner comes more to mind.'

'Winner? Don't talk to me about Winner! Fucking love the bloke, hung out with him a lot, and that cunt Cowell. D'you want a drink? I'm on the Diet Coke.' He rattles a long glass full of ice in my face. 'Been in rehab.'

'Rehab?' I am stunned.

Craig is old school. He's not quite thirty-grams-a-weekend, which is what another old mate of mine used to do, but he's not far off. He lost his wife and his kids due to his unreliable and erratic behaviour. And he still carried on regardless. In the bad old days he used to have to take a gram of speed at around five a.m. just to make sure he had enough drugs in his system in order to reboot in the morning. Otherwise there was no telling how long he might sleep. He fell asleep for three days once, only to be woken up by his brother bearing down on him, accompanied by two firemen and an axe. Apparently, Craig had overdone the downers and had missed the twenty-five phone calls and the frantic knocking on the door of his flat. Everyone thought he'd died so they called in the fire brigade and got them to smash down the door. Craig couldn't see what all the fuss was about. He was having a good time. I remember him telling me once how important it was to get the downers down before you cracked on with the coke; other-wise, he explained, your throat would be too dry to swallow. I also remember him complaining about the rohypnol abuse that was going on in the club scene a few years back. 'Don't give it to someone else!' he exclaimed. 'What is all this date rape stuff anyway? What a terrible waste of downers!'

And now he's stopped. I can't believe it.

'It was the old ticker,' he sniffs. 'It just couldn't take the crack any more.'

'Oh,' I say. Crack cocaine? Now I know why I haven't seen him for a while. That's well out of my league.

'Anyway,' he continues, 'here I am, clean, serene and bloody boring!' He throws back his large chin and laughs. 'Rehab's such a dull old place. It's full of addicts.'

'No shit, Sherlock.'

'They all had so many problems. They were taking drugs because they were raised by Alsatians. I only did them because I liked them. I didn't have any deep-rooted neurosis to deal with. I tell you, mate, I miss them. I could snort a line of ants like Ozzy Osbourne.' He sniffs. 'It's that action.' He sniffs loudly. 'I miss that.'

'I can imagine,' I say. 'Smokers miss the inhaling, don't they?' I empathize, suddenly feeling rather twitchy for a fag.

'Yeah,' he nods. 'And it's the sleaze as well, you know.'

He then goes on to tell me a story about how he and another rather famous A&R bloke met up by chance at the Sunset Marquis in LA. By way of celebration they ordered in seven grams between the two of them and had tucked into the first three after an hour. 'I'd run out of roofies,' he says, 'and he only had a couple of Valium, and then he spotted the *Yellow Pages*.' The famous A&R man decided to call up numerous escort agencies. 'It's extraordinary,' continues Craig. 'Not only does he say his real name and his room number at the Marquis, but he gets really specific. He says he wants a girl with stamina. He doesn't want a girl who's going to get lockjaw after ten minutes because, he says, he's a bit wired and it's going to take him longer to come. He says not to worry, he will come eventually, but it's going to take a while.' And with that, apparently, he left the room only to return two hours later with a smile on his face asking for more drugs.

'He's given up too,' Craig adds.

'Really,' I nod.

'Yeah,' he says, fiddling with his diamond earring stud. 'He couldn't take all the self-loathing.'

Craig fills me in on a couple of other members of his gang who can't stand the pace any more and who've hung up their credit cards and rolled-up notes. His manager pal Scrapper Harris had even been to see Beechy Colclough, but Beechy kept him waiting for forty minutes so Scrapper had the best part of a gram in the toilet in order to stave off the boredom of the Harley Street waiting room.

'The first meeting didn't go terribly well,' admits Craig. 'But, you know, he misses the fighting. He didn't really like the sex that went with the drugs, he just liked punching the pimps out afterwards.'

'Each to their own,' I say.

'How about you?' asks Craig, brushing some dust off the sleeve of his leather tan-coloured blouson jacket.

I hesitate to tell Craig about my company's downward spiral – after all, this is a business that thrives on gossip and hype and hot air. I don't particularly want him to share my increasing lack of prospects with the world, his wife and the *NME*. However, as we both walk downstairs and outside into the street for our fags al freezing fresco, I decide that Craig might have something useful to say on the subject. Which, it turns out, he does.

'Boy bands,' he says, pointing his Embassy cigarette at me. 'You should go into boy bands.'

'And not girls?'

'Absolutely not girls. Twice the trouble and half the cash. Double the hair and make-up, three times the amount of clothes. The only thing girls do better than boys is publicity. Put them in a bikini on the front of a lads mag and they'll be in every tabloid. But they still won't sell a record.'

'No one's selling records. Album sales are down ten per cent.'

'Yeah,' he nods, 'but purveyors of tat Sony BMG have seen their profits up twenty-three per cent in a market that is down by fifteen.'

I nod and smoke as I listen to him. Pop is the way forward. Pop was nominated to fuck last night at the Brits. It's just that I don't see myself as a boy band manager. I'm not gay. I don't fancy boys at all. If a sexy bloke walked into my office, other than the chewing gum finally falling out of Debbie's mouth and the sound of Paul's arse shuffling off my windowsill, I would have no inkling that he was handsome. I know of a couple of straight managers who've tried to do the boy band thing, only to dismiss some spotty bloke who was eventually put on the cover of every teen mag in the country. I know where I am with girls. I know if they're hot or not. I don't have to rely on other people to tell me. And I know how to dress them. As Dolores

O'Riordan from the Cranberries once said, 'Peel-'em-off clothes are the easy cheesy way for women, but it helps if you're crap.'

'Look, all the boy bands are back,' insists Craig. 'Take That, Westlife, even Boyzone are touring. And none of them are spring bloody chickens any more.'

'That's true.'

'I mean, fucking Gary Barlow?' Craig laughs. 'He's so boring he should be an estate agent. "Hello, Gary here from Foxtons!"' He hoots with laughter at his own joke. 'Boys,' he confirms, putting his arm round my shoulders and flicking his cigarette butt across the road. 'It's not fucking rocket science.'

2

Craig's boy band idea has been festering in my brain for a couple of weeks. Perhaps it's because he was so insistent that I am taking it seriously. Or maybe it's the tales he was telling about Simon Cowell's sodding car collection and Simon Fuller's bloody vineyard that made me think I have been far too naive about this industry and far too romantic about critical success and artistic integrity for far too long.

I have always known there's a schism between those who think that making music is a cutting-edge art form that can spark ideas and cultural revolutions, and those who think that pop is as disposable as the chewing gum stuck to the bottom of your shoe. I have always, despite appearances to the contrary, considered myself to be in the artistic rather than the opportunistic pile. I spent my early twenties playing bass in a band, only to realize I wasn't talented enough to make it. So I spent my late twenties managing my friends. I went on to use up my early thirties planning the rise of two increasingly successful bands, and now I am frittering away my mid-forties managing their demise.

During that time I have married twice and divorced twice. I have owned and lost two houses on Holland Park. I have gained a very beautiful high-maintenance daughter, Holly, who, due to my generous settlement and monthly payment plan, has an accent that cuts glass and the spending habits of a millionaire City broker's wife after the Christmas bonus has arrived. And what do I have to show at the end of almost twenty-five years in the music business? A one-bedroom flat in Kilburn, a mews office off the Portobello Road and an eleven-year-old golden retriever called Jess with a gross flatulence problem.

So you can see why the boy band idea is rather appealing. Christ, if Louis Walsh can make millions out of some dull-looking blokes from County Sligo, I must be able to cobble something together from the estates of west London. It can't be that bloody hard to find a gang of boys who can sing and dance enough to make the girls want to stick them on their walls. And the rewards . . . Lou Pearlman made a $300m fortune. Actually, maybe the ex-manager of the Backstreet Boys and 'NSync is a bad example since he was caught with his hand in the till, in his underwear on the bed and his name on the contract claiming that he was the sixth member of the band. He is currently lounging in a confined space at the behest of Florida's Orange County Police Department.

As I sit staring at my gold discs wall, my current bank state-
ment in my hand, my mind is made up. I have seen the future
and, despite all the recent doom-and-gloom predictions about
the end of the record industry, it sings and it dances and it
involves a band of boys. I run my hands over the grey stubbled
remains of my hair then clap them together so abruptly that a
sleepy Jess barks from underneath my feet. I get out from
behind my desk and march across the landing.

Paul is bulk-booking destination-restaurants when I walk in.
As an A-Gay man about town, he always books up glamorous
places to eat in and only decides whom to ask out later. That
way not only does he look spontaneous and well connected, he
also gets to be seen eating well too.

'Paul!' I say, in such a way that he takes his shoes off the
desk and hangs up on the Wolseley.

'Yup!' he replies.

It is not often that I come into his office. I normally yell
across for him to come to mine. It's a not-so-subtle pulling-
rank thing. At a 45 per cent / 55 per cent split, it's strictly
speaking mainly my company. He can do the walking.

'I've been thinking about starting a boy band.' It sounds
deeply incongruous to say it out loud.

'I've been waiting for this,' says Paul.

'Oh?'

'Well, ever since our chat about girl bands and your drinks
with Craig all you've been talking about is money and your
hatred of Simon Cowell.'

'Oh.' I had no idea I was this predictable.

'Anyway, so I've been speaking to my mate Esther who's worked on *X Factor* and *Pop Idol* and she says you're welcome to give her a call.'

'Really?'

'Yes,' he says. 'She's been at the coalface of commercialism for years and knows a thing or two.'

'What does she do?'

'She's a choreographer.'

'Right,' I nod.

'We'll be needing one of those,' says Paul.

He writes Esther's number down on a yellow Post-it note and waves it in front of me. 'You can have this,' he smiles. 'On one condition.'

'What?'

'That I can come to all the auditions.'

'Done,' I say, sticking my hand out and plucking the number from between his fingers. 'You and Holly have to be there anyway.'

'Don't tell me, gay men and teenage girls have the same taste?' he says, his eyes rolling slightly.

'Exactly.' I smile, and turn round to leave the office.

'Explain Cher!' he yells after me.

I spend the next half-hour talking to Esther on the phone. Surprisingly for a mate of Paul's, she is forthcoming and extremely helpful. She talks me through her career and credentials, which extend as far back as Take That (the first time round) via Five, Steps, Bewitched, Dee Side, Blue and various *X Factor* and *Pop Idol* boot camps. She tells me she trained as a dancer and taught at the Pineapple Studios before starting a career trying to get teenage boys and girls to dance. She has been hanging around on the pop circuit long enough to come up with some salient points. For instance, the perfect number for your average boy band is five. 'There's safety in numbers,' she explains. 'You're covered in case one of the band leaves.' Brian McFadden in Westlife or Robbie in Take That or indeed Geri in the Spice Girls – the band can carry on regardless and are hardly damaged by the irritating and ungrateful bastard's departure. 'It's a good insurance policy,' she adds. 'Boyz II Men never quite looked the same after one of them left. They carried on as a three-piece and never quite filled the stage again. It's more difficult to split up the songs if you're a four going down to a three. Having said that, the accountants prefer four because you can move them all around in one taxi.'

'Good point. Anything else?'

'They don't all need to be able to sing,' she says. 'But then you know that. All you really need are two good voices and they can carry the other three.' She laughs. 'Which is why they're known as "the passengers". In it for the ride but not much else.'

'Right.'

'Or you could be totally cynical and copy the formula. Each of the members has a sort of character, like they did with the Monkees. Easy recognition, on TV and stuff.'

'I see.'

'So you get the geeky one, the sensitive one, the cheeky one, the talented one and the handsome one – or these days the one that does the back flip. Think about it. It works for all those bands.'

Esther is right, I think as I sit back in my chair and squeeze my red leather ball, attempting to nurture my inner Svengali. There is always one with talent, one who can sing, and the rest of them are more or less interchangeable. It all stems from the Tin Pan Alley days when the music business was in Denmark Street and was an extension of the old variety shows. The idea was to find as many malleable young kids as you could, or some of those newfangled 'teenagers', change their names and exploit the hell out of them. The managers would pay them a few 'bob' a week and watch the money come rolling in, as they shelled out on another Rolls-Royce Silver Shadow. The seventies and eighties weren't much better; there were plenty of bands still on a wage. Bucks Fizz were handed a weekly pay packet and told to sing this 'Making Your Mind Up' song for Eurovision; they were shown what clothes to wear and the exact moment when they should rip their skirts off. S Club 7 were the same, a wholly owned product styled and manufactured to within an inch of their lives. At the end of the day they finished up with very little after all that singing, dancing, laughing and shiny smiling.

In Japan, they've taken the manufactured thing to a whole new level. There are singers and groups employed by record companies as they would secretaries, on a weekly wage. Some Japanese companies have dispensed with performers altogether and come up with the perfect star for any control-freak manager, the *idoru kashu* or idol singer, a cartoon pop star that sings and dances like the best of them. In a few years' time they will also interview like the majority of them, and all our prayers will be answered. We'll have an all-singing, all-dancing performer who doesn't need a cab, doesn't need hair and make-up and won't sack the manager at a moment's notice. I'm surprised Simon Cowell doesn't have a couple of them in development already.

I walk back across the landing to Paul's office.

'Thanks for Esther's number, she's great,' I say.

'Did she tell you about how they fix the shows?' he asks, grinning away.

'What, *X Factor*?'

'That's right,' smiles Paul, rubbing his hands.

'No. And anyway, they can't have. I thought they had some sort of independent adjudicator.'

'They don't fix the vote,' corrects Paul. 'They can't do that, but they do do things like give the one they want to win the best clothes, the best backing singers and the best songs. Anyone who has the full gospel choir, plus the flame throwers and the falling-petals finale is the chosen one.'

'The one who takes up all the performance budget?'

He nods. 'That last bloke, Rhydian, with the white hair, was given a five-grand silver suit, remember?'

'Not really. I have better things to do with my Saturday nights.' I pause. 'But he didn't win.'

'I know. Leon did.'

'Whoever he is.'

'That was fixed too,' asserts Paul. 'They knew Rhydian had a career anyway, so they gave Leon the one-million contract.'

'Two show ponies for the price of one.'

'Exactly,' nods Paul.

'Anyway,' I say, 'Esther was very useful. Five's the magic number, apparently. I'm thinking maybe we should put an advert in *The Stage*?'

'*The Stage*?' queries Paul.

'That's where they found the Spice Girls.'

'You really don't know anything, do you?'

Paul gets up from behind his glass desk and starts to pace the room, ticking his points off on his well-manicured fingers. But then, everything about Paul is well manicured. His bleach-blond hair is cut and treated on a bi-monthly if not weekly basis. His body is pummelled and basted in creams every week-end and he spends more money in Space NK on Westbourne Grove than a yummy mummy with bugger all to do except commute between Pilates and a girls' lunch. At £85 a pop, he has some army boot-camp trainer call round to his Paddington loft apartment twice a week to shout at him and make him sweat and haul his exhausted arse around the park. He is also very careful about what he eats. Nothing that isn't super 'orgaynic' passes his lips. He says it's organic food, but better. And by better he means much, much more expensive – like delicate leaves grown somewhere very beautiful, in wonderful soil, watered by Evian and sold in a very special private shop that only film stars and fabulous people know about. With no expensive and beloved daughter to support, Paul can afford to spend all his diminishing share of the business's back-catalogue royalties on himself. However, despite all this, and the designer suits, the special diets, the wheat-free weeks, the juice extractor and the protein shakes, Paul still drinks too much alcohol, does too much blow and has a gut that hangs over the top of his bespoke trousers. I once worked out that cost per cubic pound squared, Paul must have some of the most expensive body fat in London.

'You don't want stage-school kids,' he says. 'They're terrible and knowing and not at all sexy. Ask any boy band manager and they'll tell you what you want are ordinary working-class boys from council estates who want to be famous and who are prepared to put in the work. Tony Mortimer was that desperate to be signed he walked to Tom Watkins' house in Maida Vale from Walthamstow. Apparently he arrived with no socks on, clutching this tape.'

'How sweet. And Tom just had to take him in?'

'You don't want rich kids,' Paul continues, ignoring me. 'You don't want spoilt kids; you don't want middle-class kids who answer back. Can you think of any posh boy bands who have made it?'

'Um, Curiosity Killed the Cat? And the tall one from Busted?'

'Well, he buggered off never to be seen again. And you don't want them to be too intelligent either.'

'But Watkins is always complaining about how stupid E17 were.'

'I know,' smiles Paul. 'And look how rich they made him.'

'So, *we* want – you're doing this with me, Paul, I can't possibly do it on my own – *we* want young handsome wannabes who want to be Robbie and Ronan Keating.'

'No one wants to be Ronan Keating.'

'Robbie then.'

'Yup,' says Paul, pausing to look out of the window.

'And I'd like a couple of black kids in there too.'

'Black?' says Paul, turning round suddenly. 'You'll be lucky. There hasn't been a successful black boy band since the Jackson Five.'

'That's not totally true,' I say. 'Anyway, there are so many good-looking black kids around here. They'd be perfect in a boy band.'

'A mate of mine tried to get a black boy band together in south London and he drew nothing but a blank. Ask them to be the new James Brown and then you might get some interest. Black boys are far too cool to want to be in a boy band.'

'Now you're depressing me.'

'Listen, leave it with me, book a room somewhere, and let's see who I can rustle up.'

Two weeks later, Paul, Esther and I are sitting in a church hall round the corner from Shepherd's Bush Green. Paul persuaded me that we needed Esther's advice early on, at the choosing process. The last thing we want, apparently, is a Gary Barlow – a man with the voice of an angel, the talent of George Michael and the moves of my gran. I have also asked my daughter Holly to come along after school to see if she can lend a hand, or a viewpoint, to the proceedings. She is, at fourteen, perhaps a little old to be a member of our target audience but her memory will be a whole lot fresher than ours. Although that's not saying much in my case: I can barely remember what I did last night let alone a couple of years ago.

Paul has lined up two Formica-topped tables in a row down one end of the hall, behind which he's placed four red plastic municipal chairs. Debbie's evidently popped into Ryman on her way here as she's laid new pads and freshly sharpened pencils at each of the places. The set looks like a very low-rent *X Factor* or *Pop Idol* audition, which I suppose it is. Debbie is playing at being the breadline's Kate Thornton, who as Paul tells me is already the poor man's Cat Deeley. She is dishing out bottled water and biscuits to those hopefuls who have lined up outside.

And it's quite a line-up. Paul and his team of boys have certainly put the word out. They went round all the estates within walking distance of the office handing out flyers. They left piles of them in the local laundrette, at the gyms, stuck them in the windows of newsagents, and Paul even managed to get himself interviewed by Robert Elms on BBC London. They droned on together about this 'wonderful city of ours' before Paul managed to get a plug in for the band.

So here we all are. It's nine in the morning and we have about seventy-five hopefuls, all chewing gum and phoning their mums, waiting outside for their moment in front of the panel. Now I know what it's like to be Simon Cowell. So many expectant faces, hoping you can give them a golden ticket. It makes you feel powerful, like you mean something. It's the ultimate ego trip. No wonder the bastard always looks so god-damn smug.

The first in is a seventeen-year-old called Peter. He is slim, with dark eyebrows and a straight nose; I can't see his hair as he's wearing a thin black woollen hat pulled down over his head. He's dressed in a grey jacket and his jeans are buckled up in such a way that his arse hangs out the back. But he looks good. I think he's handsome. I glance across at Paul. His mouth is curled up into a smile, so I think he thinks so too. The first one in, and already I'm feeling good. Maybe we are going to be lucky after all.

'Hello there,' I smile, trying to be at my most charming. 'Don't worry about us sitting here. Just relax and give it your best shot.'

I lean back in my chair and half close my eyes, ready to be bowled over by some killer vocals.

'Are you lot from *X Factor*?' he asks, scratching the side of his thinly stubbled face.

'Um, no,' says Paul.

'Where's Dannii Minogue?' he asks, scanning the back of the hall. 'I only came to see her.'

'No, this isn't a show,' explains Esther, leaning over the table. 'We're here trying to put together a band.'

'Oh,' says Peter, shrugging his shoulders. He looks each of us up and down and, obviously deciding we are not famous enough to warrant further attention, he heads for the door. 'See you later.'

'Good start,' I say. 'Next!'

Debbie leads them in one after the other, and for an hour and a half we are treated to the appalling lack of singing talent that resides on the streets of west London. Not one of them could hold a tune even if it wrestled them to the floor and held them in a headlock. Christ, even my pissed-up screams in the shower are better than what is coming out of the mouths of these kids. I'm sliding off my chair with boredom, calculating the amount of money I have lost so far on this tragic and ill-thought-out adventure. I don't know what I was thinking. If Simon Cowell trawls the country with all his resources, and all his scouts, and can only come up with that fat Scottish girl, then how the hell am I supposed to put together the next Take That using £500 worth of flyers and a church hall off Bloemfontein Road?

Actually, Paul has a theory about the fat Scottish girl, Michelle McManus who won *Pop Idol* in 2003. Apparently, there were thousands of emails going round the music industry urging everyone to vote for her at the time, as a way of dis-crediting the show. Although, I did point out to Paul that the regions always vote for the act that represents them; it's only the capital and parts of the south that are non-partisan. So it was the whole of Scotland, plus a load of coke-nosed record execs, who voted for the fat girl. How they must have enjoyed the irony when her record hung on and on to the number one slot.

'This is painful,' I say to Paul and Esther as another hopeful is dismissed through the wooden swing doors.

'Don't worry, it's always like this,' explains Esther.

'I didn't know we'd have to sit through so much dross.' I yawn, and take a swig of mineral water.

'All the other talent shows filter them first,' says Esther. 'They put them into huge groups and try to find out who can hold a note, or sing a bit, and who is totally shit. And then only the good ones and the really shit ones go through. That's why some of them get so pissed off when they're told they're shit by Simon, or Louis, or Sharon, because they've been through three or four auditions to get there in the first place. So as far as they're concerned they are already the next big thing.'

'I knew they didn't audition all those thousands of people,' nods Paul, smiling away. He loves grilling Esther for any little snippet.

'They are also told any of the good back stories, so they can get the people to cry on camera,' she continues.

'What, like, "I hear your mum's died of cancer. Do you want to sing that Bryan Adams song 'Everything I Do'?"' I say.

'No,' she laughs. 'It's a tiny bit more subtle, like, "I hear this song means a lot to you at the moment." Or, "Did your mum encourage you to enter?"'

'And then they move in for the tears?' asks Paul.

'That's right,' says Esther. She stretches.

In her late thirties, Esther has one of those dancer's figures that hasn't softened or sagged with age. As she sits next to me, her arms over her head and her top riding up over her toned stomach, she reveals a belly ring, a collection of faded blue tattoos and the sort of abs Paul pays £170 a week for. She is not a tall woman but, due to her great posture and thick dark hair, she has presence. As she throws her head back in a full stretch, pushing her breasts out in her low-cut top, I think I might fancy her a bit. Paul told me last week that she's going out with some fitness instructor at her local gym, so I'm sure I'm not her type. But that won't stop me trying.

'I'm so pleased we've got you on board, Esther,' I turn to her and say. 'You are going to be such an asset. I mean, you already are an asset. A huge, huge asset.'

'Thanks, mate,' she says, looking the other way and patting me gently on my thigh. I try to squeeze my leg to make it hard and firm to her touch. But I'm too late, and all she gets is a palmful of soft flesh. Fortunately, I am saved further embarrassment by the arrival of Nick.

'Good morning,' he says, with a smile. He's the first person to greet any of us on entry. We all sit up slightly. Paul even breaks into a smile. 'How are you all doing?' he asks.

'Fine,' says Esther. 'How are you?'

'Good, good,' he says. 'Do you want me to dance or sing?'

'Well, both, eventually,' jokes Paul.

Nick is clever enough to laugh. And he's good-looking. Well, I think he is. He looks like the sort of young man they use to advertise skin creams, which is universally good-looking. I look across at Esther and she is marking a large tick by Nick's name.

'I'll dance first, if you don't mind,' says Nick, taking his long coat off to reveal a toned body encased in a tight white T-shirt. Paul nods his approval. Nick also removes his baseball cap, and runs his hands through his blond hair. I cross my fingers under the desk. Esther points the remote towards the CD player over the other side of the room and Nick immediately starts to dance.

The boy can move. He's got rhythm, he looks good, and he can do the whole break-dancing thing. He spins on his back with his legs in the air, he extends up on to his shoulders, and then, just when things look like they can't get any better, he stands up and executes the perfect back flip and back somersault. I write 'yes, yes, yes' next to his name. I look across to Esther. Her tick, reproduced twice over, has got bigger. Paul has put a neat star next to his name.

'That's great,' I nod enthusiastically. 'You can dance very well. Where did you learn to do that?'

'Oh, you know, at school, in the playground, in the park,' he says, wiping his nose on the back of his hand.

'Brilliant,' I say. No stage school in this boy, just raw dancing talent. I bite the side of my cheek with excitement. 'So, will you sing for us?'

'Sure,' he says, shuffling from one trainer to another. 'I thought I might sing, um, Boyzone.'

'Boyzone's good,' says Paul. 'Which one?'

' "No Matter",' he says.

'Go ahead,' I say.

And off he goes. Fuck me, it is all I can do to stop myself from laughing. It is so bad. No, it's worse than that. It's lamentable. And he doesn't sing it quietly, like he's embarrassed by the sound of his own voice. He belts it out at full volume, like someone somewhere has told him he sings like an angel. It'll be his mother, I'm sure of it. He has a voice only a mother could love. I look across at Esther's pad and she has written 'passenger' in large letters. I do the same. Tuneless and good-looking – we have found our back-flip boy. There are only another four to go.

By two p.m. we have the other two passengers. They are Mike and Billy, mates from the same estate. They were planning on forming a band together before we turned up; the only problem was both of them were too lazy to do anything about it, and neither of them can really sing. Fortunately, they are both handsome sods who are used to getting plenty of attention. Billy's all eyebrows and dark, the sort of boy who lost his virginity at thirteen with one of the girls in the sixth form, or failing that, one of his mother's friends. Not that I am jealous or anything. Anyway, they are both handsome enough to stand around in the back row, singing ooh and la and clicking their fingers while winking at the fat girls in the front. Neither of them even needs to exert himself in the back-flip department either.

Come three o'clock and I am seriously beginning to worry. We need a Robbie. Hell, I'd give my eye-teeth for a Gary at this point. I'd pay for the extra dance lessons. Make all the others flip around him. Anyone who can hold a note. Anyone who can sing. I don't mind what they look like, or how overweight they are. There's always surgery, or the Atkins.

The next couple of hours drag on as Debbie leads in one hopeful lad after another. My Simon Cowell complex starts to wane as I hear more and more teenage boys burst into tears in the foyer. 'But it's my dream!' they wail. 'It's all I have ever wanted!' they cry. Weirdly, they're all that desperate to sing and dance, but none of them has been motivated to do anything about it. It's like me saying I could have been the best tennis player in the world, if only some sod had given me the chance and I could have been arsed to turn up at a court.

Finally, a handsome black guy walks in and I find myself sitting up a little straighter, thinking that this could be great. He's sexy, well dressed and holds himself well. A little too well, if I am being honest. In fact, he exudes so much confidence striding around the room in his soft leather boots and tight trousers, the whole package is a little off-putting.

'Hiya,' he smiles, choosing his spot to project from. 'My name's Errol and I have been at Sylvia Young School for three years now. My favourite thing is singing and dancing, although I am good at acting too. I've brought my show reel along for you to look at, at your leisure.' He approaches the desk clutching a load of DVDs with his smiling face and his name stuck to the front.

'Errol Flynn,' says Esther, picking up a DVD and turning it over in disbelief. 'Is that your real name?'

'It certainly is,' he nods. 'My mum thought it would get me noticed.'

'She was right,' says Paul.

'I have been in numerous adverts,' Errol continues, barely missing a beat of his pre-prepared speech, 'mainly for soft drinks, and I have had a walk-on part in *EastEnders*. But my first love, as I said, is song and dance. I have prepared three numbers for you—'

'Two would be fine,' Paul interrupts.

'Or one,' adds Esther.

'Oh, OK,' says Errol, slightly wrong-footed by the lack of enthusiasm in the room.

'What would you like to show us?' I ask, trying to be nice. After all, he is only young, and at least he's got off his arse and done something about following his dream.

'I'd like to perform for you "It's Raining Men" by Geri Halliwell,' announces Errol before striding over to the CD player and popping his disc in. He then walks to the centre of the room and assumes his position.

I look down the desk. Each of us has sat back ready to watch the show. Esther hasn't even bothered to pick up her pen.

The music kicks in and Errol starts to shimmy his shoulders. 'The heat is rising,' he sings – quite well, actually. His whole body is bouncing on the spot. His head is down. His arms are slowly rising above his head. 'The street's the place to go-o-o!' he yells, and suddenly springs into action. He is all high kicks, hand claps and split jumps. The choreography is vigorous and complicated. So complicated in fact that the longer his routine carries on the less we can hear of his voice. He leaps and twirls and huffs and puffs and squeaks to get the words out. He runs along in front of our desk pointing at each of us in turn, just like the Geri/*Flashdance* video. The whole thing culminates in a sprint and a long shin slide. He finishes up as an exhausted hyperventilating heap on the floor.

Esther spontaneously bursts into applause. Paul and I join in. It is impressive, if not wholly appropriate.

'Amazing,' says Paul. 'Well done.'

'Great,' says Esther. 'Really great.'

'Errol,' says Paul.

'Yes?' he smiles.

'You could be Joseph!'

'Thank you,' he beams.

'But not a member of our band.'

'That's OK,' he nods.

'Great stuff, though,' I say, coming out from behind my table to shake his hand and hand back his DVDs. 'Good luck with the career.'

'Thank you.' He smiles again before turning to run out of the room.

'Errol?' I call after him.

'Yes?' He turns around expectantly.

'Your CD.'

'Oh, sorry.' He giggles, collects it, and rushes out of the room.

The swing doors close and we all just look at each other, genuinely at a loss as to what to say.

'Lovely,' says Esther eventually. 'But exactly the reason why you don't want anyone from stage school.'

'Mmm,' I agree.

'Knock, knock,' comes a voice from behind the swing doors. 'Can I come in?' Holly pokes her head through. 'Dad?'

'Hello, darlin'. Come in.'

Fourteen going on thirty, Holly is short and dark and very much the product of my first marriage. As the offspring of two north London childhood sweethearts, she has the legs and the dark frizzy hair that go with that. Had I managed to impregnate my second, blonde, long-limbed trophy wife rather than spend all my time drinking and doing drugs, I might have produced a totally different type of daughter. Having said that, I worship the ground Holly walks on and spoil her more than Paris Hilton. She, of course, being a teenager, enjoys the open fat wallet I provide, and after ten years of hatred following my leaving her mother she has now declared some sort of amnesty and we get on quite well.

She is dressed in her navy blue and grey school uniform, her wrists are loaded down with bangles and she has a pair of white Dior shades perched on the top of her head. She also appears to be wearing lipstick. I kiss her on both cheeks and give her shoulders a squeeze. She wriggles slightly. Too much affection is clearly not cool. So I omit to mention the lipstick.

'You know Paul,' I say. Holly smiles. 'And this is Esther.'

'Hi,' says Holly.

'Hello there,' smiles Esther.

'We're very glad you've turned up,' I say.

'We're desperate,' says Paul, rolling his eyes. 'We need a lead singer.'

'Two singers,' I correct.

'How many boys have you got in the band?' she asks, going over to the side of the room to pick up a chair.

'Three so far,' I say. 'But none of them can sing.'

'Dad!' she laughs, putting her chair next to mine. 'What's the point of that?'

'I know, I know, it's not great. Fingers crossed we can find some others.'

'Yeah, like, who can actually sing,' says Holly, her voice loaded with sarcasm.

Christ, I think as I stare hopefully at the swing doors, even my daughter thinks I'm a loser.

Another three boys bore us with their attitude and their flat, tuneless voices. 'I just want to be famous,' says one. 'Like, you know, for being myself.'

'Fame usually requires some sort of talent,' I say furiously.

The boy looks at me from across the table as if I have recently fallen from Mars and I don't understand that you can be stratospherically famous these days just for shagging some-one, showing your tits or simply talking crap on *Big Brother*. The idea that you might actually have to have a talent or have done or achieved something has clearly passed him by.

The next boy in has sandy-coloured hair and needs to walk a few more miles a day on the stairmaster, but he smiles and has something about him that makes Holly sit up and take notice. I can't see it myself. But if she is interested, so am I.

'Hi, my name is Ashley,' he says, looking down with embarrassment.

'Hi, Ashley,' says Holly, leaning forward.

'I have a few songs I've written myself, if you'd like to hear them,' he says.

'Er, no thanks,' I say. The last thing I need is to encourage any individuality at this early stage. Holly shoots me a look from under her heavy eyebrows. 'Something familiar would be good.'

'Oh, OK then,' he says, looking up, a little hurt. 'What would you like?'

' "I Believe I Can Fly",' says Paul, looking surprisingly engaged. 'It's one of my favourites.'

Ashley looks at the floor, clears his throat and starts to sing. His voice is good; not brilliant, but good. Slip it through a few computer programs and it could certainly hold its own on the radio. And he puts feeling into the words, which is saying something when it comes to such a mind-bendingly awful song. I'm impressed. Holly writes 'cute' and 'yes, yes' on my pad. Esther puts a tick on hers, and I only have to look across at Paul's face to realize that we have found one of our singers.

'Can you dance?' asks Esther.

Ashley shifts gauchely underneath his fringe. 'Um, I'm not bad.'

'Good,' says Esther. 'How about I put some music on and you just move about a bit.'

There's something excruciating about forcing or asking someone to dance. It's like the moment when you're pissed at a party and you launch yourself towards the floor thinking your mates have followed, only for you to realize you are entirely on your own in your appreciation of 'London Calling'. So Paul, Esther, Holly and I sit and stare at Ashley as we wait to judge his moves. He, in turn, looks at the floor and nods his head in time to the beat.

'Shall I dance with you?' asks Esther, making an already arse-clenching moment even worse.

'No thanks,' says Ashley, reacting as if an aged aunt had asked him out on the floor – which one just had. 'Give me a second.'

And then he went for it. Hip-thrusts, shoulders going from side to side, clicking fingers, small kicks and the white-man overbite. Why is it that white guys, myself included, always feel the need to bite their bottom lip when they dance? Anyway, he isn't as shit as we were expecting. He isn't shit hot, but then he doesn't need to be. He can move well enough. He's not Gary or indeed Geri. We aren't going to have to piss end-less thousands up against the wall trying to teach him to dance.

'You're in the band!' I say, leaping out of my seat and going over to shake his hand.

'Thanks,' he says, shaking my hand right back. 'What's it called?'

'I'm not sure yet.' I smile. 'But it'll be good. A good name.'

'OK,' he says warily. 'This isn't a piss-take?'

'No!'

'It's just that you would expect, you know, a name.'

'I wanted us all to be able to choose,' I reveal to myself and to the rest of the room. 'So that it can grow organically.'

'Oh, right.' He nods, and turns towards the exit. 'One thing,' he says, stopping and turning back. 'Can it not have "boy" in the title? Boyzone, the Backstreet Boys, Boyz II Men – it's all kind of been done already.'

'Gotcha,' I say, clicking my tongue and shooting him with

my index finger. I smile and wave him off. I have a terrible feeling he might turn out to be a bit of a pain in the arse.

Holly sighs as soon as he leaves the room. I give her a look.

'What?' she says. 'He's perfect.'

'Really? I thought he was a bit fat and sandy to be leading-man material.'

'Dad, you're missing the point. Girls don't want to sleep with the guys in a boy band, they want to cuddle them.'

'Oh?'

'Dur, it's first boyfriend stuff,' she says. 'They are ten years old. Anyone too sexy is frightening.'

'But we do want *some* sexy boys,' says Paul.

'For the mums,' agrees Esther.

'One really good-looking one,' adds Paul.

'That's Billy, isn't it?' I say, feeling increasingly out of my depth.

'Yeah,' says Paul. 'But, you know, perhaps one—'

There's a knock at the swing doors. An extremely handsome face, even in my book, pokes through. 'More,' finishes Paul, as we all stare.

'Is this the right place for the auditions?' he asks. 'Sorry I'm late, I've just finished work.'

'Work?' asks Esther.

'I'm a waiter, around the corner,' he smiles.

Not only does he have thick dark hair, blue eyes and a straight nose, he's got lovely white teeth as well. He looks like a less polished version of one of those *Beverly Hills 90210* boys that girls went mad for in the nineties.

'My name's Josh,' he says, coming over to shake each of our hands.

'You don't sound like you're from London,' says Paul, sounding distinctly flirty.

'I'm from Manchester,' he says.

'Yes!' I whisper under my breath. That'll keep the girls north of Watford interested.

'I've come to make my fortune,' he continues, with a wry smile.

I laugh a little too exuberantly. I bloody love Northern Charm.

Josh takes his place in the centre of the hall and we all hold our collective breath. Please God, let this good-looking bastard be able to sing. I don't need another passenger. We have enough of those, and anyway, this boy's too handsome to shove off to the side. He'd upset the balance of the group. I swear my mouth goes a little bit dry as the boy inhales. There is a lot riding on this – namely the future of my company and my reputation, such as it is.

Josh gets only halfway through the chorus of 'Let Me Entertain You' before I have made up my mind. The others are just as keen when I get out of my seat and walk over, saying, 'Welcome to the band!'

'That's great,' smiles Esther.

'You're great,' says Paul, vigorously shaking Josh's hand. I'm not sure if he's relieved we have found someone or just relieved that one of the longest days of his life is actually over.

'I think you're perfect,' smiles Holly, flicking her hair in a way I find a little alarming.

'This is my daughter,' I say quickly. 'She's fourteen.'

'Lovely to meet you,' Josh says, kissing the back of her hand. Suddenly Northern Charm is a whole lot less beguiling.

'Good, good,' I say, moving him along swiftly. 'This is Esther, the choreographer.'

'You can dance, of course?' she asks through her giggles.

'Of course,' he smiles.

'A proper little Billy Elliot,' she says.

'Absolutely,' he nods.

'And you've met Paul,' I add.

Paul shakes his hand again, while patting the top of his arm. Everyone seems delighted. We have found our five – Josh, Ashley, Mike, Billy and Nick. As we pack up the hall and emerge blinking into the cold, dank darkness of a March evening, I can only hope that I have done the right thing and chosen the right boys. 'You can't make chicken soup out of chicken shit.' Watkins' bons mots are ringing in my ears. Are these boys soup, or shit? Only time will tell.

The next morning, Esther's on the phone before eleven a.m. She's keen, I think as Debbie puts her through. Perhaps she wants to make herself indispensable? Perhaps she wants to talk about her deal? In fact, all she wants to know is who else is on the team. She suggests a number of stylists she will work with and a list of those she won't. She talks me through her choice of hairdresser and who she considers to be really fabulous at make-up. I start taking notes. Having only ever worked with groups that occasionally needed help choosing their T-shirts, this is taking grooming on to a whole new level. She knows the name of a great dietician they use on boot camp, and some good photographers.

'How about a plastic surgeon?' I joke.

'What?' she replies.

'A plastic surgeon?'

'Don't be silly,' she says. 'None of them last that long.'

Armed with her list of suggestions, I call Paul over from his office. He looks a little hungover and puffy-faced as he slopes in.

'Urgh,' he exhales as he flops down into the leather armchair opposite. 'I had a bit of a drink last night.'

'I can tell.'

'Met up with a mate of mine at Sony BMG and told him what we were doing,' says Paul, smoothing down the front of his black suit trousers.

'Thanks,' I say, exuding irritation and sarcasm.

'I didn't know it was a secret,' he says, putting his hands up in the air. 'Anyway, he said that they'd be interested.'

'I'm not going to sign with them.'

'Even if they offered the best deal?'

All I can manage is a petulant shivering shake of my head.

'Well, anyway, he asked if we had any boys in reserve.'

'Reserve?'

'Well, when Louis Walsh put Westlife together he had six members of the band and then had to get rid of three of the mingers before he came up with the right combination. He showed them to Simon, and Simon said he didn't like a few of them. He told Louis to get rid of four of them, but Louis kept Shane and dyed his hair blond and then showed him to Simon again with two new other members, and they became Westlife.'

'Well, fancy bloody that,' I say. 'We don't have any reserves and we don't have any hair dye, and *I* am managing this band not Simon Cunting Cowell!'

'OK,' says Paul, 'I just thought I'd mention it. And please don't shout. My head hurts.'

'Yes, well,' I huff. 'We don't even have a name yet.'

'Ah,' says Paul. 'But we are all meeting tonight, aren't we? Royal China at seven p.m.?'

'That's right.'

'Well, let's see if we can come up with something then.'

That evening all eight of us – me, Paul, Esther and the boys – pile into the Royal China on Queensway, where the lurid gold and black décor is matched by the surliness of the service. But I am of the opinion that when it comes to Chinese restaurants, the ruder the staff the better the food. And it is cheap, which is obviously one of the main reasons for us coming here. If this band is going to work I need to keep right on top of things, watch what I am spending like a hawk. So I am starting early.

'No starters, don't you think?' I say to everyone once we've taken our places at a large round table and been served some drinks.

'Are there any chips?' asks Mike, rubbing his stomach while scanning the obviously incomprehensible menu.

'We're in a Chinese,' says Ashley, over his glass of Coke.

'And?' says Mike. 'I always have chips with my chow mein. Is there chow mein on here?'

He looks at me. I am beginning to wish I had just taken them to McDonald's.

'Why don't I just order for everyone,' says Esther, taking on the role of mother. 'Much easier, don't you think?'

They all nod and put their menus down. Billy looks slightly relieved; his thick furrowed brow returns to normal. Nick sits back in his chair, puts his right hand down the front of his trousers and reaches out for a prawn cracker with his left. Josh, Ashley and Mike battle with a hot towel, chopsticks and the large china spoons on the table while Esther speaks to the hovering waiter.

'This is really a bonding exercise,' I explain, 'where we all get to meet each other properly and try to sort out a name for the band.'

'So this is all of us?' asks Josh.

'That's right,' I smile. 'You're the band.'

'Who's the lead singer?' asks Nick, removing his bollock hand.

'There isn't one,' I lie. Paul shoots me a quizzical look. 'You are all equal partners in the band. And each of you will take turns with the lead vocals.'

'Cool,' nods Nick. 'That works for me.'

'Good.' I smile.

'Is that normal?' asks Ashley.

'Perfectly,' I say. 'Most boy bands take it in turns.'

'Take That didn't,' Ashley persists.

'That's because not all of them could sing.' I smile again. A little more tightly this time. 'But you guys can all sing. I auditioned you personally.'

'Absolutely,' agrees Esther, snapping a cracker in half and then eating only half of that.

'Anyway, tonight isn't about who's singing and who's standing where, we've got years of that. Let's just get to know each other. Billy?'

'Yeah?'

'What sort of music do you like?'

'Linkin Park, Kaiser Chiefs,' he answers.

'Great. Interesting. Mike?'

'Well, you know, the Arctic Monkeys. Oasis, they're OK.'

'Good. Nick?'

'I don't really like music very much,' says Nick. 'Actually that's not true. But, you know, I find it hard to remember the names. Whatever's on the radio, really.'

'So none of you like boy bands then?' I ask.

'Will Young's OK,' says Nick.

'He's not strictly speaking a band,' I reply. 'Although he is a boy, I grant you.'

'I like singer-songwriters,' says Ashley. 'David Gray. Amy Winehouse is great.'

'Yeah,' agrees Josh. 'And Mariah Carey.'

'She doesn't do much writing,' says Paul.

'Really?' says Josh. For the next ten long minutes the conversation continues in this enlightening vein, during which time I learn quite how musically challenged some of the members of the band are. Then Josh looks over Paul's shoulder and finally announces, 'Oh look, here's the food.'

The boys leap on the food as if no one has fed them in a decade. They all assiduously avoid any semblance of green and go for the noodles and the meat.

'Excuse me,' says Mike, waving his hand at a passing waitress, 'do you have any ketchup?' The waitress looks at him with a totally puzzled expression, shrugs her shoulders and walks off. 'I need ketchup,' insists Mike, flicking the noodles about on his plate. 'You can't have a Chinese without ketchup.' The rest of them continue to trough through their food in silence. Mike holds off for a full five minutes before he joins in.

'So,' I say, looking around the table at this motley collection of boys I've gathered together, each with their faces stuffed full, 'anyone got any ideas about a name?'

3

We sat around that table for several hours trying to come up with names. The boys, I have to say, were not that helpful, or inspiring. Nick came up with some not entirely useful ideas like 'Sex Machine', 'The Shaggers' and 'My Place or Yours?', which didn't leave any of us guessing as to why he might have decided to join a boy band in the first place. Each artless suggestion elicited sniggers and giggles from Mike, Billy and Josh; only Ashley was a little more circumspect. In fact, he appeared to be somewhat shut off and spent the best part of the evening knocking back Diet Cokes and exchanging text messages with his real friends.

Paul tried his best. He came up with a whole load of camp sparkling names like 'Chaps and Claps' and 'Fun Boy Five' but none of them went down very well. 'I have never been terribly good at this,' he said, belching slightly into his Beck's beer. 'But anything's got to be better than Kick It, which was the original name for Take That.'

In the end it was Esther who came up with Band of Five. No one liked it too much to start off with, but in the absence of anything better, that's what we're sticking with for the moment. We're hoping it's got a sort of 'us against the rest of the world' feel about it, as well as a touch of that Spielberg series *Band of Brothers*, and a not so subliminal link to the old pop group Five, who were very successful, if not fantastically long serving.

Two weeks later, at midday, I'm waiting for the boys to turn up at the office to sign their management contracts and hopefully be impressed by the number of out-of-date shiny records I have on the wall. Interestingly, Debbie appears to be rather excited by the idea that Band, as I'm now calling them for short, are arriving imminently. She's been on the phone all morning alerting her mates to the good news. It's amazing what a frisson of success can do to one's appeal. I remember being introduced to some sexy girl in the Astoria a couple of years ago, before Road to Reality played. She smiled and nodded at me. I was just another overweight middle-aged bloke giving her the eye. At the end of the gig, however, she was all over me like a social disease. It wasn't that she wanted to shag either me or any of the members of the band. It was just that I was with the hip crowd, where the action was, and she wanted to be there.

So despite the fact that she held their hands, helped them audition and gave them water and biscuits and sympathy,

Debbie is now a hair-flicking, gum-chewing ball of energy, because the boys are due any minute.

'Do either of you want a coffee?' she shouts up from the bottom of the stairs. 'I thought I might go and get some croissants and danish, for the boys,' she adds.

'A skinny double shot latte,' comes Paul's voice from across the landing.

'An espresso,' Esther shouts down from my office.

'A normal full-fat one,' I add.

I hate all this coffee choice. When I first started out in the business no one bothered with this coffee and danish rubbish. If you wanted refreshment during a meeting there was usually a bottle of Jack Daniel's rattling around in someone's top drawer. Sometimes when I go to record company offices now they've got that many cakes and biscuits and little bottles of water I have to pinch myself that I'm not at some meeting with the WI.

I have a mate who hates 'fashion coffee' even more than I do, but he's got good reason. When he was working with Adam Ant a few years back he ended up travelling from LA to San Francisco to drink a cup of coffee. It was Mr Ant's idea, apparently. He'd heard about this place that did amazing coffee and on his one day off during a six-week tour he was determined to go and sample some. My mate felt sorry for him and thought he shouldn't go alone, so they left the hotel at 7.30 a.m. and drove for eight and a half hours to get to this place. They drank their coffee sitting on the bonnet, then got straight back into the car to drive another eight and a half hours back again. Adam was of the opinion that it was the best cup he'd ever drunk in his entire life. My mate said it was a Starbucks and was so put off coffee he didn't drink a drop for two years. He now only touches the stuff if it's cheap and shit and instant. I kind of understand how he feels.

'So is the deal all ready to be signed?' asks Esther, leaning across my desk and picking up my stress ball. If her backside weren't so pert in her skin-tight black trousers I might just punch her lights out. No one plays with my ball and gets away with it. But with her I just grin and bear it and think of shagging her one day.

'Well, it's been with the boys' lawyers,' I say, 'and come back, so we should be OK.'

'They've got lawyers?' she asks.

'We sort of have to do that these days,' I say. 'The days of screw-you-and-your-mother deals are very sadly over.'

'No more deals like the famous Tom Watkins contract with Bros where he got twenty per cent of everything,' she says, squeezing my ball.

'Well, that deal was twenty per cent of gross,' I say. 'It's always between fifteen and twenty per cent of gross, it just depends on what the word gross means. A Watkins gross, that's everything including expenses; gross after touring expenses have been taken into account; gross without expenses and minus VAT. There are many nuances of gross.'

'All the competition winners I've worked with have to sign contracts as soon as they get down to the last ten, or twelve, or whatever it is. As soon as they get on the telly, basically they sign the lot away.'

'Really?'

'Yeah. Well, it is the telly that got them there, or at least that's what they argue.' She smiles. 'So you gave them lawyers?'

'I gave them a list: Russells, Clintons, Sheridan's – they all know the tricks, so it's not even worth trying. Anyway,' I add, stretching and then patting the wad of contracts on my desk, 'they all went for Russells, which makes it easier for us. It's kind of annoying to have to deal with too many people. Also, it means there's only one invoice to pay and recoup back from the boys when they make some money later.'

Esther walks over to the window and looks down to the street below.

'I see they've finished outside,' she says.

'Paul's gutted,' I say.

'I heard that,' he shouts from his office.

'Eavesdroppers only hear ill of themselves,' I reply.

'Fuck off,' he shouts back.

'Here they come,' says Esther, pressing her face against the window. 'Or two of them anyway.'

I move over to the window and look down. Billy and Mike are walking up the street in shades and baseball caps, like they're being trailed by the paps. They've got their baggy jeans on and there's a swagger in their hips.

'They look the part,' says Esther.

'They're the style-over-content element of Band so at least I've got something right,' I say.

'*We* have got something right,' agrees Esther, untactfully reminding me that last week I gave her 2 per cent of the deal and that she has a vested interest. For that I get her choreography skills, her hair and make-up mates, and, if push comes to shove, me with my back against the wall and a gun against my head, I also get her access to Sony BMG via her contacts with Cowell as well as Paul's mate. This business is all about money, and nothing buys loyalty more than a percentage.

Debbie is running along the street carrying her paper tray of coffees, a bag of buns and croissants under her arm and the office keys in her mouth. If she were hoping to impress these new pop stars on the block, this is probably not the look she would have gone for. They both stand around while she fumbles at the door. It takes the late arrival of Nick on his bicycle before either of them help.

'One of you give the girl a hand,' he shouts as he pulls up, looking fit and handsome and just what we wanted.

There then follows a bit of a scrabble as both Mike and Billy go for the coffee and the buns. The keys are dropped, the coffee fortunately isn't, but a danish is lost in the process. I contemplate coming down the stairs to meet them but decide against it.

'Up here!' I shout before sitting back in my chair and waiting for them to troop up. I quickly arrange my feet on the desk in a manner that I hope exudes power and importance.

'How are you all?' I say when they come in.

'Fine, great,' they say as they file in and sit in a row on the maroon leather sofa. The sofa is a little too small and they sink slowly down as they stare back up at me.

'Morning!' It's Josh, arriving downstairs.

'Up here!' I shout.

'Sorry I'm late,' he says, bounding up the stairs. 'The bus was late.'

'That's the last time you'll be on one of those!' says Nick.

I let the boys indulge in a bit of banter while we all wait for Ashley to arrive. I silently rehearse my *Fame* lecture, which goes something along the lines that there is a lot of hard work to come which will involve long hours and dedication and might not be as lucrative as you think to start off with and 'right here is where you start paying – in sweat'. Or some such inspiring and intimidating rant.

I am interrupted by the sound of a loud female voice in reception.

'I want to talk to the manager,' she says.

'He's busy at the moment,' says Debbie, doing her job for once. 'He can't be disturbed.'

'I know my rights!' says the woman. 'Come on!' she orders, and two sets of feet come stomping up the stairs.

Ashley enters my office. Even though he is looking at the ground, his cheeks and ears are glowing bright red with mortification. He is followed by a large woman with scraped-back hair in a ponytail, wearing a pink terry tracksuit and white T-shirt. She has rings on every square-tipped finger and earrings climbing up the sides of both lobes. Her body is badly out of shape, but her face is quite pretty. She looks about thirty.

'You the manager?' she asks, pointing a finger at me.

'That's right,' I nod.

'Well, I'm Ash's mum,' she says, her head wobbling from side to side as if she were expecting some sort of confrontation.

'Lovely to meet you,' I say, getting up out of my seat and coming round to shake her hand. 'You have a very lovely and very talented son.'

'Oh,' she says, stroking her gel-smoothed hair with the padded palm of her hand. 'Right.' She stands there, looking round the room, taking in the gold discs, the framed magazine articles, the leather sofa and the leather-topped desk. 'So, you been doing this long?' She has very clearly been wrong-footed by the set-up. I have no idea what she was expecting but it was very obviously not this.

'I have been in the industry for a while, yes,' I say.

'You any good?' she asks.

'I have had my moments. I have had a few hit records as you can see.' I point towards the golden wall of achievement.

'Yeah,' she sniffs, walking over and taking a cursory look to see if there's any name she might recognize. She draws a blank, puts her hands on her expansive hips and turns round.

'You gay?'

The other boys in the room burst out laughing. Whether it is out of excruciating discomfort or the fact that they all want to ask the same question, I'm not sure. Ashley goes redder than anyone I have ever seen this side of a full coronary. His mother just stands her ground and stares.

'Um, no,' I say. 'I am heterosexual.'

'I am,' says Paul, standing in the doorway.

I roll my eyes slightly. Does he need to be quite so out, quite so proud just now?

'Oh?' says Ashley's mother, turning her attention on him.

'I have a daughter,' I continue, trying to draw back the heat.

'Whatever.' She dismisses me and turns back to Paul. 'Will you have anything to do with my son?'

The whole room looks at Paul. He glances up towards the sky, pretending to think. 'Um . . .' Ashley's mother takes a step towards him. 'In the day-to-day scheme of things . . . no.'

'Right,' she says. 'Where do we sign?'

'We?' I say.

'Actually, he's not my type anyway,' continues Paul. 'Why do some people think that gay men find all other men irresistible when in fact some of us—'

'Yeah, we,' she replies. 'Ash is fifteen; there's no way he can sign anything. He's underage.' She shoots Paul the sort of look that could actually kill a man less orgaynically nourished.

'Chubby sandy-haired teenagers don't do it for me,' says Paul, putting his hands up and turning to leave the office. 'I can't say it more succinctly than that.'

Or more tactlessly, I think as he leaves and everyone else in the room checks out Ashley to see quite how fat and ginger he is. The band has yet to form and there are already problems.

I pick the contracts up off my desk and hand them round. The boys sit and squiggle away, signing on the dotted line without reading them again. Meanwhile Ashley's mother takes hers and slaps it back down on my desk. She takes up a position in the leather chair and, licking her thumb, proceeds to flick through every goddamn page of the thing, muttering to herself.

Fuck! I shake my head slightly. I can't believe none of us bothered to ask Ashley his age. Fifteen! *Fifteen!* I can't believe he is bloody fifteen! I am going to have to ask the council if he can perform. I am going to have to get permission for him to go into certain clubs. I have got to make sure he doesn't get pissed and that he doesn't have sex. I have basically got to be his bloody father. Worse than that: I have got to be his involved and caring father. I do, after all, own 20 per cent of him. I had a mate who used to look after Billie Piper and he said it was a nightmare: so much paperwork involved, and gigs cancelled as children can only work something like twelve hours a week. Simon Fuller had a similar problem in New York recently when 19 Touring company were fined for contravening child labour laws; the recent *American Idol* winner Jordin Sparks and one of the runners up, Sanjaya Malakar, were both under eighteen. They failed to register them when they were on the road and singing live and had to cough up some paltry $5,000 fine, which hardly broke that over-stuffed bank. But the US laws are tough: they also state that children under the age of eighteen must keep at least 15 per cent of what they earn in trust until they are eighteen.

Ashley's mother sighs and scratches her head with a white square-tipped nail. She turns another page of the contract. I look at her, and my heart sinks further. What makes all the other problems pale into insignificance is that I am not only managing five boys, I am also looking after Ashley's mother. If

I had wanted to manage a middle-aged woman I might have given Madonna or Lulu or, hell, even Kylie a call. But I'm not stupid and I value my bollocks.

'Looks OK to me,' she suddenly announces, pushing the pile of paper back towards me.

'Good,' I say with a tight smile, 'it should be. It's been through two sets of expensive lawyers three times, so it should read OK.'

'Don't mind me,' she says, holding out a hot pink hand for me to shake. 'Dionne, my name's Dionne, and Ash is my eldest, so I want the best for him. This is his one opportunity to hit the big time so I want it to work.'

'No, I agree,' I say, my teeth clamped together. 'That's good parenting.'

'Yeah, well, at least one of us gives a shit. His dad, on the other hand, is no fucking where. Ran off, you know,' she nods, 'as soon as he found out.'

'Oh, I am sorry,' I say, watching poor old Ashley, still longing for the ground to swallow him up as he stands there, his dirty laundry flapping in public.

'Yeah, well, you pick yourself up, don't you?' continues Dionne. 'You got a pen?'

Dionne finally signs, and I wish I could reach for my Valium. A friend of mine once said to me that the thing about managing boy bands is that you also always end up managing the families as well. I didn't actually think he was being literal.

After sharing a few more of her family secrets, mainly that

she was fifteen when she had Ashley, Dionne leaves in a puff of Victoria Beckham's new perfume and we crack open the champagne – not to celebrate her departure, although by the look on Ashley's face, the moment when her pink terry backside finally left the building would have been enough for him to pop a cork. When Paul comes in to join us Ashley grovels some sort of apology, although quite why he needs to after Paul had called him a fat ginga in public I don't know.

Talk soon moves from mortifying mothers to the future of Band of Five and what exactly our next move is.

'It'll all be down to the song,' says Paul, knocking back some warm champagne from his plastic cup.

'Yeah.' I nod in agreement.

'Are you going to go with a cover?' he asks.

'Well, I'm not sure.'

'What sort of cover?' asks Josh.

'I'm not sure,' I say again.

'Do we have to?' asks Ashley. 'Isn't that what all boy bands do?'

'There is a reason why all boy bands do it,' I say, 'and that's because it works. Take That, Boyzone, Blue – they were all very successful with covers.'

'*Very* successful,' says Paul, supportively. 'In fact, I think one of the few times Westlife didn't have a number one was when they sang their own song.'

'I remember,' I nod, although I don't, of course. Who remembers anything Westlife have sung?

'Apparently, they had a bit of a to-and-fro with Cowell when he wanted them to sing "Mandy" and they said they wanted to do a song of their own. He said it wouldn't work. They released a single called "Bop Bop Baby".'

'It sounds rubbish,' says Ashley.

'It was,' agrees Paul. 'And I love Westlife and all they touch.' He has clearly been drinking too much champagne because that's the first I've heard of this affection for those Irish songsters. 'Anyway, it peaked at number five or so, which is low for them, and Simon said, "I told you so." He then asked, "Do you want to be at number one all the time?" And they said, "We'd quite like to be at number one all the time." And he said, "Sing bloody 'Mandy' then." And that was it.'

'Have they not sung one of their own songs since?' asks Josh.

'Nope,' says Paul, taking another swig of champagne.

The great cover debate goes on long into the afternoon; the boys kick back on my sofa and chat. We get through six bottles of champagne and a similar amount of cigarettes. Strange how everyone becomes a drinker and a smoker when their mums are nowhere to be seen. And the longer they hang around in my office, the more they begin to feel like a real group rather than a load of handsome waifs and strays I have picked up off the streets of the capital – and Manchester. Mustn't forget to keep mentioning Manchester. It's going to sit well with the press that they aren't all from London, particularly when we tour.

As they sit with their feet on my magazine tables telling jokes and putting their fags out in their champagne, there is certainly a rapport developing in the group. Ashley is the baby, and everyone is treating him as such, ruffling his hair and trying to shock him with stories. And since his secret is out now, he has relaxed a little more and had a drink, which I remember he didn't do at the Chinese restaurant. Mike is clearly the cheeky one. He has the gift of the gab and the stories to match. He's one of the best-looking too, and has probably been the worst behaved so far. For a good-looking bloke Josh is a little bit more mature and focused in comparison with the others. He strikes me as less laddish and a bit of a mummy's boy and does admit halfway through the session that he was in the local church choir. 'I'm an Irish Catholic from Manchester,' he says. 'It's the law!'

He and Nick seem to get on the best. Perhaps it's their square jaws that seem to bond them; whatever it is, they get pretty chatty. Billy is quietest, which is surprising because I had him down as one of those boys who go out on a Saturday night and have to flick away the women like flies. Then again, as my track record has shown, I know very little about the female of the species and how they tick. I'm told they go for sensitive types. Possibly. They certainly don't go for overweight middle-aged music biz types who drink and smoke and coke too much, that's for sure.

As I sit down at nine p.m., with a modicum of room spin, to tuck into my microwave 'bistro chicken meal' for one, I can't help but think I've done well today. I've signed a band that I formed, they're good-looking, which is unusual for me, and they seem to like each other. And some of them can sing.

*

The next morning I'm in bright and early at 10.45 a.m., looking for songs. Overnight I decided to put the cover idea on the back burner and see what sort of talent there was out there and who would be ready to sell us a song.

Although this isn't the first time, it has certainly been a while since I last did this. Also, if I am going to get my hands on the Holy Grail I am a tiny bit late out of the blocks. I am referring to the Christmas number one, of course. I wouldn't be a boy band manager worth any weight in naughty salt if I didn't have my eye on the festive chart. These days, however, Cowell is the Grinch who ruins Christmas, the winner of his piss-poor talent show pressing their over-hyped ballad on or around 16 December, thereby raining on everyone's yuletide parade. And it used to be a bit of a parade, with every record company releasing the big guns, the novelty guns and an old fave or two. There would be a flurry of betting; serious money used to pass hands. Even old indie bores like me used to get involved, writing out fat cheques to fat mates who always managed to pick the winner. But Cowell and co. have changed all that. The *X Factor* winner is more or less guaranteed the top slot. But you can live in hope.

I should have been a little more organized, though. There is still time to get a band together, tour it, get a fan base up and running and get to number one by the end of the year, but I have rather missed the boat when it comes to songs. There's a season for selling Christmas songs. The music publishers start touting them around soon after the previous year's have bitten the dust and become roadfill in China. Come March most of the best songs have already been snapped up by the best singers. There are A-list and B-list songs and A-list and B-list songwriters, just like there are A-list and B-list stars to sing them. If I am lucky there might be a few B-list songs left, but the As will most certainly have gone. Still, you can never tell what might happen. I did hear there was a rather undignified rush recently for Britney's songs. No sooner had the girl been strapped down and carted off to rehab, or the asylum, or wherever she went, than music publishing phones were ringing off the hook in LA as managers, producers, acts and A&R men tried to get their hands on all the top-flight songs she won't be singing for a while. Don't be surprised if Beyoncé, Mariah and Shakira have a few more hits than usual this year. It is hard, as they say, to keep a good song down.

I have a look through what EMI Publishing and Chrysalis Music have rattling around in the cupboard. Sadly, the two writers I have my eyes on – Greg Kurstin, who wrote 'Wow' for Kylie, and Savan Kotecha, who has penned for and with Gary Barlow, Westlife and Gareth Gates – are both otherwise engaged. I amuse myself for a minute on their websites, where you can punch in various moods, genres and ideas you might want to find in your song, including 'life affirming', 'Sunday', 'happy', 'hope', 'heart', 'dark/brooding', 'cry/tears', 'colour', 'numbers' and 'work'. I type in the last two hoping to come up with the old Sheena Easton song 'Working Nine to Five', but it doesn't seem to be on EMI's books.

I am sitting contemplating reviving the track for Band of

Five and running the sad-versus-kitschy/amusing argument around in my head when Paul comes into the office.

'All right?' he sniffs. His face looks red and his champagne jowls look well and truly re-toxed.

'I'm good,' I reply. 'I've been thinking about a song for Band.'

'Oh, right,' he says, scratching his cropped hair.

'But I have a feeling we are too late for any of the A-list songs.'

'I think so,' he says. 'But we probably wouldn't get them anyway with a new untried band. Who's going to give us their highest earners when they could get Madonna to sing them?'

'I've heard Madonna asks for a writing credit and fifty per cent of the publishing,' I say.

'Fifty?' he asks.

'So they say. She changes "a" to "the" and takes fifty for her creative input. And still they queue up to work for her.'

'She can make a dud a hit, I suppose,' says Paul, taking a sip of his latte and burning his lips. 'Shit! Why do I always do that?' he asks, licking and sucking his lips with his thick hungover tongue. 'I never bloody learn.'

'My mate once burnt his bollocks on an apple pie,' I say, by way of trying to make him feel better. 'He went to a drive-thru McDonald's, bought an apple pie and put it on his lap. It slipped out of the bag and between his legs and he ended up having serious ball ache and had to apply cream to his nads for weeks.'

'That must have hurt,' Paul smiles.

'Talking of bollocks,' I continue, 'I had another mate whose job was to dry Axl Rose's nuts.'

'What?' Paul frowns.

'Yeah,' I nod. 'He was employed to stand by the side of the stage with a hair dryer in each hand, and while Slash was doing his solo and the rest of Guns N Roses were playing away, Axl would come to the side of the stage, pull down the front of his cycling shorts and my mate would hair-dry the bollocks. Apparently, it was to stop the chafing.'

'Ouch,' agrees Paul. 'I suppose that is only marginally better than blowing coke up Stevie Nicks's arse with a straw.'

'D'you think?'

'I'd prefer the bollocks to the arse – wouldn't you?'

'Not sure,' I say. 'It's surely one of life's imponderables. Anyway, d'you know any good songwriters?'

Paul stands and thinks for a second. 'There's always Suzy what's-her-name.'

'Is she any good?'

'She's had a few hits,' he says. 'She is now NA, AA and CA.'

'Right.'

'The only thing she can't give up is the sex,' he continues. 'She's got the masturbating down to four times a day though.'

'I'm amazed she's got time to do any work,' I say, watching Paul walk out of the room. I am left with the image of Suzy going for it hell for leather every four hours or so. It must be exhausting. I am slightly loath to tax her further. But needs must, as they say, so I get the number from Paul, call and leave a message on her phone – something along the lines that I have a hot new boy band and I need some material. I also decide to give an old friend of mine, Jerry, a call. Jerry's been in the music business for a while. He recorded a few earnest albums no one was that interested in and was dropped by his record company, but I hear his publishing deal is going well. His is not an unusual situation. The music industry is full of failed performers who make money out of selling songs, and failed writers who make money out of other people's lyrics. And then there are of course failing record companies that seem to be able to make money out of old rope, and everyone.

Then again, the music business is a bizarre beast. There are so many people taking a slice of the record pie it is a wonder anyone can get rich or fat, but the labels still somehow manage it. Take the price of a CD album, which is, let's say, £10. They immediately take 15 per cent off the price for 'packaging', which is one of the many ways in which the record company likes to siphon off a little extra when it can. Packing will only ever really cost a maximum of 5 per cent, so the label pockets 10 per cent straight off. The remainder of the tenner is divided up between the label, the publisher, the distributor of the record, the retailer, and finally the sucker who sang it. The sucker then has to give 20 per cent of that to his or her manager, and if there is more than one sucker, then the suckers have to divide that equally between themselves. So, out of that £10, £1.50 is packaging, then the retailer takes about 30 per cent, the distributor has around 9 per cent, the publisher has 6 per cent, the label bags 30 per cent, and the artist is left with about 10 per cent. In Band of Five's case, they would therefore make a pound per CD, minus my 20 per cent, which comes to 80p. Divide that by five, and each of the boys will pocket 16p per CD sale.

Those record execs are so canny. Record deals are still written as if the end result were a pressed piece of vinyl, even though until very recently CDs were twice the price of an old album. Fans would think nothing of shelling out up to £20 a CD, whereas LPs were never over a tenner. Artists were getting the same 50p-a-copy royalties as before, even though the price of the end product had doubled. Royalties were effectively halved. In the States they had the additional hangover of keeping 10 per cent back for breakages. The original shellac and vinyl were obviously quite fragile; CDs, on the other hand, are supposed to be unbreakable – or at least that's what they told us on *Tomorrow's World*.

When I get through to Jerry he sounds like he is on good form. Turns out his career is very much on the up, and he's been doing well in the US.

Breaking the US is, of course, what every band and act wants to do. Anyone who tells you different is lying, or, like Robbie, has had their fingers burnt through trying and is now pretending, much like a surly child, that they were never that interested in the first place. There are obviously many ways of doing it: hoping you get lucky, like James Blunt, and have a number one record; touring your arse off like every other UK band usually rather unsuccessfully tries to do; winning five Grammys, like Amy; or by creating heat or a buzz and a story over here and taking it back to the US. Gnarls Barkley broke

'Crazy' in the UK before the US, and the Scissor Sisters were successful over here way before they were over there.

Whichever way you try to do it, radio play is one of the most important elements of a song's success. There are something like three thousand radio stations in the US – about half as many as there were in the old days when two thirds of them had their playlists in the control of the Mafia and you needed cash, coke and other forms of payola or backhanders to break a hit. 'Payola' is a term from the late fifties, and comes from the contraction of the words 'pay' and 'Victrola' (an old LP record player). The first court case involving payola was in 1960 when Alan Freed was indicted for accepting a $2,500 'token of gratitude', which apparently did not affect airplay. He paid a small fine and was released. His career faltered, and in 1965 he drank himself to death. Before the Freed case payola was not illegal, but commercial bribery was. After the trial, however, it became a crime, punished by up to $10,000 in fines and one year in prison.

'Can you believe they're playing my song?' shares Jerry over the phone. 'I'm getting fifteen thousand spins a week and I get fifty cents a spin.'

'That's amazing,' I say, wondering if I should try to persuade him to come over to me. Although judging by quite how well he is doing at the moment I shouldn't think he wants to muddy his waters at all.

'I'm being played on AC and Hot AC,' he continues, 'which is amazing.'

The US divides its radio stations into categories that include

AC (adult contemporary) and Hot AC (a bit edgier); then there is Urban (mainly black music like Jay-Z), Rap (which includes hip-hop) and Pop (which can mean anything from Kylie to James Blunt). However, before your record is played on any of these stations they research it.

'Apparently, I went down well with the bored housewives in the Mid-west,' Jerry laughs.

He's not wrong. A Jerry song would've appealed to the testing panels they use where the taste-makers, such as they are, are asked various questions about how 'familiar' a song is, whether they find it 'offensive' or 'appealing', and whether they would listen to it in their car. Jerry's song was clearly bland enough to slip through the net; he tested well so he gets spun. After that it is all about calls into the station, requests and, of course, the occasional expensive dinner for the radio producer, some concert tickets and maybe even a free car. It's just a question of trying to be subtle about payola as the days of suitcases of cash and firm handshakes containing fat cheques are gone.

Despite his success in the States, Jerry assures me he is keen to meet the boys and adds that he might have a few songs hanging around. He says that he's happy to pop in tomorrow to see if we can come up with something together.

As I hang up, Debbie puts another call straight through.

'Hello there, it's Suzy,' purrs a provocative female voice.

Shit, I think, is it ethical to flirt with a sex addict over the phone?

'Good afternoon,' I say, squeaking slightly as I try to sound as much like a bank manager as I can.

'I've been on hold for a while,' she says.

'I'm sorry.'

'Don't worry,' she says, 'I kept myself busy.'

An arousing image comes to mind. I try to blank it, but it won't go away.

'I am sorry,' I say again.

'Why?'

'Oh, sorry, that's good – keeping busy,' I stammer.

Why did Paul have to tell me about Suzy's problem? It makes all communication with her full of double entendre, and I'm easily flustered when it comes to that. In a manner that is as businesslike as I can muster, I try to talk her through the boys and the idea behind the band and ask her to think about it.

'I'll sleep on it,' she says. 'I have always liked the idea of doing a boy band.'

'Good, good,' I cough. 'Talk soon.'

I hang up and loosen the belt of sweat that has gathered around my waist. I am not sure I can work with Suzy; my worse nature might well get the better of me. I am tempted to look her up on Facebook to check to see if she is good-looking. After all, I'm sure we could use one of her songs.

Paul comes in and mentions he's got Des Adams on the line asking if we'd like to meet up and discuss the album.

'Has he got one yet?' I ask.

'He says so,' replies Paul.

'Great,' I say. 'I'd love to hear it. Tell him to come by this afternoon.'

Des drops in at three p.m. with his guitar over his shoulder, wearing his worn leather jacket, his low-slung jeans and his faded green T-shirt. His brown hair has just the right amount of bed-head ruffle for a rock star, and at five feet five inches he is suitably short. He's good-looking enough to do a photo shoot for the *Observer Music Monthly* magazine, but he's not really front cover or girl's bedroom material. As a result his audience is mainly male.

'Hey guys,' he says, coming over to slap the palm of my hand and click his finger like I'm a mate from his hood. 'How's it hanging?'

'It's hanging fine, thank you,' I say.

He unslings his guitar, sits down on the sofa, puts his Converses on the mag table and waves a CD at me. 'D'you want it? D'you want it?' he teases.

Not that much, you twat, I think. 'So much!' I smile through my caps, doing one of those overexcited shivers. 'Sock it to me, Des, the suspense is killing me!'

I spend the next forty minutes listening to the biggest pile of dross I have ever subjected my ears to. It is so bad I actually begin to doubt my own music taste. Is this so bad that it's good? Or am I now so old and out of the loop I just can't hear the tunes any more? And throughout it all Des nods his head, flicks his turquoise foot and half closes his eyes at his very genius. Every so often he says 'Oh, oh, oh – here' and indicates with a pointed finger that this bit is to be appreciated for its sublime qualities. When it's all over, I don't know what to say. Tumbleweed and a gust of wind blast through the room. This album could almost be as uncommercial as one of Bob Dylan's born-again Christian offers, which is saying something. They were so bad that Dick Katz, Dylan's record boss, apparently renewed his $20 million deal only after shouting at him, 'No Torah! No Bible! No Koran! No Jesus! No God! No Allah! No fucking religion! It's going in the contract!' But this is worse. It is sub-Robbie Williams with a bit of Jeff Buckley thrown in to try to make Des sound like he has soul. Which he clearly hasn't. It feels as if he's driven around LA in his Rentawreck convertible thinking he's the man, cherry-picking bits and pieces and mixing them together into a hideous, piss-poor pile of crap.

'So?' says Des, sitting upright now, his foot tapping with excitement.

'So . . .' Do I tell him it's shit and risk losing him? Or do I pass it on to the record company, let them deal with it, and keep my client? 'It's great!' I say, passing the buck. 'I think we should send it to Dave at Warner's and see what he thinks. But I'm sure he will think the same as I do.'

'Wicked,' says Des. 'Because, you know, I was a bit worried you wouldn't like it.'

'I can't think why.'

'It's a little different from the last one.'

'Different is good,' I say, getting out of my chair. 'Different is so, so goooood.'

We exchange more platitudes as I slowly edge him out of the office and down the stairs. I'm not sure how long I can keep the whole charade going. I pat him on the back and send him out into the street, promising to bike off the CD to the record company today.

As I walk back upstairs I am reminded of the time when the whole of the Polydor A&R department were too nervous of Level 42 to tell them their new album was below par. They were a hugely successful band – their album *World Machine* had been an international hit – and rather than tell the band their next album needed work, everyone insisted it was marvellous. It wasn't. Later, Mark King, the lead singer, came back to the company to tell them they were a bunch of arse-holes. He said he'd been with them for a long time, he'd come to them for advice, and they had let him down.

It normally takes huge amounts of success before the balance of power shifts and people start to lie, I think, as I sit back down at my desk. You're normally a few platinum albums in before you can deliver what you like. But I can't risk losing Des. Let Warner's play bad cop, and then I can pick up the pieces.

The next morning, Jerry's at my desk regaling me with stories about trying to work with Mariah Carey on her new album $E=MC^2$. 'She is literally imprisoned by her millions,' he says.

Macrobiotically thin and in his late thirties, Jerry's a pot-smoking hippy who has through his songwriting been dusted with the golden glow of success. His hair is blond and glossy, his skin is a little bit too tanned, and his leather thong neck-laces and beaded bracelets look like they've been picked up in an expensive boutique rather than the usual gap-year hippy markets.

'So you get flown to the yacht,' he says, 'because she can't come off it for tax reasons. She's only allowed a certain amount of dry-land days a year. It's so bizarre. But when you know her last tax bill was something like twenty-one million dollars, you can see why.'

'I can't believe you've been working with her,' I say.

'Well, no one works *with* her, it's *for* her. And all that happens is you do the work and she lies on a divan and says yes or no with a wave of her hand.'

'Did you get any tracks on the album?'

'Sadly no,' he says. 'Do you think I'd be here if I had!'

'So what do you have for the boys then?'

'Let me meet them first,' he says.

Half an hour later, Band are gathered in the office. Jerry's shaking their hands, checking them out, and they are doing the same.

'You're a songwriter?' sniffs Nick, looking Jerry up and down.

'You writing for us?' asks Mike, shaking his hand.

'Who have you written for?' quizzes Josh.

The mere mention of Miss Carey seems to allay all their fears. Josh's face lights up as he grills Jerry for every available detail. What was she wearing? What did she eat? What was the boat like? This is clearly the closest to fame he has ever got.

They all gather round and jostle for position when Jerry brings out his mobile phone and starts showing them poorly framed snaps of the boat.

I suggest that they all move across into Paul's office. He's out to lunch this afternoon. He's wining and dining the boys at Warner's, trying to smooth any ruffled feathers in anticipation of the reaction to Des's album. His office is as good a place as any for the boys to bond with Jerry, and for them to start throwing some ideas around. Or whatever Jerry wants to do.

I can hear them laughing and chatting through my shut door, so I decide to go through my emails. I fire one off to Suzy, just to make sure she is still on the case and that my eggs are not all in Jerry's basket.

'Hello there – you OK and working hard?' I send.

'I was just thinking about you,' she replies straight back.

'Business or pleasure?' I return.

'Pure pleasure.'

'Really?'

'Yes, really.'

'I hope I wasn't too rough with you?' I write.

I pause before I send it. Fuck it. I hit the button.

'You were very thorough,' she immediately replies.

I sit back in my chair. A volley of laughter emanates from Paul's office. This is going to be an entertaining afternoon.

4

Fortunately, Jerry and the boys had a more successful afternoon that day than I did. Only I could manage to turn off a sex
addict. What's wrong with me? What did I do? Maybe I was
just that little too forward? Or that bit too needy? Or, let's face
it, out of practice. But somehow, somewhere, I overstepped the
mark in our emails and Suzy told me to piss off in no uncer-
tain terms. She's told Band to piss off as well. Which makes me
all the more grateful that there was so much healthy bonding
going on next door while I tried to type with my left hand, my
Jockey Y-fronts around my knees.

   She obviously meant it too. These last few days a small part
of me has been hoping for a reconciliatory call or email from
her, but it seems I've burnt my bridges completely. Jerry is a different matter. He's here now, keen as anything, his skinny arse
sitting on the corner of my desk.

'OK,' he says, 'so, as you know, I spoke with them and asked them loads of questions, trying to draw things out of them – their life experience, such as it is. I often think I should offer my services as a shrink, because that's what it's like.' He picks up his pad of paper. 'Josh has been in love and had his heart broken. He won't say by whom, but that's one of the reasons he left Manchester.'

'Oh?'

'And Ashley says he's never been in love but he knows what it feels like. Mike's had no one special. Billy has had two, and nothing seems to touch Nick particularly at all.'

'OK,' I say. 'None of that surprises me.'

'Nick did rather hilariously say that he loves his dog better than any girl he's met.'

'And you worked with that?'

'I love you, I love you, but I love my dog better – that's not exactly the best trope you've ever heard, is it?'

He's right about that, but then tropes are tricky things. They are what makes an OK song good, or something dull interesting. They are lyrical twists, turns, surprises. So, 'you're beautiful, and I'll never be with you' is better than 'you're beautiful, and I'll always be with you', which was how it was supposedly originally written. Portishead's 'Nobody loves me, Nobody loves me, Nobody loves me – like you' adds a twist to the expected. 'I love you, I love you, but I love my dog better' doesn't quite have the feel-good factor I am after. Girls don't pay to hear that sort of thing.

Pop songwriting tends to be a formulaic, non-spontaneous

exercise. There are usually verses and choruses and, normally for boy bands, lyrics that are too bad, too negative or too sad. Upbeat is our name and feel-good is the game. However, there are always exceptions to the rule. One of the greatest hit records of all time is universally acknowledged to be 'Bohemian Rhapsody', and it breaks every rule. There's no chorus, no verses, and it is twice the length it should be. Three minutes is deemed the perfect length for a pop record; 'Bohemian Rhapsody' is nearly six. For lesser mortals than Freddie Mercury, if you can't say it in three minutes, you're not doing it right. It is something about the way the mind traditionally concentrates, and boy bands are nothing if not traditional.

Jerry talks me through his ideas, his hooks and his thoughts. He has put three songs down on tape and wants me to listen to them. It's just him and his guitar – no frills. Or he could sing them right here for me.

'All three are ballads?' I check.

'Nearly,' he says, clearing his throat and picking up his well-worn guitar.

'Cowell always goes with a ballad.'

'Does he?'

'Always. Especially for the Christmas number one. There's always some power ballad about how "this time it will be different", "it's all change now I've won", "it's my perfect moment", or some such bullshit.'

'Wasn't that Martine McCutcheon?'

'Christ, what happened to her?'

'Isn't she on the telly?'

'Back where she belongs,' I smile.

'OK, so this is the first one,' Jerry says, getting off my desk as he begins to strum away. 'This is called "Brief Love",' he announces over the opening chords.

I sit back, stare out of the window at the clear blue sky, and listen. It's a good song; it's beautiful, it's powerful. It's about young love and how transient it is. The chorus has a hook and a line – 'I love you my melting rose'. I can see girls liking it. I can hear mums singing along to the radio. More importantly, I can hear it on Radio Two. Radio Two is crucial to my plan as it is where most of our airplay will be. Radio One doesn't play pop any more; they are not overly fond of the boy band. If it's in the charts and it makes it into the top ten they'll be forced to playlist it, but they certainly won't champion it. Unlike, I hope, those nice boys on Radio Two.

The second song, 'To My Manor Born', is a little bit more rocky and perhaps a little less successful. It's a sort of cheeky-chappy sound, a bit too Brit pop for me, but it might be a good one for the pot, make them sound a bit edgier later on. It's about growing up on an estate, and Jerry has miraculously managed to slip in Nick's dog. 'My dog's sexier than yours, look at its lovely white jaws,' he sings at one point, and smiles at me, before taking up the melody. It is a toe-tapper, but my instinct is that it's not the first single, and it may be a bit too hip to make the album.

'The last one's totally slushy,' says Jerry, looking rather

embarrassed. 'You told me to let go of all my inhibitions, release the lovesick boy out of the boy band.'

'I did,' I nod.

'OK. This one's called "When You Find the One".'

'I'm loving it already.'

Jerry's face turns soulful. He stares at the floor, runs his fingers through his hair, and starts. It begins slowly; you can almost hear the growing strings, the building drums. And then the chorus: 'Let me kiss your sadness, let me ease your pain – you are the one, and I'm in heaven again.'

Fucking brilliant. Not a great trope, but packed with longing and misery. I think only Enrique Iglesias could say it better. Actually, maybe not even him. It's got weddings and first dances and first snogs and first shags written all over it. I can feel my heart beating a little faster, my hands growing clammy. This one is cheesier than a fucking Swiss fondue, but it's a hit – I am sure of it.

'Brilliant, brilliant,' I say, coming over to shake Jerry's arm off. 'Bloody, bloody brilliant. You're a genius!'

Paul and Esther agree with me when I play them Jerry's tape later that afternoon. They both seem delighted.

'The last one's got number one written all over it,' says Paul. 'I can see that playing well at G-A-Y, which as you know is the litmus test of everything boy band.'

Esther nods. 'What do the boys think?'

'Who cares!' I say. 'This is what they're singing. Jerry's a well-known songwriter, he's doing brilliantly in the States, and it's only because we're mates that I have managed to get hold of him. They're bloody lucky to get anything this good.'

'Of course,' she smiles, 'but it would help if they liked it.'

'They will,' I say.

And they do. Or at least I present it in such a way that none of them is stupid enough to suggest that they don't. They all sit around the office nodding their heads in time to the music. Josh half closes his eyes and really feels it, thereby confirming his lead singer status. Mike and Billy sway from side to side clicking their fingers. They think they are joking, but little do they know that will be their role for the next eighteen months. I can see Nick frowning slightly, wondering where his back flip might fit in. He clearly doesn't realize this is not what the record is going to sound like at the end. Only Ashley is a little bit nonplussed. But he knows that since his mum signed his contract his family are expecting him to bring home the new car, the plasma, the BMX bikes and the Dolce & Gabbana handbags. He is now the family cash cow and he has fifteen long-lost relatives lining up to milk him.

'So this is it, guys,' I say. 'This is the band, this is what we're singing, and this is where all the hard work starts!'

There is much whooping and clapping and high-fiving.

'Yeah!' says Josh. 'Band of Five!'

'Band of Five!' says Mike, slapping palms with Josh.

Paul comes in. 'Congratulations!' he enthuses. 'Band of Five!' He clenches his fist, giving the air a small punch. 'Group hug!' He flings his arms open, expecting everyone to nuzzle in. Except they all stand back. No one wants a man-cuddle from

Paul. The moment has suddenly turned a bit sticky so I come over to do the honours.

'Come here, you fat bastard!' I say, slapping him playfully on the back. 'Thanks for all your help. What a team!' I walk up to each of the boys and slap them heartily too. Paul walks round and gives each of their shoulders a quick squeeze.

'Next stop—' he starts.

'The rehearsal room!' I finish.

A week later I turn up at Pineapple Dance Studios on Langley Street in Covent Garden. These sprung floors and large mirrored walls have seen more exhausted pop stars than the toilets at China White. Anyone who is anyone in the world of show has had their routines honed and their abs toned here, and Band of Five are no exception. Esther's had them thrusting and kicking and clapping and shaking their shoulders here for two days already. They've been practising some moves and singing along to Jerry's tunes. Paul and I had a brief conversation last week about trying to get in someone like Take That's choreographer Kim Gavin, or even *Strictly Come Dancing* judge Bruno Tonioli, who Paul knows well, to come and put them through their paces; but even at mates rates these guys are going to be at least a couple of grand a week and at the moment we are deal-less and penniless. I am forking out for everything. And anyway, Esther's got her percentage to think of, and if she's good enough for Simon and Louis, she's good enough for me. Plus she got us a bit of a discount at the studios, normally between £32 and £45 an hour. Every little bit helps.

I walk in to find them all covered in sweat, knocking back bottles of water. They have been on the go since eight a.m. this morning and now, at eleven, Esther is allowing them their first break. They all look very pink-cheeked and tired. Except Nick, of course, who is in his element.

'All right, boys?' I catch sight of my gut hanging over the top of my tight jeans. I try to pull it in, but my white shirt resolutely refuses to deflate. Now I know why Cowell favours the high waist: it helps keep the rolls in check. 'How are we all doing?'

'Great,' says Mike, wiping his mouth with the back of his hand.

'It's coming together,' says Esther when I join her. 'Some are more natural movers than others. But Josh is really working hard.'

'Josh?' I ask.

'Yes,' she says, her voice sounding a little tense. 'He's working hard.'

I look her in the eye. Is she really trying to tell me that Mr *Beverly Hills 90210* can't dance? She meets my stare with a round-eyed, slightly distressed look. Fuck, she is. We were all so excited to hear his voice and so admiring of his handsome bloody face and lack of body fat that we never asked him to move his arse. He looks like a dancer; he's got the body for it. He can't be as bad as she is making out.

'OK, guys, break over.' Esther claps her hands and paces around at the front of the studio. Dressed in a pair of tight black leggings and soft leather pumps, her dark hair scraped back into a ponytail, Esther looks the business and means pretty much the same. 'Get your arses down the front here and let's show the boss what you are made of.'

The boys file to the front and stand in a line, heads down, legs slightly apart, hands by their sides. Josh is in the middle at the front, flanked by Ashley and Nick; Mike and Billy are on either side of them. It is the first time I have seen them together like this, as a band, and they don't look shit. In fact, they look good. Well, not Hear'say embarrassing anyway. As manufactured bands go, they really were the bottom of the food chain. I don't know whether it was the Shrek boy or the chubby dark one who did it for me, but somehow they didn't look like they belonged with those relatively attractive women. They were unwatchable. Yet Band of Five look like they work.

Esther turns on the music. It's Beyoncé's 'Crazy'.

'OK, one, two, three, and . . . Oh, oh, oh, oh . . .'

Esther's shoulders are moving up and down. The boys copy her. I look on. They are all in time, except for Josh. They jump up and down in time to the beat, moving three steps to the left and three to the right. Josh goes the wrong way on the wrong beat.

'Left! Left! Left!' shouts Esther. 'It's not fucking rocket science, Josh. It's not like I've changed the steps. We've been doing this since eight this morning.'

'I'm sorry,' he says, shaking his head wearily. 'I just panic and go the wrong way.'

'OK!' she says, clapping her hands together again and striding back to the sound system. 'Get back in line.'

There's some sighing and shooting of fucked-off looks towards Josh before they line up again. Heads down, arms by their sides.

'And, ready? From the top.'

Cue Beyoncé. Cue the shoulders. Cue the jumps to the left and the right.

'Good! Josh, great! Keep going! Keep going!'

Josh is so goddamn pleased that he's managed to get over the first hurdle, he forgets what he is doing next.

'Slides, Josh! Slides! To the left. To the right. Arms, Josh! Arms!'

Poor bastard. I have seen enough. I don't know what is going to break first today, Josh's will or Esther voice's. It is very obviously going to end with someone in tears. I walk over to Esther, put my arm around her and steer her over to the side of the room. In the mirrors I can see the boys anxiously staring at us.

'So, what d'you think?'

'Well,' she says, stroking her forehead and looking at the floor, 'four of them can dance.'

'Right.'

'Josh is about as mobile as my Labrador, and she's got degenerative arthritis.'

'Can you fix it?'

'That depends on him,' she says. 'He's worse than the Barlow, you know.'

'I think he's looking quite good these days.'

'He's worked his arse off,' she mutters. 'They're in ice baths every night, those guys. Straight off stage into freezing water. To stop the build-up of lactic acid.'

'What, in those jaded thirtysomething joints?' I say sarcastically.

'Exactly,' she nods.

'God, what happened to the days of coming off stage and relaxing over a groupie?' I smile.

'What?' she asks, looking at me like I'm an arse. 'There's far too much money involved these days to twat around like that. They can't afford injuries and things like that. Look what happened to Howard.'

'Look indeed,' I say with a shrug.

'He broke a rib?' Esther prompts. 'Doing a back flip on stage.'

'Anyway – Josh,' I say.

'Well, if he is willing to work I am sure I can teach him the routines. But he's got to want it.'

'Josh?' I say turning round.

The boy goes white. His face looks hollow and haunted. 'Yes?' His voice cracks slightly.

'Come over here.'

He walks over as the others gather together and whisper behind him.

'Right, listen,' I say, putting my hand on his shoulder. 'We have a bit of a problem here.'

'Yes.' He sounds quiet.

'You are not the best dancer in the group,' I say.

'No.'

'So, if you are going to stay in the group, you've got to make the effort, put in the extra hours and practise, practise, practise.'

'OK,' he says, his shoulder hunching underneath my hand.

'So, will you do it?'

'Yeah,' he nods.

'You've got to be sure.'

'No, right, yeah,' he says.

'Because if you don't really want it, I can find someone else.'

'No, I do want it,' he says, turning to look at me, his blue eyes flashing with determination. 'I really want it.'

'You've got to want it badly, Josh, because you are going to have to be working your arse off when Micky here is sitting with his feet up watching TV.'

'Micky?'

'Mike, I mean Mike. You're not a natural mover.'

'No,' he says.

'But you can sing, which is the hard part.' I smile, and pat him on the back. 'So get back there and nail the dancing.'

'Right,' he nods, turning back towards the others.

'Don't let me down, Josh.'

'You won't regret this,' he says, walking back to the group, clenching his fist at me.

'He looks determined,' I mutter out of the side of my mouth.

'He's going to need to be,' Esther replies.

A week later Josh still seems determined. I have booked the band into a recording studio in Soho to get a demo tape and a backing track together, and he is the first to arrive. We are booked in for five twelve-hour days, and so far, at the ten a.m. call time, he's the only one who has turned up. As we both sit on the pale purple sofa staring at the matching pool table, I try to do a few sums.

I'm subbing each of the boys £50 a week at the moment, basically so that they can get to and from work, eat a sandwich and not get pissed. Craig, whose reckless idea this was in the first place, insisted that I should keep them on a budget 'as tight as a gnat's chuff'. He went on to explain that, in the tradition that is Take That's ex-manager, Nigel Martin-Smith, Walsh and Watkins, if you keep your band just above the breadline, they will behave like good worker bees and turn up for work; shower them with cash and they'll be down China White and knocking on the door of Boujis before you can say 'one-hit wonder'. The studio is costing me £600 a day plus VAT, including the engineer, and the dance studio set me back a couple of grand too in the end. By my calculation, including legal fees and other sundries, I'll be in about £10K on Band of Five and I have yet to make a squeak. I have been putting my feelers out, but I have got to get something together for people in the business to hear and see before we can dream of meeting our currently disinterested public. So this week is about getting some tracks down, working out some harmonies for Jerry's songs and putting something together to show to a tour manager. It is time my show ponies started to earn their keep. Or at least not cost me so goddamn much.

The rest of the boys are not far behind Josh and are

brimming with energy and excitement. The look on each of their faces when they take in the pool table, the football table, the Xbox, the drinks, the snacks, the magazines, the sexy velour upholstery and the dark lighting is priceless. They can't believe their luck.

'Oh my God!' says Mike, running his car-thieving hands all over the soft furnishing. 'Feel this shit!'

'Look at the snacks,' says Ashley. 'Crisps and everything.'

'And games,' grins Billy, raising his thick dark eyebrows.

'Not that there will be time for that sort of thing,' I add hastily. 'Studio days are expensive, lads, and the clock is ticking.'

Normally, as a manager I wouldn't spend much time in the studio with one of my acts, but that presupposes they know what they're doing. Usually they know what they want to sing, they've written or at least co-written the songs, and they spend as long or as short a time as they want recording their album. If the studio is close by, I will pop in and out, occasionally offering my support, ideas or ears. If it is out of town, I wouldn't normally bother them. I'd only offer my extremely valuable opinion when the track is emailed, or biked over to my office.

It is, however, in bands' interest not to dally too much in the studio as they have to pay for their own recording costs as they are recoupable against any future royalty payments on album sales. And then, in a quirk that is peculiar to the record industry, it is the record company and not the artist that owns the masters. One artist once complained to me that it was akin to the bank still owning the house after the mortgage had been paid, or indeed movie stars having to pay for the cost of a film they'd appeared in and then giving the rights to the company that distributed it. And everyone wonders why the record business is in a bad way at the moment, when they treat their assets with such obvious 'respect'.

Having said that, I am planning to be just as mercenary. I am paying for these recordings so the rights to them at the end of the week will be mine and mine alone – with Jerry, Paul and Esther taking their percentages, of course. But at the moment we all have a cut of nothing, which is worth less than nothing.

Jerry arrives with his guitar over his shoulder and beanie hat pulled over his head. I always think there is something rather suspect about a man beyond the age of thirty-five who still tries this hard to be hip. The band, however, give him the full backslapping, finger-clicking, high-five welcome and we all head off to Studio One.

The boys and Jerry crowd in on one side of the glass while I settle down on the other side with the engineer. In his early thirties with long lank hair in a centre parting, he seems an amiable enough chap. He shakes my hand and introduces himself as Rob.

'What are you after?' he asks, flicking various switches and buttons up and down on what looks like the flight deck of the starship *Enterprise*.

'They're a boy band,' I say, gesturing towards the glass at the boys, who are wandering around the soundproof room saying things like 'Woo! Wow! Can you believe it? So this is what it's like'.

'This a microphone?' asks Nick, going over to tap the top of it.

Rob flicks a switch and barks, 'Step away from that!', his voice booming through the speakers. 'This is delicate equipment.'

Everyone stops and stares at the glass. They squint in the light and cover their eyes.

'Can you hear us?' asks Mike.

'Yes,' says Rob. 'We can hear every word. It's you who can't hear us.'

'Oh,' nods Nick. 'So that's how it works.'

'The room is soundproofed,' continues Rob, leaning forward and tucking his long hair behind his ears, 'so we can make as much noise as we like in here and no one can hear us. Equally, we can't hear the street outside.'

Jerry is setting up his guitar and getting into position behind a mike.

'You ready in there?' he asks. 'I think if I just lay down a quick vocal with the guitar then we've got something to run with. Yeah?' He nods towards me.

I lean forward and flick the switch. 'Good idea, Jerry, and then I think it would be helpful for you to come this side. Then we can get going on putting some stuff together.'

Jerry lays down all three tracks with professional speed. He does have a nice voice, but it is not powerful enough to fill an arena. Then again, the same goes for some of the biggest stars around. There are plenty of big names who are excellent lip-synchers; just ask Madonna, Justin Timberlake, Britney Spears and 50 Cent. I remember a mate of mine who went to the Spice Girls gig in Istanbul telling me he was having a chat with one of the sound engineers who showed him the six mike feeds for the show – one each for the girls and one for 'live studio' atmosphere that was to be played over the bits that weren't live. They'd book-end each song with a bit of live chat, cut to the recording with live studio atmosphere, then cut back to the girls at the end. It's an old TV studio trick used the whole world over. Especially when your acts have to sing and dance as much as the Spices did, or indeed do. It's hard work singing and dancing for two hours without puffing and panting down the mike.

As Jerry packs up his guitar and moves over to our side of the glass, I resist the temptation to ask Rob what he thinks of the songs. Recently my shrink has been telling me to stop being so needy, seeking the approval of the wrong people while ignoring the needs of those closest to me – i.e. my daughter. And anyway, he's a middle-aged bloke. He is bound to hate what we are doing.

Jerry pushes his backside against the heavy door and enters.

'Thanks, man, that was great,' says Rob, not bothering to look up. He is flicking switches and checking red lights and making sure he's storing it all somewhere. 'OK,' he nods to me, 'what would you like to do first?'

'I'm thinking "Brief Love" first,' I say.

'Is that the first one he sang?' he asks.

'That's right.'

'A ballad, then?' he asks.

I nod.

'Are they all singing?'

'Nope,' I say. 'The two lads on the end are on dead mikes.'

'Which two?' he asks, looking down at mission control.

I point Billy and Mike out. 'Dark moody handsome one and the short cheeky one. The tall sporty one will need a lot of filters and tweaking.'

'OK,' he says, switching them off.

'Christ,' mutters Jerry.

'What?' I say, turning round.

'That's a bit harsh,' he says.

'They'll learn,' I reply. 'Craig told me that half of Boyzone are off playing golf when they record their albums; someone else does backing vocals. I think that's kind of a good deal myself.'

Jerry shrugs and cracks open a can of Coke. What does he care? Anything to make the thing a hit.

The boys line up behind their mikes. Rob plays out the melody using Jerry's guitar.

'Can we add some drums to that?' I ask.

'How about that?' asks Rob as a tsk-tsk-tsk disco beat starts up.

'And strings?' I suggest, looking at Jerry.

'That would be nice,' he says, over the top of his can. 'And maybe some brass? You know, jolly it up a bit.'

'D'you think?' asks Rob, looking decidedly turned off by the idea.

'It's worth a go,' Jerry responds with a shrug. 'But then, you know, I only wrote the thing.'

About forty minutes later and Rob, Jerry and I have come up with some sort of backing track for the guys to sing to. It doesn't sound fantastically sophisticated but then what else can you expect in such a short period? Anyway, we're only after demo quality at the moment. When Band of Five are signed and sealed they'll get the full sexy Mark Ronson remix treatment.

'OK?' I announce through the intercom.

The boys leap to their feet, itching to get on with it. Their expectant faces peer through the glass.

'Yes?' asks Josh. 'Are we ready?'

'Yup,' I say. 'OK, so for this song I thought we'd try out Josh in the middle and Ashley and Nick either side with you other guys on the end, and we'll see how that goes. Then we'll move it around and mix it up.'

They all nod and smile.

'What d'you mean, mix it up?' asks Jerry as I sit down.

'You've got to make the passengers think they've got a chance at the top,' I say. 'It's good for morale. You can't say the line-up is fixed, otherwise no one would try.'

'I see your point,' he sniffs.

'Ready?' asks Rob. The boys nod. 'Here goes.'

'So, Josh, just to make it clear, you're lead vocals and, boys, you're on the la-la-las,' I say.

'Here goes, then, again,' says Rob, rather pointedly. 'One, two . . .' He nods the three and cues the music.

We spend the whole day trying to nail 'Brief Love'. Josh was great and gave his all at each and every take; the other boys faded and lost interest as the day wore on. We filled them full of junk food and fizzy drinks in an attempt to keep their energy levels up and every so often we let them loose on the pool table to sink some balls and let off steam. Twelve-hour shifts are long and arduous if you aren't used to them; it's hard to keep people focused on the job. Jerry fell asleep at one point during late afternoon only to be caught snoring loudly by Mike, who managed to get three balls of paper into his open gob before he woke up in a fit of choking.

It's eight in the evening now and not even Red Bull can stop them from yawning, so I decide to call it a day. There is only so far I can push them and expect them to bounce back the next day.

'D'you think we've nailed something?' I ask Rob as he chucks a load of crisp packets in the bin.

'It's hard to tell,' he says. 'I won't know until we mix later in the week.'

Tuesday passes in a similar fashion, except we have a go at 'To My Manor Born' and the atmosphere is a little more subdued. Come Wednesday and the passengers are beginning to get well and truly bored. It's clear there is only so much oohing, aahing and yeah-yeah-yeahing you can do before you lose the will to live. I'm amazed they've managed to get to day three before beginning to dick around. But it's now hard to get Mike off the sofa, Billy is just shovelling in crisps for want of something better to do, and Nick's mobile is bleeping either with messages he's sending or games he's playing.

'OK, then,' I say, 'time to mix things up a bit. Nick, you're on lead vocals. Mike, you're playing second, and Josh and Ashley, you're backing.'

Billy looks at me, his mouth full of cheese and onion crisps. 'What about me?' he asks, crumbs flying everywhere.

'You're next up.' I turn and look at Rob, sitting beside me. Checking that the open mike is off, I add, 'This should be fucking awful.'

Actually, it's worse. Nick can't hold a note, Mike can't find one, and when I let Billy have a go, Rob loses all decorum and ends up sniggering quietly into his long lank hair.

'Jesus,' he says to me, 'I've heard some crap in my time, but they are bad.'

'I know,' I say. 'But they look good, and they can move.'

Thursday evening is the lowest point. Band of Five practically hit the floor. No amount of e-numbers, cheap sweets or line-up changes can lift their spirits, so I resort to another form of spirit – namely, alcohol. I call Jerry and get him to bring in some beers. He is on strict instructions not to be too generous as exhaustion, teenagers and booze are not the most creative combination.

We all gather round the purple pool table and attempt a

bonding game, sipping our beers and chilling out before one last attempt at 'When You Find the One'.

'I had no idea people worked so hard in pop music,' announces Mike, bent over the cushion, one eye closed. 'I thought it was sex, drugs and more sex.'

'You lot have barely started,' says Jerry. 'I've got this mate who was working for Simon Fuller in the States and he said you should see how hard they work those *American Idol* guys. Jordin Sparks was doing ten a.m. to three a.m. trying to get her album done. They had two weeks to do it and get it out as it was dropping on November twentieth, which was the Friday before Thanksgiving.'

'Black Friday, the most lucrative day of the year for sales,' I add.

'That's right,' he nods. 'It's the day everyone from Puffy to Prince releases. If you mean business, you're a Black Friday release. And Jordin means business: they had pre-orders for over a million records.'

'That Simon Fuller is so fucking clever he even managed to sell the Americans back the American dream,' I say. 'I mean, that's the all-American dream, isn't it? To come from nothing and make it big and famous with loads of money. No wonder they love it so much.'

'I know,' agrees Jerry. 'And the acts have got to love it too. Otherwise you'd never be able to put up with the dietician, the nutritionist, the pushy mother doling out Ritalin . . . I know of one star who worked so hard her tongue swelled up from singing and she couldn't hit a note. So they ended up having to inject her tongue with steroids to bring the swelling down.'

'Shit!' says Josh, covering his mouth with his hand. 'That's disgusting.'

'Think yourself lucky.' I smile. 'Now, finish your beers, we've got one more track to finish.'

The beer and Jerry's talk do the trick. The boys pull something a bit special out of the bag. Josh actually manages to get the hairs on my arms to stand up – either that or someone's turned the air con up too high. All I know is that Rob says 'yes' under his breath and punches the air gently before saying to me, 'That's the one.'

Come ten o'clock the following night I have the masters in my hands. Rob is looking exhausted, having spent the whole day at his mixing desk, tweaking the vocals and adding beats and flourishes to make our demo tapes sound like something that could actually chart. He's also given me a digitally mastered backing track that the boys can sing to live.

As I walk out into the cool night air and on to the beer- and vomit-stained streets of Soho, I can't control the grin on my face and the spring in my stride. I am beginning to feel that this boy band thing could be possible. Cowell doesn't have the monopoly on putting things together. Fuller, Martin-Smith, Walsh, the whole lot of them will be taking notes when they hear there's a new Svengali on the block. I march around the corner to Soho House and order myself a very large vodka to celebrate. Next stop, the tour.

'Croydon is a good place to start,' declares Tony, scratching his balls in my office early the following Monday. 'I need to hear the lads first before I take them on, but failing them being a complete unmitigated fucking disaster, I don't see why not.'

At five foot three Tony's a small lad with a big personality and a totally bald head. He's an ex-security guard turned tour manager who's been in the business for years. He's packed with energy, stories and scams. He's always got a sparkle in his eyes and a couple of grams in his back pocket, and he's the perfect bloke to take Band of Five on the road.

'We'll start with the schools,' he sniffs, putting his bloody great boots up on my desk.

What is it about tour managers that they always have to dress as if they're 'on tour'? Tony's wearing boots, shorts (even though it's early May and still freezing), some shit promotional T-shirt, a khaki waistcoat covered in handy pockets; and a pair of reflector shades sit on top of his shiny head. You can practically see the backstage laminates swinging around his neck.

'Schools?' I repeat.

'Where did you fucking think we'd start, Wembley fucking Arena?' he asks, throwing back his domed head, laughing loudly and clapping his hands.

'I thought maybe gay clubs?'

'Gay clubs?' He laughs and claps again. 'Well, we can do the gays, but they tend to need a bit more of an act, something slick, whereas teenage girls will scream at bloody anything. Don't get me wrong. I'm sure your lads are fine and that, but the schools tour, as you know, is all about learning, honing, gelling, and then you're ready for the gays, when you've got a bit of an act – d'you see what I mean?' He belches. 'Jesus, don't you just hate it when last night's curry repeats on you?'

Rather than hang around and discuss Tony's digestive habits, I suggest we go down to Pineapple Studios to watch the boys do a small set so that he can check them over. There is a small possibility that Tony might refuse to take them on tour, but it is slight as I know he's between bands at the moment and for £500 cash a week plus expenses he'd quite frankly tour my accountant.

'I'll tell you what I miss,' he says, his head just poking over the top of the steering wheel of his people-mover. 'The *Smash Hits* tours. Those were the days, eh? Screaming girls, boy bands, no one being able to hear a thing. It was the best way to launch a new band. D'you know, after a Take That concert in the early days they used to have to sluice down the seating as so many girls had wet themselves?'

'Jesus,' I say, in response to both the anecdote and Tony's driving.

'I really do miss them,' he says again. 'It's much harder now, you know. The *X Factor* tour has sort of taken over the teen-scream stuff. You've still got the Girl Guides at Wembley Arena, I suppose. The noise is deafening.' He grins and looks at me.

'Careful!' I shout as he narrowly misses a cyclist.

'Thing is,' he continues, barely acknowledging his near-murderous experience, 'you think your band has made it until some fat-arsed roadie comes out on stage to change the mike and they scream just as loudly for him. They're hormonally crazy!'

I grip the edge of the velour seat all the way into Soho. The knuckles on my hands glow white as I listen to Tony tell me about the matinée performances he's done with Steps and Blue. The shows would start at noon and babes in arms would be brought along to listen.

'I mean, this is the big pop conundrum, isn't it?' he says, Braille-parking his car into a space outside the studios. 'How can you be cool when you're playing to a one-year-old in a babygro on a Tuesday afternoon? Then again, do you need to be cool when you're selling out Wembley Arena?'

'Mmm,' is all I can manage as I sit rigid in the front seat. I'm not sure I'm going to survive a week with this nutcase at the wheel.

Inside the studio the boys look great. Esther has managed to borrow some baggy jeans and sweat tops from a mate of hers who's the PR from some trendy clothes line or other. All I know is that they look like they might mug you, but perhaps with a bit more style than the usual crack-smoking hoodie you find hanging around the off-licence. Anyway, Tony seems impressed.

'Good, good,' he says, striding around in front of them, eyeing them up and down like some sergeant major. 'You look great,' he smiles, standing in front of Josh, coming up to his chest. 'But can you sing?'

'Of course they can,' says Esther, nodding to each of them, turning on the CD backing track and counting them in with her index finger.

Josh starts to sing the opening lines to 'Brief Love' and the others do the bouncing shoulders and slides. 'La, la, la,' they sing, clicking their fingers as they move into a quick hitch kick and then stand with their legs slightly apart. They all join in the chorus: 'My love for you in heaven grows, I love you my melting, my melting rose.' They've got some sort of thing going on during the chorus, with their arms above their heads. It's a simple enough move that even Josh can join in with. Esther's done me proud, I think as I lean against the mirror in the studio. They're shit, but they're good shit.

They finish in a line with their heads down. Tony starts to clap, and laughs loudly. 'Great, lads, great,' he says. 'I don't know what the fuck a melting rose is, but the girls will lap it up. Lap it up!'

Band go on to perform the other two songs. 'When You Find the One' works better than 'To My Manor Born', which is still a little too upbeat for my liking. But Nick pulls off a neat back flip back somersault which makes Tony whoop, and out of the corner of my eye I swear I see his foot tapping along. But 'When You Find the One' is definitely the best song, even if Tony checks his watch halfway through it.

'Great, great, great,' he says, shooting a fake punch at each member of the band. 'This is gooooood,' he says to me. 'No problemo.'

That afternoon Tony comes back with some ideas and figures for me to play with. He is proposing between three and five gigs a day for a week. He'll collect the boys between five and six a.m. in his people-mover then drive to, say, Wolverhampton where they'll do a gig during morning assembly. It'll take between ten and fifteen minutes to do, and then they'll be back in the car to get to another school for mid-morning break, and then lunchtime, and then one more after school. He says he can slip in a few local radio stations while they're at it. By the end of the week he's hoping the boys will be slick enough to take in an underage disco in a church hall or community centre, and perhaps a couple of gay clubs on a Friday and Saturday night.

Over the phone he talks me through a list of schools where he's got permission from the head to perform. 'They're all state,' he says. 'Comps mostly; the privates tend not to let you in. The lads might be asked to do some Q and A after the show, you know, to sort of pretend it's, like, educational, and then what we're after is emails.'

'OK,' I say, not quite understanding what he's saying. 'Emails?'

'Yeah, email addresses, so that we can get the girls while they're young and bombard them with shit about the band. Who's doing what. What Josh's favourite colour is. You need blogs.'

'They won't have time to write blogs!'

'Of course they won't. You write them, Paul writes them, your receptionist writes them. My old assistant used to sign all Posh Spice's fucking headshots or autographs when she worked for an old plugging company. "Dear Sick Child, Get better soon – love Posh". Simple.'

'I see,' I say.

'And then, when you've got your first single ready to go

you've got a fan base that's gagging for it.' He inhales. 'Do you have a MySpace page yet?'

With so much to think about and so many bases still to cover, I am pleased to be snoozing in the front of Tony's people-mover on the way up the M1 to Wolverhampton, despite the quality of his driving. I have successfully managed to delegate all the computer stuff and the viral marketing to Paul, Debbie and her mate Gordon, who is apparently brilliant with websites and blogs and creating a buzz on MySpace, which has become as much a music biz staple these days as trying to get bands to play on *Later . . . with Jools Holland*. Who'd have thought it?

All the boys are fast asleep in the back. Tony jigs up and down in the driver's seat, having downed too many espresso shots or one too many lines of cocaine.

'They need media training, you know,' he says. 'You've got to have media training these days.' He pauses briefly before continuing – not that he needs any response from me. 'Kate Thornton used to do it, you know. When she was the editor of *Smash Hits* it was one of her sidelines helping groups fill in those tricky questionnaire things. She did Westlife and Boyzone but refused to do Take That because she was so busy. Of all the groups to pass on, eh?' He laughs and claps one hand on his thigh. 'Do your boys have any skeletons in their closet?' he asks. 'Have you had a rattle around? I mean, you don't want a Kerry Katona whose mother gave her lines of speed when she was fourteen and who slept with her boyfriend and beat him up just to prove how bad he was.'

'I suppose not,' I say, suddenly feeling a little worried. We haven't checked out the boys or where they come from at all.

'Or you could have a Shayne Ward.' Tony roars with laughter. 'Imagine the amount of shit that hit the fan that day at fucking Syco Records when the press discovered that Shayne's father and cousin were in prison for raping an OAP. Not one gerontophile rapist in the family, but two! You couldn't make it up.'

He pulls up outside what appears to be a large inner-city comprehensive. There's graffiti on the walls, rubbish on the streets, and CCTV cameras everywhere. It looks rough. The building is a sixties mess of glass and steel and inner-city planning, the antithesis to Holly's cosy private school palace in North Hampstead. I am tempted to tell Tony to forget it and drive on. This is not the sort of place that is going to appreciate five boys disco-dancing to a backing track.

'Wake up, lads, we're here,' chivvies Tony over his shoulder. 'We've got about half an hour to set up and get ourselves together.'

There's some moaning, stretching and yawning coming from the back.

'We here then?' asks Mike, looking out of the window.

'Looks like it,' says Ashley.

'Come on, guys,' says Tony, 'it's show time!'

He gets out of the people-mover, stretches his legs and opens the boot. He takes out a gym bag, unzips it, and pulls out a handful of something.

'Here you go,' he says, sliding back the side door.

'What's that?' asks Josh.

'Socks,' Tony replies.

'Socks?' asks Nick.

'Yeah,' says Tony, handing them round. 'I've got you a pair each. Pop them down the front of your trousers.' He winks. 'Gives you a great big cock.'

5

Against all the odds, Band of Five were not murdered at the comp in Wolverhampton. We set up during the headmaster's address in main assembly and, I think due to the fact that the usual God squad proceedings were cut short and they didn't have to sing 'Onward Christian Soldiers', the audience were appreciative. There were a couple of pockets of resistance at the back, where groups of surly, pimply lads sneered and jeered, but they were drowned out by the cheers and screams of their female contemporaries. And while the boys sat at the front answering questions that ranged from 'What's it like being famous?' and 'Have you met anyone famous?' to 'Do you have a girlfriend?' I passed round a clipboard and pen to collect anyone and everyone's email address. I shook hands with the headmaster before leaving and promised to bring the boys back once they'd made it. Our first gig without Esther.

Our first gig outside the studio. Our first gig as a real band and they weren't absolutely terrible. I feel a small glow of pride as we leave.

Walking out of the gates, I have to say, I'm not sure I'd be too pleased if my child attended that school. I left with the personal emails of a hundred-odd children to whom I am about to try to flog all sorts of shit. Then again, I thought as I sat back in the people-mover, with Holly nearly grown up and my input having been a big fat zero, it is kind of late in the day to come over all responsible parent.

We moved on to the next school and things were a little easier. I think the boys were less nervous and the school was altogether a little less threatening, less populated by hoodies. I collected another fifty or so email addresses and we got back into the car and pressed on.

Throughout the week, Tony was amazing. It's far too expensive to put an unsigned band up anywhere for the night, so not only did he drive us everywhere, he dropped us all off at our homes every night. He also never lost his temper once. And just when the boys were flagging, thinking they couldn't get all excited about singing the same three songs with the same moves in front of another group of embarrassed, squealing schoolgirls, he'd come out with some sort of story.

'Freddie Mercury's party was the best I've ever been to,' he'd say out of the blue. 'They were legendary, mainly because there were so many drugs going down. I remember going once and they had these shaven-headed dwarves handing round the coke on little silver platters like vols-au-vent. There was piles of the stuff, and they handed you this silver straw to help you snort it. By the end of the night – well, the next morning – Freddie was telling people to do it off the top of their shiny heads.'

'At last, a use for your big slaphead,' I said.

'Good idea,' he agreed, pulling up outside a radio station.

There were only two glitches on the tour. One was when the backing track broke down completely during the second song; the boys had to carry on singing regardless of the lack of music. And the second was radio. For a group of chatting lads there was nothing more guaranteed to shut them up than the red glow of a studio light. Happy to talk endlessly about themselves in the car, but as soon as anyone asked them anything a little more tricky than what their names were and where they came from, they all clammed up. We did four local stations, one hospital radio and a download that I'm sure will be languishing in cyberspace for some years without so much as a sniff of interest. And all the results were the stammering, monosyllabic same. Media training is definitely something I am going to organize as soon as I get these boys signed. I could always ring up Ms Thornton, now that she is a little less occupied these days, but I think it's something the record company can fork out for.

Friday night was the pièce de résistance of the week. Tony managed to blag us a spot just before midnight at Loving It, a gay club night in a place in Birmingham. Backstage in a changing room that was similar in size to the people-mover we'd been in all week, the boys were nervous and exhausted. They shoved in their sixth or seventh Big Mac meal in so many days and listened to Tony trying to gee them up.

'Just enjoy it,' he said. 'You know it now, so enjoy it. That's the main thing. Also, you should flirt with the boys in there.'

'Really?' said Mike.

'They know you're not gay, but that's not the point, is it? I know I'm not going to get to fuck Kylie, but I still want her to shake her arse at me on stage and fill me with promise. It's all about promise.'

'OK,' nodded Nick, taking it all on board. 'Is there room for me to do a back flip?'

'I haven't managed to have a look, but if not, improvise.'

'Improvise?'

'Here,' I said, producing a bottle of vodka and handing it round. 'A couple of swigs each should do it.'

And it sure as hell did. They were great. We changed the order of the set so that they started out with 'To My Manor Born' and ended on 'When You Find the One'. The dancing went to pot. Josh forgot entirely what he was doing, but Mike just went for it and flirted and toyed with the punters at the front like a pro. Nick didn't manage to get his back flip in; there was barely enough room for them to stand and dance in a row, let alone for any of his acrobatics. They were as high as Pete Doherty when they came off stage. Their faces shone, their eyes were luminous, and they couldn't stop talking. 'Did you see that?' 'It was amazing.' 'I can't believe I did that, and then you did that.' It was like all the shouting and the hard work and the sitting in the back of a car for a week had been worth it. They were loving it, and it was great to see. The club promoter was so pleased he asked us out front for a drink and to meet some of the crowd. He even gave me a £50 fee, which of course I pocketed. There is no point in sharing that with the band.

'There'll be groupies next,' said Tony when we were driving back down the motorway in the early hours. 'God, I remember a story about Mötley Crüe. They were always surrounded by groupies, and there was this particularly fat one who followed them around in the early days. She was obsessed with Tommy and would hang around every night wanting stuff signed, that sort of thing. Then one day, as they were getting back into the bus, they saw her driving off in her own red Ferrari. No one could believe it. So the next time she came to a gig and asked them to sign something Tommy said, "I'll shag you if you let me drive your car." So the woman said yes and Tommy and she went off together backstage. As he left, Tommy said to the bass player, "I won't be long, come and get me in twenty minutes." Half an hour later the bass player went backstage to see this fat woman riding up and down on Tommy's cock, yelling "Ahhhh!" And just as she came, Tommy put his hand out and said, "Keys." ' Tony laughed and slapped his thigh. 'Keys!' he repeated.

I turned round to look at the band's reaction. They were all fast asleep.

It was around five a.m. when Tony finally dropped me off. The birds were breaking into song, the sky was turning pale and my eyes were stinging with tiredness. I gave Tony his £500 in cash and thanked him for a great week.

'Drive carefully,' I said.

'Yeah,' he yawned. 'This is always the dangerous bit, at the end of it all, when you've got no one to talk to, no one to keep you awake. A mate of mine died recently doing just this. Drove himself off the road.'

Despite my exhaustion I didn't manage to relax until I got Tony's text telling me he'd arrived home safely. I can see why this touring is addictive, I thought as my head hit the pillow. You can get quite close in a week.

It's Monday now, and quite frankly the weekend's not been long enough. I have yet to recover. I am practically hosing myself down at my desk with double-shot lattes in the hope of waking up my brain. I am checking and re-checking my emails, all of which seem to be about Viagra, pile cream, laxatives and cheap Rolex watches. Unsurprisingly, I'm at an age when these bargain offers are beginning to pique my interest. I am on the point of purchasing a $25 starter pack of purple pills when Paul rushes into my office to tell me the new Band of Five website's gone 'mad'.

'Mad?' I say, slouching forward over my desk. 'How mad?'

'Oh my God!' he says, clutching his chest in excitement. 'We've had forty hits this morning!'

'Forty?'

'I know!' he nods.

'That's hardly going to launch us to number one, is it?'

'Well,' Paul says, sounding a little bit hurt, 'I thought it was rather good.'

'It is, it is,' I say, trying to be nice. 'Well done.'

'There's definitely a buzz happening,' says Paul, turning to flounce out of the room. 'Check out the MySpace page if you don't believe me. Everyone's playing the records.'

It turns out it's not quite everyone, but 'Brief Love' has been listened to forty-three times; 'To My Manor Born' is in the hundreds, and 'When You Find the One' is almost one thousand. Could that be construed as a buzz? Are Band of Five the new Sandi Thom? The new Lily Allen, who had garnered so much interest she just had to be signed? Or could I just spin it that way? There is surely enough of an interest to get a show-case together. The boys are no longer totally green; they have some experience under their low-slung belts. I decide to give my A&R friend Craig a call to ask for advice.

That afternoon he saunters into The Electric looking exactly the same colour as he was the last time we met. Except this time, due to the tiny pair of white shorts he's wearing, there is more opportunity for me to appreciate the profound depths of his mahogany colour.

'Mate, mate, mate,' he says, waving his hips and swinging his tennis racket, 'check this out.' He takes a step forward with one neon white shoe and executes a swift backhand motion, narrowly missing a passing waiter. 'Isn't that the best action you've ever seen?'

'Very good,' I say, holding my temples. Craig's already giving me a headache.

'Good?' he exclaims. 'It's fucking brilliant! And so it should be. It's cost me five grand.'

'Five grand?'

'Tennis coaching, mate. It's the thing these days, and it's fucking addictive.' He stands upright and sniffs, tensing his arms. 'Everyone's doing it. In fact I'm thinking of chucking in the music biz towel and opening up a tennis centre in Marbella. What d'you think?'

'Try not to do it before the end of today,' I sigh. 'I want to pick your brains about Band of Five.'

'Band of Five? Haven't you come up with anything better yet?' he asks, plonking himself down on a purple velvet pouffe in front of me. His legs are wide open and I can see the string bag that contains his balls.

'Pop 'em away, Craig,' I say, nodding towards his bollocks.

'Oh, sorry,' he says, looking down and tweaking his jewels back into his shorts. 'They've been seeing some action, these babies,' he grins. 'I've been dipping my pen in the company's ink. Now that I am no longer chemically challenged I can't get enough of it.'

'You should hook up with Suzy,' I suggest.

'Oh, songwriter Suzy,' he says, like he is seriously thinking it might be a good idea. 'Did she give you anything good?'

'Sadly, no.'

'Oh. She's good. Cranberry juice!' he barks at a passing waiter, before stretching his hairy brown legs towards me. 'So, how can I help?'

Craig spends the rest of the afternoon wading through the contents of his BlackBerry and SIM card. He suggests a whole load of A&R mates he says might be interested. The boy band market is obviously very different from the indie scene and any of the usual contacts I have are far too hairy and earnest for such a venture, and they would also not take me seriously. Craig comes up with the slightly retrograde idea of Nomis Studios around the corner for the showcase.

'I can't tell you how many times I've been there after a big fat lunch and a bag of nose candy.' He laughs so enthusiastically his white trainers leave the floor. 'It's all so fucking political. You go in, one at a time – Sony, EMI, Warner's, Island, Polydor – then the poor bastards sing, and then you walk straight out again. Or if you're Tracy Bennett you walk straight in, and straight out again.'

'What, the bloke who ran London Records?' I ask.

Craig clicks his fingers at me over his fourth cranberry juice.

'You don't need to do a showcase if you don't want to,' he says. 'There are other ways. I remember one girl and her manager coming to my office. She took all her clothes off and everyone gathered round to listen as she sang totally starkers.'

'Did you sign her?'

'No, don't be stupid,' he smiles. 'She had a cracking pair of Harveys, though.'

'Didn't the Spice Girls showcase at Nomis?'

'I think so,' he says. 'I think it would be a good idea. Show that you're serious. Put a bit of effort into it. You can control things a bit more than if you take them to a gig.'

'There is always something so goddamn depressing about showcases though,' I sigh. 'I mean, you sit there looking at this pretty girl and this nice-looking bloke and they are dancing away fronting some band and you think, You've got two singles in you, one shit album, and maybe a few TV appearances. You can see it in their eyes – this is my moment, this is my moment – and part of you thinks, No, love, why don't you do us all a favour and fuck off home?'

Craig just stares me, a puzzled look on his craggy face. 'Have you been at the gear?' he asks.

'What?'

'Is it come-down Monday or something?' he asks. 'I have never heard such a load of depressing old nonsense in my life. Everyone knows you can't get music on TV these days.'

I laugh. He's absolutely right. Half the problem with trying to break a new band these days is that there is nowhere to promote them. *Top of the Pops* is dead, and Saturday-morning kids TV is no more; the days of rock bands staying up all night doing coke, Es and acid only to be interviewed by a giant pink bird are over. Even MTV, which pioneered putting music on television and worked out a cunning way of making bands give them their videos to play for free, have given up playing music in favour of reality TV and comedy shows. And those television spots were so important. The Cat Deeley interview, the second-last song before they played out *Top of the Pops* – all these are now confined to history's bin. They ranked up there with getting your band on the front cover of *Smash Hits* and *Top of the Pops* magazine. Somehow a spread in *Heat* just doesn't quite cut it. I suppose this does slightly explain the undignified scrum to get your act on shows like Ant and Dec and *Strictly Come Dancing*, guest training slots on *The X Factor*, or dueting with Kylie on her 'Aren't I Fabulous?'

tribute show. There is just nowhere else for pop to go. There are only so many kids who watch Lorraine Kelly on *GMTV* or Fern and Phil on *This Morning*. And the audience slumped in front of Jonathan Ross on a Friday night don't exactly rush out and buy records with their pocket money on Saturday morning.

'Pop is about selling sex,' sighs Craig, 'and when you've got ugly boys playing ugly tunes to ugly girls, it's no wonder the industry is on its last legs. Fucking hell, mate,' he says, holding his hands up. 'Look! Now you've managed to make *me* depressed.'

But he is not half as miserable as I am after I spend the next three days calling up Craig's list of connections and contacts, all of whom say no to a showcase at Nomis. We can't even get our boy band seen, let alone arrested. Maybe this is the worst idea of my life so far. Perhaps I should quit while I'm only £10K down. I wonder how Leanne is getting on with her album. Maybe Chris from Road to Reality has fallen out with Terry and now plans to go solo? Has Dave at Warner's had any thoughts on Des's album yet?

'There's always Sony BMG,' suggests Paul, helpfully, through the door.

'I'd rather eat shit.'

'Yeah, well, there are plenty who've done worse for a career in showbiz,' he points out with a shrug of his shoulders. 'They've got Westlife, Take That, Leona, Will Young. It's the right place to be. And remember, Boyzone were turned down by everyone; no one would take Walsh's calls. And Cowell only took Westlife because Worlds Apart weren't working and he wanted someone to take on Take That. You never know. Call them.'

'As I said . . .'

My head falls into my hands. I stare at the Sony BMG number on my pad. Shit or humble pie? I wonder which one tastes worse.

I get to taste neither. I am passed around the switchboard leaving messages on voicemails until I am finally told by some secretary, or assistant's assistant, that Sony BMG are not interested in coming to a showcase, or in boy bands in general.

'I always knew they were a bunch of cunts,' says Paul when I call him back into my office. 'Anyway, they've got no taste.'

'It's such a shame,' says Debbie as she walks in with two paper cups of coffee and one iPod earphone swinging free. 'I played them to my mate Lily and she thought they were great.'

'Lily?' I ask.

'Yeah, Lily Allen. You know, the singer. She loved them. She thought they were so bad they were cool, or something like that.'

I could kiss her. In fact I do. I shift my large arse around the desk, give Debbie a big smacker on the forehead and squeeze her shoulders so tightly she protests.

'What's that for?' she says.

'You're a genius,' I say. 'Is there any chance of her putting that on her website? Or even getting them on her show?'

'And a link to our MySpace thing,' adds Paul.

'Don't see why not,' shrugs Debbie, getting out her mobile phone.

*

Now, the thing about the music business is that it's controlled by a bunch of middle-aged men who enjoy a lunch and a bottle of wine and have the flocking instinct of lemmings. A mention by a groovy taste-maker girl with her own TV show whose every night out is hosed down by the paps, and suddenly my calls are returned and the showcase is rescued from total doom and disaster. There's not exactly a herd of A&R men ready to knock the door down, but a gang of them have agreed to see the band at Nomis and they are booked in for this afternoon.

One of the more famous rehearsal studios, Nomis (Simon spelled backwards) is a huge warehouse in a very un-prepossessing street in west London, yet it has played host to the great and the good from pop's hall of fame. Prince, Oasis, George Michael, Kylie and Paul Weller have all used the rooms to work on shows, tours and one-off gigs.

'This is it?' asks Mike as we pull up outside. 'I've ridden past here a thousand times on my bike.'

'This is crunch time,' says Paul, helpfully fuelling their nerves. 'This is where it all gets decided.'

'Or not,' I say. 'There are always lots of other people to see.'

Esther chivvies them all through the doors, along the corridor and down the stairs into one of the ten rehearsal rooms. Inside are five mikes set up in a row facing an array of decrepit seating, including a biodegrading sofa and a couple of club chairs. It looks more like the remnants of a car boot sale than an audition room. A jeans-clad technician is laying cables and tapping the mikes, making sure everything's live and ready to go. I pull him over to one side just to check that the two mikes on each edge of the row are not switched on. The last thing I need is the passengers joining in and buggering things up.

Paul and I spent the whole of yesterday discussing tactics. Do we have the A&R guys come in one at a time, make them feel special and sort of try to butter them up? Or do we get them all in together and make them think there is a bit of a buzz going on, that they need to act quickly and strike while the band is hot? After much argument over the pros and cons, we decided to go for the big show, get an atmosphere going to encourage, in my fantasy, a bit of a record exec fistfight, with me as the umpire.

It is one o'clock, an hour and a half before the show, and the boys have already been through their set three times. Esther's fine-tuned them down to the last hand clap and they are pacing around the studio, tweaking their hair in the wall of mirrors, like a troop of caged monkeys. I can't bear the tension any more and pack them off to the canteen, telling them not to eat chips but to get something macrobiotic down them, and to keep an eye out for Kylie, or Prince, who might well be in the building. They all look at me like I'm nuts. I'm not sure if it's Kylie or the macrobiotic meal that's floored them. Either way it's a blessed relief when they go. It gives Paul and I a chance to tuck into one of the warm beers and glasses of wine we've laid on for our guests, as well as a couple of fistfuls of peanuts.

'I hope this is going to fucking work,' I say, my mouth full of dry-roasted.

'Relax,' says Paul, pacing up and down, exhaling. 'It's not like we haven't done these things before.'

'Not like this I haven't. I usually invite them down to a gig, ply them full of booze and drugs and tell them where to sign. This whole Kids from Fame thing is a totally different story. And I am sober.' I grab another beer. 'I need to take the edge off.'

Come two thirty I am three beers down and feeling a whole lot better. Sadly, Esther's reminded me that I can't smoke inside the studios, but otherwise the alchemy is nearly complete. I have told the boys they need to talk a bit between the songs, jolly it up, like they're at a real gig. All we need now is for the A&R men to arrive.

It's a quarter to three before they start swanning in, a whole tense, nervous fifteen minutes late. EMI are first through the door, a junior from their department who tells me his boss Tony Wadsworth is on his way. Sony BMG and Island arrive at the same time. There's quite a gang of them, including Nick Gatfield, Nick Raphael and Sonny Taklar. They are swiftly followed by Jason Iley from Mercury and Max Lusada from Warner's. All of them studiously ignore the beers and snacks, settle down in the seats and the sofa and get out their BlackBerrys. There is little in the way of conversation or indeed buzz. The atmosphere is as upbeat as a wake. You would have thought they'd all been dragged here by the hair, kicking and screaming, away from their nice lunches at Chez Christophe.

We can't start because we're still waiting for Polydor to show. Colin Barlow said yes when I called him yesterday. I left a message with his assistant this morning. But it is now ten past three, he still hasn't shown, and everyone else is beginning to sigh and yawn and look at their watch. Christ, a couple of them are so bored they've even sampled the crisps. I look across at Paul, who's looking tense, and I can see Esther's face straining through the glass panel on the door. Paul gurns something at me, which I take to mean 'let's get started'. I nod at Esther through the glass and walk over to the mikes.

'Good afternoon,' I say. 'I'd like to thank you all for coming down here today.' I cough. 'Some of you may know me from my indie days and it's good to see some new faces here.' I nod towards the sofa; no one looks up from his BlackBerry. 'Anyway, rather than tell you all about the band and how I found them, I am going to let them speak for themselves. Ladies and gentlemen, I give you Band of Five! Enjoy!'

I nod towards Paul to start the backing track. The boys come in whooping and clapping to zero applause.

'Come on!' cheers Josh. 'Let's get this party started!'

'Yeah, wa-hey!' the other boys enthuse.

'Come on, everyone, let's go!' adds Nick.

There is no reaction in the room. A sea of stony faces look on. Someone's mobile goes off and he takes the call. The music fades down and the boys take their position in front of the mikes, but still the exec chats away, and as the boys start 'Brief Love' he puts his finger in his ear and carries on his conversation. Amazingly, none of the boys is fazed by this. They have clearly got their eyes on the prize and no discourteous garrulous twat is going to ruin it for them. I am reminded of what I said to Craig the other day. There is something about the hope in their eyes. This is my moment. This is my moment.

The team from Polydor arrive just in time to distract everyone else from the carefully-worked-on harmonizing in the second chorus. If only I could send them packing. Instead I grin and shake their hands and gesture silently towards the beers. Colin hasn't shown, so I have to content myself with one of his many juniors, but I grin away, making sure the disappointment doesn't show.

The song trails off to a resounding silence. A couple of sniffs; someone coughs uncomfortably.

'I'd like to thank you all for coming here this afternoon,' says Josh. 'We're Band of Five, and we're delighted that you could all make it.' He is trying his charming best to engage them, and I have to say a few of the female elements in the crowd are sitting up and paying attention. 'I'm Josh, I'm twenty, and I'm from Manchester. I came to London because the streets were paved with gold.' He laughs. No one else does. A couple of the girls smile. 'OK. Good. Um, let me introduce you to the rest of the band. This here is Ashley, who's the youngest at fifteen.'

'Hello,' says Ashley, his pink cheeks flushing pinker.

'This here is Nick,' continues Josh.

'All right?' says Nick, pushing his thick blond hair off the front of his face.

'And down at the ends are Mike and Billy,' says Josh, indicating either side with his hands.

'Hi,' the two boys say down their microphones.

Shit! No one can hear them. The boys look puzzled. Mike taps the end of his mike. I pretend to be surprised that it's dead, rush over and start to play around with the wires like there's a sound problem, while a couple of people in the audience snigger into their sleeves. The techie rushes over, his face puce pink, thinking he's made a mistake and misheard me. In the fuss and commotion I manage to convince him to turn the mikes on and then immediately off again when Band start to sing. He tells me not to worry, he's done this many times before. I send Esther round with a bowl of crisps and a bottle of wine while I calm the boys down, and then we get ready to start again.

They get through the other two songs without a hitch, or indeed a round of applause. Josh keeps the Northern Charm thing going between songs and by the end, although most of the execs head straight for the door, a couple of girls do stay behind to chat to him. The lad has certainly got something, I think as I watch the room empty quicker than a green room running out of free booze. A couple of guys pat me on the back or the arm and make a telephone gesture with their finger and thumb as they leave, but quite frankly that was about as successful as a fart in a wind tunnel.

I try to rally the troops after everyone's gone. The boys do look deflated. Paul's started to bite his fingernails again, which doesn't bode well, and Esther's pissed off outside for a fag – and I didn't even know she smoked. The only way to get through this is alcohol. I ring up Debbie and tell her to get her arse down the off-licence; we need beer, vodka, Red Bull and anything else she thinks might help teenage boys come to terms with their first real brush with the mean and hard world of show business.

An hour later and we're all back at the office listening to some crap on Paul's iPod, knocking back the beers and Bacardi Breezers. Ashley is already pissed after his second Beck's: he's gone all round-eyed and floppy and he keeps giggling and belching. I fully expect the wrath of Dionne tomorrow morning. The other boys are complaining about the Nomis technician, and Paul's nodding away in agreement. Esther's got me pinned against the wall, blowing smoke into my face. She's on a bit of a roll.

'Cunts,' she says. 'They're all cunts. Did you see them? Sitting there on their phones and their BlackBerrys like they had somewhere better to be while my boys danced and sang their socks off. Cunts!' She exhales in my face before nibbling on one of her burgundy nails. 'No wonder this industry is going to the dogs.'

I wake up the next morning with a blocked right nostril surrounded by bottles, butts and Red Bull cans that have been used as ashtrays. I slept on the office sofa again and my back's killing me almost as much as my head. I move slowly towards my desk, whipping the old coke residue off the leather top with the palm of one hand before searching in my drawers for some Resolve. While I sit and watch the powder dissolving at the bottom of my Evian bottle, I sweat at my desk and hope that I have got away with it.

The boys went their separate ways at around midnight, but

LIMERICK COUNTY LIBRARY

not before Ashley had puked in the office loo and fallen asleep on the stairs. Debbie very kindly took him home, while Paul and I cracked out a gram of coke and Esther called a cab. Paul and I talked at each other about what is happening at EMI and whether the arrival of Guy Hands was a good or bad thing. He's the CEO of Terra Firma, the private equity company that has taken over the business. 'The music industry is being run by accountants,' Paul kept on complaining as he chopped out line after line – which is obviously a bit rich seeing as he's one too. When Esther's cab arrived I took it upon myself to escort her downstairs and stick my tongue in her ear. I was aiming for her mouth but she pre-empted me and moved, hence my hitting the wrong orifice. She hit her head on the side of the cab door as she climbed in, so I'm secretly hoping she was too pissed to remember.

Before I can dwell on the excruciating embarrassment of it all, my phone goes.

'Hi, it's Gavin here from Polydor,' he says. 'How yer doin'?' He does wait for me to respond before he continues. 'So, we'd like to see Band of Five again, with the whole of the A&R department, plus publicity – the usual. Could you set up another showcase, just for us?'

'You're interested?' I can barely speak.

'We're interested,' he confirms. 'There are so many old boy bands doing the rounds at the moment, we think there's room for something new, a bit fresh.'

'You do?'

'Yes, we do. So can you set it up? We'd like to send everyone down to have a look. Lucian Grainge would also like to come.'

Oh my God! Is that the sound of a heavenly choir? Lucian Grainge would like to come? Lucian Grainge, the lord of all music, the chairman of Universal? The man who had Take That play at his son's bar mitzvah while he and his pals took over the whole of Nobu wants to look at my band? Paul is going to scream the house down when I tell him.

And he does. His reaction is so loud that I worry he'll bust a blood vessel. Esther's excited enough to pretend not to remember that a matter of hours ago I launched myself at her like a sex-starved Exocet. The boys are all delighted too. Josh cries, Nick, Mike and Billy cheer, and Dionne is pleased enough not to shout at me for filling her underage son so full of booze he had his head in a bucket half the night.

Three days later and we are all back at Nomis Studios. The boys are pacing, Esther's smoking outside, Paul's eating, and I'm obsessively calling Gavin to make sure they're on their way.

'Lucian's coming?' I check again.

'He's coming,' confirms Gavin.

I punch the air and do a little spin.

'This is like meeting Madonna,' says Paul through a mouthful of cheese and onion crisps. 'It's that goddamn exciting.'

At midday the rehearsal room is packed. I've met Andy in publicity, I've met Dave in marketing, the lawyers are here, the whole of the A&R department has turned up, and Colin Barlow's on the sofa next to the MD David Joseph; all we need is for Mr Grainge to arrive and I think my head might explode.

147

I put my face outside into the corridor where the boys are going through their routines in hushed whispers. Hands up, spin, turn, kick – they are just trying to think of something to do to allay their nerves.

'OK?' I ask, patting Billy on the arm.

'All right, boss,' he says. His face looks so white against his black eyebrows.

'Good luck, break a leg.' I smile. 'Remember, you are all fucking great and talented. I personally chose you from a cast of thousands. I know you won't let me down.'

They all seem so young today, staring back at me. I am beginning to appreciate the odd dichotomy in this boy band business. The manager's role is paternal as well as exploitative. If anyone laid a finger on any of these boys, I'd punch their lights out.

I walk back into the studio and Gavin approaches me.

'Mr Grainge sends his regrets,' he whispers in my ear.

'Oh,' I say, stopping in my tracks. Wanker, I think. 'Shall we get on with it then?'

The boys come out, I give them a bit of a build-up, and they give the performance of their lives. By the end of 'When You Find the One' there are actually smiles on a few faces, and a couple of people clap. The band bow and the room explodes into chat. 'We could do this?' 'We could do that?' 'Are there any more songs?' 'We should get recording?' 'When can we meet?' 'How long have they been together?' 'Who's the oldest?' 'What shall we do to market them?' 'I think we can do a deal.'

*

Three weeks pass and we are still doing the deal. Their lawyers are talking to our lawyers and the negotiations drag on and on. Polydor are looking to sign us up on one of these new so-called 360-degree deals that Robbie Williams famously signed with EMI for £80m (although I've been told it was more like £30m), after which he shouted at a press conference, 'I am rich beyond my wildest dreams!'

The idea is that since the arse has fallen out of the CD market, and even downloads are down, and music is everywhere – on the radio, in the car, in the shopping mall, on adverts, in dramas – why bother to buy it? So the record company thinks that having promoted an artist, built up their career and made them a star, they should be allowed a slice of their performing revenue. Or, as one lawyer put it to me recently, 'They've fucked their business and now they want a piece of yours.'

I know that many people think that's true. The record industry is in decline, and they only have themselves to blame. They spent so much time in the late nineties trying to work out how to sue their own customers who were downloading from Napster that they forgot to work out a way to embrace the new culture, and how it could work for them. Instead they buried their heads in the sand like a bunch of Luddites and carried on investing in CDs while treating their artists with high-handed contempt. Boardroom talk was never about the music, only ever about units sold. The product was not the musician but the CD. Ten pence' worth of disc was selling for £10, which is a mark-up of 10,000 per cent – the most impressive in all of retail. Even then nine out of ten acts fail. Any record deal only ever has a 10 per cent success rate.

And what deals they are. The *Wall Street Journal* recently investigated the business and concluded that 'for all the twenty-first-century glitz that surrounds it, the popular music industry is distinctly medieval in character: the last form of indentured servitude'. No wonder, then, that a huge star like Prince ended up writing 'slave' on his face in protest at the fact that even having earned out, or having paid back his advance, Warner Bros still wouldn't allow him to leave the company to record elsewhere. George Michael had a similar experience when Sony wouldn't let him go. He ended up buying himself out with an override deal, which means that the record company still takes a slice of him wherever he goes.

Whatever happened in the past, the record companies always seemed to win. They would hand out these advances that artists seemingly never managed to earn out on. The band would pay for the studio, the recording, the cars that took them there, the food they and everyone else ate; they paid for the publicity, the adverts, half the videos, the tour, the manager – everything was recoupable against the royalties. MC Hammer learned the hard way that if you surround yourself with two coachloads of hangers-on (fifty-eight of them in his case) you can end up with nothing. Morris Levy, MD of Roulette Records, would shout 'You want royalties? Try Buckingham Palace!' at any artist who enquired about payment.

And if they ever did recoup, they would have to wade

through some fairly creative accounting to work out the route of the cash. Services are routinely double-invoiced for. One record exec told me that in three thousand audits done on a company, in some '2,998 of them the artist was underpaid'. Another industry insider remarked that it 'makes Enron look like amateur hour'. For some artists the only way to get their cash is to threaten to audit the company. Or, in the case of the Dixie Chicks, sue them: they did Sony for 'systemic thievery'. It's either that or wait years for the money to come through. While the record company makes money on the interest, you work out how to pay the mortgage.

But you can't feel too sorry for these rock stars; some of them are just as profligate as the companies they complain about. John Taylor from Duran Duran was famously doing an audit of his accounts when he came across invoices for a lock-up garage of which he had no recollection. When he went to the lock-up he found two DeLorean cars he had forgotten about, each with eight miles on the clock.

But you can kind of understand why some artists have given up on record labels altogether and are releasing their records through other means. Like Paul McCartney, who has signed up to Starbucks. They have 7,500 outlets and give you a fifty-fifty deal on a CD that they sell for a proper amount of money, £14.98. They don't discount like everyone else selling CDs, at £5.98 or £6.98. What is the point of a record company that wants you to sign up to a six-album deal and then doesn't look after you? It is hard to live off 5p per iTunes download.

If you're a big band like Radiohead you can afford to give

away your album on the net for free because you make £20m on a three-week tour of the States. Why make an album for a couple of million that will take two years to recoup when you can make £20m in a month? It's the same idea behind Prince giving away his album on the front of the *Mail on Sunday*; the record is no longer a means to itself, it is only a calling card for future O$_2$ Arena ticket sales. However, if you don't fill stadiums, if you are much further down the pop food chain and you don't have a body of work the fans will pay to see, you need nurturing and promoting, and this sort of big-gun behaviour will piss you off. It devalues the price of music – it makes it worthless. Why pay full whack for an album when Radiohead are giving theirs away for free? It's the sort of 'I'm all right, Jack' type of philosophy that buggers it up for the rest of us.

The same could be said for the 360 deal. The record company isn't just buying your music and your performing rights, it's buying you as a brand. And as brands go there is no one bigger than Beyoncé. She is a singer, an actress, a fashion label, a perfume; she endorses Pepsi, L'Oréal, Armani, American Express, Ford, McDonald's, and Walt Disney theme parks dressed as Snow White. Everyone wants a slice of her. She is one of the most marketable women in the world. She is beautiful, slim and bootylicious. However, if you are none of these things and won't make a great 'product', how easy will it be for you to get a record deal, no matter how great your songs are or how brilliant your voice? There are many who think that the days are numbered for girls like Beth Ditto. What the labels really want is a pretty pouting pop star who is pure product and can endorse a range of duvets and panties, like poor dear 'Brave Kylie'.

Then again, the halcyon days of the record business when people would leave their desks on a Tuesday and not return for the rest of the week are unworkable now. The idea that you can charge the company for coke as 'fruit and flowers' to the tune of £200,000 a year, or put hookers down on the label's Amex card, just doesn't work in a corporate world. A recent audit of EMI accounts made for some interesting reading: £20,000 was blown a month on 'candles' to decorate the LA apartment of an artist plus entourage, as well as the £5.6m apartment that was used twice a month by a former manager.

I remember there used to be a flower shop in Kensington, where they dealt coke along with bouquets. All bouquets were sixty quid and they'd shove the gram in with the posy. At one record company, everyone was claiming £59.99 for flowers on their expenses. Personnel apparently found out and were not amused. They said it was a joke that people were doing drugs in the building. Then, at a morning meeting one of the execs chopped out a large line on the desk, snorted it and said, 'So fire me.' When someone complained about finding two lines chopped out in the loo at work, left for someone else, the argument was put that they shouldn't have gone into that loo in the first place.

Somehow we were allowed to get away with it. In those days even the pop stars seemed to be more extravagant. You had Freddie with his dwarves, and Elton with his high heels and stratospheric bar bills. Elton used to have trolleys of champagne parked outside his suite at the Ritz, while inside he snorted most of Bolivia and disappeared up his own fundament so far that he once rang up his manager early one morning to complain about the weather. 'It's windy,' he said, 'do something about it.' Bowie and Rod Stewart had entourages that numbered over twenty, and wherever they went a tsunami of liggers – or hangers-on – would follow. Even the money was bigger: Dire Straits made £40m in 1986 during their Brothers in Arms tour, which is worth double in today's terms. That is all the more extraordinary when you realize they didn't spend it on coke, hookers and first-class travel. Like good eighties capitalists they invested in some fine pension funds.

So, as I said, it is nearly a month since Polydor said they wanted us to sign and we are still negotiating, although it looks like we are nearly there. I have been debating whether or not to sign the boys up to me as a production company, then for me to sign with the record company, and then license them the music, rather like a few other managers of manufactured bands have done. They were paid by the production company that signed them which was owned by their manager. Some would say that's a conflict of interests; others would say it's just clever accounting. The lucky manager took a cut on both sides of the equation. Sadly, I am not that sharp.

At last I get a call from Gavin to say that all the papers are ready for us to sign and would we like to come to their High Street Kensington offices for our champagne moment. On the way there I talk the boys through the deal: £100,000 advance for two albums with no 360 element. It doesn't sound much, because it isn't. After I take my 20 per cent it will be even less, and then they have to divide it between the five of them. Esther's cut is negligible, and Paul gets nearly half of mine. So he and I have made £20,000 between us, with outgoings that will amount to pretty much the same. The boys, however, can't believe the enormity of the figure and are mentally spending it all as we drive through the traffic. I don't have the heart to explain to them that they will be living off £100 a week pocket money for the next year or so, working their backsides off doing PAs – personal appearances – to try to make some extra money. Now is not the time to piss on their parade, so to speak.

We pull up outside Universal towers, opposite the Bristol garage on Kensington High Street. The boys stand and stare at the impressive building – seven floors of music, with Lucian Grainge presiding over the lot from the penthouse office plus balcony at the top.

'I wonder if we'll make it to the rooftop retreat and Lucian Grainge's office,' says Paul. 'I hear Mrs Cowell, as he calls him, is always up there comparing cars with the big man – and that's when they're not at the Sandy Lane together.'

'I don't think Gavin said we were going to the top floor,' I say. 'It's reserved for hit record celebrations only.'

'You never know,' smiles Paul.

The atrium is all glass and corporate with two sets of security and television screens blaring out the label's latest video release. Gavin comes down to meet us. He is all smiles and shaking hands.

'Welcome, welcome to Universal,' he says, running his hands through his thinning hair. 'This way.'

We walk past the coffee bar on the ground floor and head towards the lift. The boys follow like a school party struck silent with awe. Gavin ushers us into the lift and sadly doesn't press the top-floor button. Paul and I look across at each other. So near, and no cigar.

We get out on the Polydor floor and Gavin directs us along a corridor towards an empty office. Inside is a large black ash table surrounded by chrome and leather chairs. Gold and platinum discs grace the wall, and in the middle of the table there are two bottles of champagne on ice, a box of dainty Marks and Spencer party sandwiches and an assorted collection of glasses.

'I am sorry, Lucian sends his regrets,' says Gavin, picking up a bottle of the champagne. 'It's Friday afternoon and everyone's left early. Houses in the country.' He smiles.

While he hands around a glass to each of the boys, I notice a pile of contracts sitting on the desk behind him.

'First things first,' Gavin says, following my gaze. He pops the cork and bubbles fizz down the side of the bottle. He fills the glasses, and by the time he gets to me there is only a drizzle left. 'Oops,' he says as he realizes his mistake. 'Oh well,' he shrugs, making no move towards the second bottle on the table. 'Cheers, everyone!' We all clink our glasses. 'Welcome to the music biz!'

6

The champagne moment improved somewhat towards the end. Even if Lucian didn't grace us with his presence, eventually some of the lawyers and marketing guys wended their way along the corridor for crisps and a glass of bubbly. But it wasn't quite the Grand Prix-winning experience Paul and I have been working towards. Fortunately, the boys were so overawed by the size of the building, its history, the fact that Take That are signed to the same label and that they are in the same stable as Boyzone, they didn't notice the dearth of revellers. They happily signed away their recordings, voices and toned backsides for practically zip while knocking back tepid champagne.

The only person to be less than impressed by the deal is Dionne when she signs on behalf of Ashley in the bright light of a June morning. As she sits at my desk going through the papers with me, I can see the realization slowly dawn across her heavily made-up face that Ash's first monthly wage will barely cover the down payment on the enormous plasma she's ordered for their lounge, let alone half the other showbiz trappings she's about to feather her nest with.

'So when will they be making real big money?' she says, pen poised, looking at me through her turquoise lashes.

'I won't lie to you,' I reply, economizing with the truth. 'Not for a few months, maybe next year.' I smile encouragingly. 'But you never can tell. Maybe sooner.' I nod for her to sign.

In the old days, maybe, when sales were good, records were expensive and Japan was double bubble, a good boy band could easily make several hundred thousand each in one year. If Dionne only knew that these days someone of the calibre of Britney Spears only got around $150,000 from 1.54 million downloads of two singles – 'Gimme More' and 'Piece of Me' – from her last album *Blackout*, she might consider curtailing her home-improvement spending somewhat.

But the boys are happy. They are living the dream and are back in the studio re-recording their three songs with a live band, two dead mikes and plenty of fuss. There's talk at the label of getting in Cathy Dennis, who wrote 'Fever' and 'Can't Get You Out of My Head' for Brave Kylie. Paul is pushing for Guy Chambers, the man who wrote Robbie Williams' hits, and Gavin is muttering about getting some covers down on the album.

Covers are, after all, a nice, cheap and quick way to get a band something to sing as you don't actually have to pay the songwriter for the song, you just pay for the use of it, as it were. So we just give away the publishing (which we would have done anyway, as Band of Five don't and can't write their own material) and we hand over 50 per cent of the Performance Rights Society money. Amazingly, once a songwriter has published their song they have no say over who records it – just so long as they don't change it in any way. Keep the melody and the beats the same and don't bugger around with the words, and Gareth Gates can record U2 without U2 being able to stop him. Just as an author can't stop anyone from reading their book, so a songwriter can't stop a band from singing their songs. There are plenty of songwriters who pace around in the dark swigging meths and spitting feathers at boy bands pilfering their material. Tracy Chapman was supposed to have been none too pleased about Boyzone covering 'Baby Can I Hold You Tonight', but other than huffing and puffing and sulkily cashing the cheque at the end, there wasn't a lot she could do about it. Remixes, on the other hand, can get you into all sorts of trouble. The songwriter and the publisher have to approve your innovative and creative tweaking, otherwise the recording cannot be released.

Gavin is mooting the idea that Band of Five cover the David Dundas single 'Jeans On' – it's catchy and easy and perfect for a quick summer release. It just might capture the imagination of the youngsters while at the same time reminding the record-buying middle youth of their earlier youth, or at least their parents' youth. The whole project could have a bit of a retro aspect to it. My jury is still out on the idea as Fat Boy Slim has already sampled it and Seat used it in an ad for some un-inspiring run-around a couple of years ago.

In the meantime, I call Jerry in the hope that he might have a couple of album fillers in his bottom drawer. When he finally picks up the phone, he tells me he's got jetlag having just flown in from New York.

'God,' he says, yawning, his duvet crackling in the background, 'you wouldn't believe the week I've had. I was working in a studio where some poor sods were hanging around for Whitney Houston.'

'Whitney? I didn't know she was recording again?'

'First album in four years,' he coughs. 'Everyone who's ever had a hit has been asked to pitch ideas and songs for her. Clive Davis is holding court in his offices on Central Park West.'

Clive Davis is another A&R legend who has been immortalized in song, film and by the Rock and Roll Hall of Fame. His career began in the late sixties and he has signed and delivered some of music's most successful artists, from Janis Joplin, Santana, Springsteen, Billy Joel and Aerosmith to Justin Timberlake, Christina Aguilera, Alicia Keys and Kelly Clarkson. He has also had the pleasure of working with Leona Lewis. So I suppose if anyone can resurrect Whitney's career, Clive can.

'But I hear the voice has gone,' Jerry continues. I can hear him lighting up a cigarette.

'Hers?'

'That's what I hear. All I know is my mate was working in the same studio where she was supposed to be recording and she didn't show all week. From ten a.m. to six p.m. they sat every day waiting for her to show up and every day they changed the cut flowers, and ordered in the Cristal and the caviar. The studio's three thousand dollars a day and they waited for a week. At around five p.m. every day an assistant calls to say that she's not coming and then the next day they order in from Cipriani again.'

'The Cipriani? What is it with that place?' I've heard that Jay-Z and his gang at Def-Jam Records and Roc-A-Fella have Blini Fridays where the barman from Cipriani mixes the champagne with white peach juice flown in fresh from bloody Italy. What is it about the Americans that they love the place so much?

'Fuck knows,' Jerry says. 'Sharon Osbourne practically holds court in the London restaurant.'

'It's a celebrity haunt,' I say. 'Paul's in there all the time, eating a thirty-five-quid bowl of pasta.'

'That and Cristal. Mariah Carey's engineers tuck into the stuff at the end of every recording session she doesn't turn up to.' He yawns again. 'Anyway, how can I help you?'

Turns out that Jerry does have another couple of songs we might be able to have for the album, if we cross his palm with enough silver and percentage points. However, he doesn't have a whole album's worth.

Just when I am beginning to think that Band won't be able to get an album out before Christmas and I might not be making a single penny from record sales this year, Paul saunters across the landing into my office.

'Why don't we ask Leanne or Des Adams if they have any songs for the boys?' he suggests. 'That way we could make a few quid each way, as it were.'

For a man who spends most of the day thinking about himself, his social life and his abdominals, Paul does occasionally engage his brain on something a little extra-curricular and comes up with a good idea.

I put a couple of calls in to them both. Des bores on for half an hour about the lack of reaction from Warner's to his album before I realize that his stuff is all a bit too LA and angst-ridden to be of any use to an upbeat and handsome boy band. Yet Leanne, for a pubescent from Harpenden, is surprisingly on the money. She has one happy disco number about partying on a Saturday night, amazingly called 'Saturday Night'. Perhaps even more amazingly, when I play it to Gavin, he likes it.

'I think this would be a great addition,' he says, nodding away, his limp hair flopping forward. 'It's got a good vibe to it and it's not at all edgy or alienating.'

I smile back at him, encouragingly. I think he means that it is suitably bland for Band, which I am inclined to agree with.

Leanne is delighted when I tell her and gives a little squeal down the phone. She has a publishing deal with EMI and they are only too thrilled to see themselves finally make a bit of money, even if they know in their hearts it will never make a single and will hardly keep any of them in drinking club memberships.

Two weeks later all the songs on the album are finished: the original three tracks, 'Saturday Night', Jerry's other two album-fillers, plus four covers and 'Jeans On', which I finally relented about. Gavin calls me to tell me that they are sending them to Stockholm for remixing. 'All the boy bands are doing it these days,' he says. 'These guys are good and quick and cheap, which of course makes them doubly good.'

'Yeah,' I agree, thinking that the last thing we need to do is start shelling out more cash for producers and remixers which can, if you're using the likes of Timbaland – currently Mr Hot and Happening and doing Madonna's new *Hard Candy* album – cost $160,000 per backing track.

'Don't think the only thing to come out of Sweden is Abba,' adds Gavin.

Another two weeks pass before we get eleven radically remixed tracks back and a claim for a credit and 25 per cent of the publishing. Clearly the other thing to come out of Sweden these days is daylight robbery. I kick up a fuss with Gavin, who shrugs and tells me that's the way it works these days. Records are being carved up like small bits of pizza; white music is becoming more like black. Traditionally it was only rappers who had track writers – the guys who sat on the computers and came up with the beats – and then topline writers – the guys who came up with the lyrics and the melody, the stuff you sing along to in the car. Rock and roll was all about one person in a room on their own with an acoustic guitar, and the music would be recorded and written and perhaps played around with in the studio by a producer who would get a flat fee. But now it is all about percentages.

'Think yourself lucky,' he adds. 'Beyoncé Knowles takes twenty-five per cent of the song and even her dad Matthew sometimes gets a cut and a production credit.'

'Why do they care about the credit?'

'I don't know,' he says. 'They want to be thought of as songwriters, I suppose. But, you know, that's the way it works – everyone's on a cut. There was one record exec who used to take ten per cent of everything that crossed his desk. Then again, he did control everything; he controlled the gateway to working in music. His connections ran all over the city, and if you didn't play ball, you wouldn't work. It's *Sopranos* stuff. Even right down to what you'd release when. If he said "This is your first single" then it was your first single. He was the president, and every act paid.'

'Swimming with sharks,' I sigh.

'That's about the sum of it. Do you want me to talk to Jerry?'

Ever the coward, I let Gavin go ahead and share the good news with Jerry. There isn't very much the poor bloke can do about losing 25 per cent of his songs. He calls me up, rants and raves and asks me my advice. I tell him to swallow it, as 75 per cent of something is better than 100 per cent of nothing. He agrees.

'All you get as a songwriter,' he moans, 'is people trying to take away your credits and hammer down your percentages. You have to fight for every small goddamn thing, and it's exhausting. D'you know a good mate of mine ended up with thirty-five per cent of her song recently after everyone had taken their cut? Thankfully it became a number one record all over the world, so she made some money. But, you know, in any other profession that wouldn't be business, it would be just plain bullying.'

Leaving Jerry to nurture his inner wounded artist, Paul and I set about trying to get a release date out of the record company for the first single. We both trade calls with Gavin for nearly a week. Neither of us is sure if he is avoiding us, or whether he is genuinely tied up in meetings with other acts. I spend several sleepless nights shit scared they are not going to release us at all.

Record companies do this all the time. They sign an act, they help you to produce an album or a few songs, and then they say something like, 'We've spent a couple of hundred thousand on you, in the studio, with the musicians and paying for the post production, and we've played it to a few producers at Radio One and they're not feeling it, so we're going to cut our losses. We're not going to waste good money after bad promoting you. You're dropped.' And being dropped isn't like making a film that bypasses the cinemas and goes straight to video. Getting dropped means the song is never released. The only positive outcome from this piss-poor situation is that you are released from your record contract. You pay them nothing and you are free to take your songs with you, and if someone else signs you then they have to pay your old record company an override deal, a small cut, or a couple of percentage points on the record. Most of the time you wander off into obscurity. Very occasionally you become James Blunt, who was signed and then dropped, walked off with his record, and then went on to sell over eleven million albums – the best-seller of 2006.

However, it is more usual for the record company never to let you go and also never to release you. They can keep you there for ever. One of my bands, whom I no longer manage, is still signed to a record company and they have yet to release their second album. They signed, did their second album, the company hated it, and they won't let them go. Every so often they throw a couple of thousand pounds at them and pop them in a studio for a week, so the boys can pretend to be working. But it is like a pair of golden handcuffs. They won't promote you, they won't release you, and they won't let anyone else have you either, just in case they make you a success and you become James Blunt and they're embarrassed. My old band signed up when they were all about eighteen, and that's it. They're stuck in musical purgatory and there is nothing they can do about it.

Paul and I have been sweating for days now. I've had phone calls from Josh and Dionne asking what's going on. I am half tempted to get the boys back out there again into the clubs, perhaps try to attach them to someone else's tour, to try to get some money in while we all sit around waiting to hear how our fate has been decided. Then, finally, late on Thursday afternoon, just as Paul and I are contemplating sloping off to the local pub to drown our sorrows and call Franco the local line merchant, I get the call.

'OK,' inhales Gavin. The knowledge of his own importance means he no longer has to introduce himself on the telephone, he can just dive straight into conversation. 'Right then, the news is good. In fact the news is excellent. Lucian is behind you.'

'Lucian is behind us!' I repeat loudly for Paul's benefit across the landing. A snorting, stifled squeal precedes his grinning arrival in my office. 'That's excellent news.' I nod, smiling at Paul, who minces his hands with delight.

'He thinks boy bands are back, particularly for summer.'

'Boys *are* big for the summer,' I say, still nodding at Paul, who gives me the thumbs up. Boys are big all year round as far as I'm concerned. But if Lucian says they're a summer thing, what's a season or two between friends?

'And he wants you to go with the David Dundas cover.'

'Oh,' I say. 'That's a little un . . . um, unexpected.' Paul looks concerned. 'The Dundas, you say.' Paul frowns again and shrugs. Fuck it. Whatever Lucian wants, Lucian gets, right? 'How very clever of him.'

'And he's got some great ideas for the video,' enthuses Gavin.

'He has? I can't wait.' I'm trying hard not to sound disingenuous.

Ten days later, Josh is walking around in a pair of white boxer shorts and white ankle socks in a mocked-up laundrette in the Riverside Studios in Hammersmith. The idea behind the shoot is a revisit to the Nick Kamen Levi 501s ad. Back in the day, over twenty years ago now, Nick and his pants got a whole generation of young ladies all hot under the collar; he not only launched a pair of jeans but a piss-poor pop career too. The hope here is to do the same, only better.

It's a question of glamour by association. Record companies are always hoping to tweak your visual memory, or sell you a story, like the images that accompanied Duran Duran's 'Rio' or Wham's 'Club Tropicana'. Sometimes they call in hot artistic types like Andy Warhol. His Curiosity Killed the Cat video was cutting edge and copied later by INXS, but it still didn't manage to make 'Misfit' a number one. But it is mostly about the money. These days record companies no longer have the cash to send bands to Antigua, which is where 'Rio' was filmed; they can no longer afford thousands of dancers, or sets like those in many of the Madonna shoots. The iconic videos that launched a thousand conical bras are over, unless of course the artist pays for them.

Perhaps the artist most famous for picking up a tab is Michael Jackson. He hired Martin Scorsese to direct 'Bad' for $1m, but I guess his most profligate moment was when he splashed $8m on a promo for his *HIStory* album, which for under four minutes turned out to be one of the most expensive pieces of footage ever shot. A teaser where Michael commanded an army of soldiers and a fleet of helicopters in the streets of Budapest was filmed at the stage in his career when he was married to Lisa Marie Presley and was being piped into meetings at Epic along a red carpet with trumpeters either side, and had an understandable mini Hitler complex after seeing Leni Riefenstahl's *Triumph of the Will*. The shoot involved a £40,000 giant statue of Michael and half the

Hungarian army, who refused to play ball, prompting the producers to fly in two hundred soldiers from 3 Para, to be taught the routine by twenty dancers. Jackson was five hours a day in make-up, which made his artist and prostheticist the most important person on the shoot – apart from a Hungarian dwarf who was picked up on the way. Fans were flown in from all around the world and there were four Michael body doubles, one of whom had to vomit to keep his weight down. And there were strict instructions to keep the air conditioning on full blast so that Michael's make-up didn't fall off his face. What with Lisa Marie refusing to come out of the trailer until she'd had the perfect tuna sandwich, and thousands following his every move having received daily tip-offs from his security teams, you can see how the costs mounted.

Sadly, there is no room for such fun and games on our shoot. The budget is as tight as Josh's boxers. Nick, Mike and Billy have also been given various pairs of pants to wear, ranging from the Peter Stringfellow-style leopard-print thong Nick is sporting to Mike's skin-tight white Armanis, last seen on Goldenballs' balls in every magazine and on every bus in the country. Billy's in a pair of black Calvin Klein boxers. Only Ashley has been difficult to costume. His six-pack is more like six packets – of crisps a day. No amount of Esther sending him to the gym or trying to advise him about diet appears to have worked. So he is currently suffering the embarrassment of an all-in-one granddaddy romper suit, as worn by insane elderly gentlemen carrying shotguns in Westerns. He is trying to hide this embarrassment behind a veneer of jolly cowboy japes, but it has taken the director, some Colombian called Carlos, most of the morning to work out what to do with him. While the other boys have been lounging around drinking Coke, flirting with the dancers and having their toned bodies oiled and sprayed orange, Ashley's been standing around in his under-wear with everyone prodding him and sighing, muttering among themselves about how they can best light his puppy fat. I am only glad Dionne is not here to see it all. I'm sure she would have had the director's nuts in her vice-like grasp before you could say 'Ashley's eaten all the pies'.

'It's interesting, isn't it?' says the make-up girl standing next to me as we watch the boys file past to take up their positions by their respective machines. 'When you do a girl band you can't believe how thin the girls are. They get this competitive anorexia thing going. All it takes is one fat shot of one of them in *Heat,* or an article about how they should be "proud" of their curves, and the whole band goes running for the laxatives. I know one girl band that actually split over who'd eaten the last square of laxative chocolate. D'you know, some of them get so thin they get that hairy-faced gerbil look when their whole body gets covered with downy fur to keep them warm.' She looks at me and snaps her chewing gum. 'It's a nightmare to cover all that up. But with boys' – she's nodding at Ashley – 'they just don't seem to care. Some of them even seem to get fatter. I mean, have you seen Boyzone recently? They're not ageing well, are they? So' – now she's looking me up and down, taking in the jeans, the white shirt and the Cuban-heeled boots – 'what d'you do?'

'I'm the manager,' I say. 'And I am paying for half this shoot.'

'Oh,' she says, her voice rising an octave. 'That's nice.'

Actually it's not particularly nice. I'm now another fifty grand down, and counting. This boy band idea is becoming one of the greatest loss leaders of all time. I am beginning to regret my chronic coke overdose at the Brits and the onset of my Simon Cowell complex. Fortunately, just as I am feeling totally disheartened about this whole sorry game I'm playing, I spot Cowell's smug mug looking at me from the pages of the *Mirror* one of the technical guys is reading. He's looking so pleased with himself at having bought yet another fat car to add to his fat car collection. A friend of mine spotted him recently weaving his way through the crowds in the lobby of the Four Seasons in LA; he had a balloon of Bailey's in one hand while the other was wrapped around his mother. I kind of wish he'd punched his lights out. But then, you know, what doesn't kill you . . .

'OK!' shouts Carlos from the confines of his canvas chair as he stares at the small TV monitor in front of him. 'Quiet on set!'

'Quiet!' yell a couple of other lesser-paid but more self-important individuals dressed in black.

A lanky, hairy teenage boy with the sort of forward-blown bouffed hair I last saw on Lulu claps the board together and the director shouts, 'Action!' The playback track kicks in, and for the first time I hear what 'Jeans On' sounds like at full blast, on a poor sound system, with a room full of people

171

– which is how, out of the confines of the studio, most people will hear it. And it's not bad. Perhaps Lucian was right about this being the first single. It's upbeat, it's simple, it's entertaining, and the 'ch ch' sound in the chorus is immediately catchy. The make-up girl is already nodding in time to the music. Her mouth is slightly open as she tries to sing along, picking out one word in five, and playing verbal catch-up between the verses.

The boys, meanwhile, are sitting in a row in their underwear, each of them opposite a fifties-era tumble dryer, watching their jeans go round and round. There are various hot girl dancers in short pants peppered around the 'laundrette' who eye each of them up as they get off their chairs, take their jeans out of the machines and slowly inch them up over their hips. This is obviously an excuse to show the boys' bodies off, and the passengers are rising to the occasion – or at least one of them is. Mike's erection is so obvious in the first take that we have to film the whole opening panning shot again. He disappears off to the dressing room for a 'private' fifteen-minute break, and returns in five with a much more video-friendly profile.

The rest of the afternoon's filming goes without too much of a hitch. Carlos gets all the glossy, greasy, toned torso shots every boy band needs these days, and Nick doesn't seem too fazed by the make-up girl putting another pair of socks down his thong. He seems totally at ease with his arse hanging out all afternoon and doesn't react to every passing hand tapping his buttocks. Actually, I think he is loving the attention, as are the rest of them. Interestingly, during the breaks it is Josh and, surprisingly, Ashley who seem to get the lion's share of the female attention. Mike and Billy stand around looking handsome and taking the piss out of each other, something I suspect they have done together since they were about six. Nick flexes his muscles and dances around, being patted on the arse, while Josh and Ash do the talking. Perhaps Holly was right after all: Ash is the one the girls will like, despite his crisp-packet belly and his sandy hair. He is certainly the most ordinary looking and the most approachable.

It is nearly midnight when we finally get out. More cans of Red Bull have been quaffed in the last couple of hours than at an underage party. As we all pile into the people-mover to drop everyone off, they are still talking and laughing and taking the piss out of each other. Esther's sitting in the front, seemingly happy with how it went. I am hoping it's all going to come together in the edit. As a straight middle-aged guy, most of the bumping, grinding and auto-frotting just goes right over my head. There are only so many close-ups of Josh's washboard or Nick's buttocks I can really cope with. The last couple of frames of them all rolling around in their pants was very reminiscent of Take That being covered in jelly and having it swept over their naked arses – which was a particularly low moment of the nineties, I thought. However, everyone else on the set seemed to find it hilarious and it's just what the audience wants, so who am I to say anything? I am sure even Cowell delegates sometimes.

I look out of the window at the passing shops. It has been a long and exhausting day. Billy suddenly lets off the most enormous fart and shoves Mike's face between his legs. Mike screams and protests, while the rest of the band roar with laughter and applaud Billy for his hilarious joke. God, I think as we pass the Shepherd's Bush Empire, this had better be worth it.

A few days later, Gavin is walking me and the band into the office of Spin It, a record-plugging company just off the Earls Court Road. A converted church full of blow-up furniture, cluttered desks and young people with bleached hair, multiple piercings and neon-coloured T-shirts, it is obviously a temple to cool and happening stuff.

'We've used these guys a lot before,' says Gavin as we stand by a tank full of tropical fish waiting for a guy called Daniel to get off the phone. 'Now that you've been made a priority act, you're getting the full VIP treatment.'

I have never quite known what particular alchemy makes the difference between languishing in signed development hell and becoming a record label priority act. All I do know is that one is a slow form of suicide and the other means that all their contacts, their money, their expertise and their enthusiasm are at your disposal. And by the grace of Grainge we have been put into the priority box.

'Hi, sorry about that,' says Daniel. 'Danny,' he says, vigorously shaking my hand. 'Have we met before?' He narrows his blue eyes at me.

He is tall and slim with spiked grey hair and baggy jeans. A thick key chain hangs out of his pocket. We are definitely of the same generation.

'You look familiar,' I lie, a little. All these guys look the same. They dress like overgrown teenagers who are clinging on to their PlayStations and refusing to grow up.

'I know,' he says, clicking his fingers. 'I worked on one of your records a few years back when I was at Warner's.'

'Right!' I nod, clicking my fingers back at him.

'Road to Reality,' he says.

'Oh, right.'

'They're a great band,' he says. 'Great songs. How are they doing? Such a nice group of lads, and very talented. What are they up to?'

'Um, I wouldn't know. We parted company.'

'Oh, OK. And now you're into boys,' he says, looking a little puzzled about what the hell I am doing here flanked by a troupe of handsome youths.

'Boy bands,' I correct.

'Boy bands,' he smiles. 'So, Gavin.' Danny rubs his hands together. 'Do you want me to get Richard in on this as well and we can have a chat about what you want us to do?'

'Good idea,' says Gavin.

'Lads!' says Danny. 'Come into the office, make yourself at home.'

We all follow Danny into the inner sanctum and cram up on the white leather sofa and transparent pink plastic chairs that fill his office. Through the glass divide I can see another fifteen or so hipsters going about their groovy business, their feet up on their desks, or hunched over computer screens. There are posters all over the walls advertising concerts or featuring bands and groups endorsing soft drinks. The place is buzzing with chat and the constant trill of phones.

'Yeah, yeah,' Richard is saying into a mobile phone, 'I agree it's a shitter, but you tell Ant and Dec if they want to book Sophie Ellis-Bextor, they have to take the other cunt too. I don't care what you do with him – gunge him, spin him around, fill him full of pizza. You play fifteen seconds of the record and you can have him, OK?' He pauses and acknowledges the group in the room. 'Well, ask them and call me back – later.' He turns off his phone. 'Sorry,' he says, blinking behind thick Buddy Holly specs. 'I'm Richard.'

'Hello,' I say, getting out of my pink plastic chair to shake his hand.

'We've met,' he says to me. 'At the Brits. I'm a mate of Terry's.'

'Oh yes, of course,' I lie again.

'It was quite late, you might not remember.'

'Oh no, of course, Richard! I remember.' It really doesn't sound very convincing. 'Nice to see you.'

'Likewise.'

'So, this is Band of Five,' announces Danny.

'You're a good-looking bunch,' says Richard. 'Can you sing?'

There's a ripple of laughter around the room.

'Of course they can,' says Gavin. 'Lucian's made them a priority act.'

'Well, then,' smiles Richard, 'hold on to your hats, lads, you're in for one hell of a ride.' His mobile goes. 'What?' he barks. 'Becky – yes? Ant and Dec have said yes. Good. That's the correct decision. I'm in a meeting, I'll have to call you back.'

We all sit, or perch, while Danny talks us through Spin It's enthusiasm for plugging the band. He starts suggesting ideas for 'the plot' or 'the buzz', which he and his team will try to get together to promote the band to radio and TV shows. Gavin and I nod our way through the meeting, but both of us know everything is dependent on how much money the label is prepared to put behind the band.

In the good old days, when I was making money rather than spending it and hammering gold discs on to my office wall, record companies thought nothing of spending £12K on taking one random old tosser from Radio One off in a private jet to watch a football final in Amsterdam for the evening and then fly him home again. And that wasn't just to plug a particular single, that was to keep the 'special relationship' going. Plugging budgets were never discussed as such; prices were considered a little vulgar. It was all about taking executives out to the most expensive restaurants, quaffing the finest wines and cuddling up to some high-class hooker. I had a mate who would take Bananarama to Venice on the Orient Express or fly a whole load of DJs first class to San Francisco to stay at the Coliseum to see U2 and Oasis. It got to the point of finding out where the band was playing and then settling on the best and most glamorous way to get there and the most expensive place to stay, and then you could justify the trip by inviting a few useful people along. Sometimes they dispensed with the band altogether and just went for a piss-up at Gleneagles, drinking their bodyweight in whisky and Benedictine.

Radio One bosses would occasionally clamp down on these freebie trips. There are, after all, only so many times a producer can accompany a superfan to Tokyo after agreeing with a record label to a special Elton John week. But I do remember hearing of one BBC Radio exec sitting in tears in the airport in Paris, surrounded by garlic and *saucisson*. He'd been on a freebie weekend courtesy of a record label and had got so stoned with the sexy plugger girl that they'd gone round and round Paris stuck on the *périphérique* and missed the last plane to London. It looked like he would miss the Monday-morning playlist meeting where the station's weekly music policy is decided, and have to own up. Fortunately, a late-night flight to Manchester was found and he was shoved in a taxi back down to London. He made the meeting practically with his pockets full of foie gras and a string of onions round his neck, only to suggest this lovely little tune he'd heard over the weekend.

Other plugging methods were not so subtle. Grams of coke sellotaped to singles were delivered to radio stations all the time. There were a few famous DJs who would even accept complimentary ladies of the night courtesy of the label, or just a quick blowjob or handjob before going on air. Indeed, there were some who said they could make your record a hit for the paltry sum of £50K. There is one old radio producer whose palm was so greased it is said the foundations of his swish house were made of vinyl.

Anyway, the days of naked girls sitting outside Radio One astride white horses while handing out a single are over. There are some lucky bastards, like James Blunt, with enough cash to splash on flying a planeload of press and party liggers over to Ibiza to listen to his new album, and to relax in his hilltop villa, kicking back to a private acoustic session. But more usually, due to financial constraints, the plugging and the PR has to be a little cleverer and a little more targeted.

So you can imagine how much my heart sinks when I am introduced to Lucy, a skinny, pretty blonde who will be in charge of Band's publicity.

'Hiya,' she says, holding out her limp hand for me to shake. 'I'm going to be doing your boys.'

In more ways than one, I think, as I watch her fawn and flick her hair as she flirts with each and every one of them. I find her obviousness more than a little irritating, but, as Paul tells me later over a few drinks at the long bar of the Soho Hotel, this sort of behaviour is what is expected of her – all part and parcel of the PR world. And he's asked around and she is much better than she looks.

'I've been told she's great with the male hacks,' he says, leaning against the bar with his finger in the air, trying to attract attention. 'She gives good wine and dine.'

'And head,' I add, a little the worse for wear after a couple of what Paul calls 'loud' vodkas.

'Probably,' agrees Paul. 'But, you know, that's the way it works. She puts her tits on the table and they put her band in the tabloids. And as she leaves, she slips them the CD.'

'That's where she's going wrong,' I say, rattling my ice. 'It's a bit harder to slip them a download, isn't it?'

'Anyway, she's asked me about tapping into the gay mafia. She says that radio DJs don't like putting boy bands on their shows; they prefer girls and think the boys are a little bit sissy. So she's going to go after a few late-night girl DJs and she's asked me about my gay contacts. Who do I know in the world of TV, radio and magazines? You know us queens, we love a boy band. Two more vodka and tonics,' he says to the barman.

'But why don't DJs like boy bands?' I ask.

'They lack credibility,' says Paul.

'There's that,' I nod. I take a large swig of melted ice. 'Fuck it, Paul, we have one bite of this cherry, we should pimp them properly.'

There are plenty of stories of boy band members being whored around, either with or without their knowledge. Most of the time there was nothing particularly predatory about it; it was more like a general bit of teasing within the gay community. There's the story of one manager deliberately sending the prettiest boy in his band to the house of a gay record exec on a Sunday with their new demo tape. The boy band member then sat on the bed while the exec listened to the music. It was like a joke between the big boys: here's something a little special for you, enjoy, and listen to the music at the same time. The boy band member either played along or was blissfully unaware, but he put on the tight trousers just the same.

However, there were a few Lou Pearlman-type characters –

the manager of 'NSync and the Backstreet Boys – who did reportedly cross the line, although he's always denied it and he's never been charged. On one occasion Pearlman is said to have summoned a potential boy band member to his door at two a.m., answering in his dressing gown. After a long argument the boy in question finally beseeched him, 'What do I have to do to get into this band?' To which Pearlman lay back in his chair, spread his legs, exposing his white pants, and replied, 'You're a smart boy, figure it out.'

There are plenty of other stories closer to home about managers shagging members of their band, or telling them that sexual favours can get them hits. And there were, and are, plenty of boys who used their looks and appeal to get what and where they wanted. Much like the acting profession has its casting couch, there are some in the boy band business who have the attitude 'one up the bum, no harm done'. It is seen as an occupational hazard that is inextricably linked to career advancement.

'Get out your BlackBerry, then,' I say to Paul. 'Let's see what you've got.'

While Paul and I come up with a list of boy-band-friendly producers and writers, Lucy and the Spin It boys also get together a plan of action. The production team sort out the album cover and publicity photos, and before long the whole machine is ready to be unleashed on an unsuspecting public.

'We are just finalizing the cover,' Lucy tells me when I phone her.

'Great,' I say, smiling to myself.

I had a mate who worked in the design department of a record company who always used to complain about the signing-off process on the cover. In the end he would design what he wanted and then move it about a bit before handing it over to the marketing director, who'd suggest a few tweaks, only for my mate to put the cover back to how it was in the first place. The marketing guys just wanted to have some input so that they could say to their girlfriends, 'See that George Michael cover? I did that.'

All I know is that the photo shoot of the boys in jeans went well. It was decided to keep it simple. Take their shirts off, grease up their chests and have them lounge over a white Cadillac. And they all turned up, which is more than can be said of UB40 for one of their album cover shoots. A member of the band went missing only to be replaced by a techie with a paper bag on his head. I have to say it didn't look that bad.

'And we have a list of radio stations we're hitting next week,' adds Lucy. She tells me she's already had a few people work on the secretaries of a couple of shows. These secretaries famously guard the portcullis to the DJs so it is always useful to placate them with U2 tickets and backstage passes, or indeed employ them on a record – as Mickey Most did when he needed a party atmosphere for 'Some Girls'. The record was a hit and all the girls received platinum records for their contribution.

Lucy, Danny and Richard appear to have pulled more strings than puppeteers on speed over the last few days, for the boys and I find ourselves on our way to a late-night session at one of the capital's top radio stations. I am not sure how they managed it. There was talk of us turning up to some music industry drinks party and monstering a few DJs, forcing the boys to corner them and sing a cappella in the corridor like the Spice Girls used to do. But fortunately there's clearly some old queen somewhere who's saved us the trouble. All I know is that it's not the presenter, who meets us with the disinterestedness of a dog revisiting a day-old turd in the street. His name is Shane and he gives us a sniff with his septum-challenged nostrils before returning to his desk and the late-night requests.

I suppose for an old skinny geezer like Shane a boy band doesn't hold much curiosity, but then neither does much of his show. All the records are decided in advance. On a popular station like this you come out of the news and go straight into a hit, and from then on the hour, or 'clock', is decided by a program called Selecta, which offers up pre-programmed suggestions for a producer to put in the show, depending on the tone, the age group and the time of the night you are broadcasting. Before being programmed the music is tested, much like in the US, by a playlist group sitting in a room deciding if they like it or not, if they have heard it too much, or indeed too little. Then the records are classed as A-list, B-list and Recurrent – that is, a hit we like to hear again and again, such as 'I Can't Get You Out of My Head' or 'Angels'. Although I've been told that Kylie and indeed Robbie are 'burning' a bit at the moment, which means their hits are not going down as well as they used to, and therefore they're coming off the Recurrent list. As are songs like 'Bad Day' by

Daniel Powter and 'You Give Me Something' by James Morrison, both of which have been played to death. However, all you need for your star to be in the ascendant and for your record no longer to be burnt is another hit, of course.

The boys are sitting around drinking the complimentary beers, and I am having a plastic glass of cheap red wine, while the harassed producer talks through the mike at Shane. 'This one's three and a half minutes, Shane,' she says, 'if you want the toilet. And then we've got the news.'

Shane comes out, pulling up his loose grey slacks as he approaches us.

'This your first interview?' he asks.

'That's right,' says Lucy.

'Look and learn,' he says, walking past on his way to the lavatory.

'What does that mean?' asks Billy, looking a little nervous.

'Don't worry,' says Lucy. 'He's an old has-been who used to shag his secretary over the desk while reading the news.'

'Really?' I ask, somewhat impressed.

'Happens all the time on these late-night shows,' she says. 'A DJ mate of mine once had two girls under the desk blowing him and the newsreader at the same time. They were fans of some US rap band and thought this was the best way of not getting kicked out of the studio.'

'They were probably right,' I say.

'Mmm,' agrees Lucy. She looks at the boys. 'So, are you all happy you know what you're saying?' Lucy's been running the boys through some questions this afternoon in the hope of helping them negotiate the perils of the radio interview. But looking at them now biting their nails and bouncing their knees, they are not exactly exuding confidence. She looks at the producer, 'Any jingles and links you'd like us to do would be great,' she smiles.

'That would be brilliant, if you would,' says the producer, sipping a thin-looking coffee from a Styrofoam cup. 'It's always good to have a few idents in the bag.'

Shane walks past me rubbing his nose and itching his arse. He clicks and points his finger at me.

'All right, chief?' he says. 'In you come, lads.' He nods at the boys and they all follow him in to the studio.

They settle down in front of their mikes; there are only three so Mike and Billy, and Nick and Josh share. A young bloke in specs reads the sports results, and then they go straight into the new Take That record. The record finishes and the red light goes on.

'Take That,' announces Shane. 'And now, get this. I am joined by a new boy band who want to follow in the footsteps of those boys, and their name is Band of Five!' Lucy whoops in the back of the studio. 'That's the sound of their publicist shouting there. Well, you have one fan, boys.' They laugh.

'Small beginnings,' says Josh.

'I suppose you have to start somewhere,' says Shane. 'Why don't you tell us all your names?'

The boys introduce themselves around the table.

'Excellent, excellent,' continues Shane. 'So, which one of you is gay?'

7

Despite all Lucy's protests to the contrary, Shane's show was not a great success. Firstly, the boys were thrown by the gay question. Instead of laughing and saying something crass like 'Are you asking?' they became defensive and serious, saying that there was nothing wrong with being gay and that some of their best friends were gay. But, you know, you live and learn. I think perhaps we should have given them a bit more media training than a couple of hours with Lucy before sending them into the old cokey's lair. It's not often I say this, but where's Kate Thornton when you need her?

And the rest of the interview was a little dull. Josh did most of the talking, while Mike cracked a couple of gags. Nick said that he was really proud of the album but then managed to let slip that they hadn't written a single track on it. But at least 'Jeans On' was played after the interview, and that cheered the boys up a bit. Then, when we were all in the lift on the way out of the building, Shane asked his listeners to ring in and place a bet as to how long they thought Band of Five would last. An outraged Paul called me on the mobile on my way home.

'The man's a homophobic tosser,' he said. 'I can't believe he hasn't been taken off air. He's an arsehole.'

'He's an old coked-up has-been,' I replied. 'The industry is full of them.'

'Well, I'm never listening to that show again.'

'That'll learn him,' I laughed.

'I can't believe you're not more pissed off,' he said.

'It's one in the morning, mate, it's a hot sticky night in July, and I've had one glass of shitty Shiraz. There is only so much energy I can muster.'

The next day must be slow on news – either that or Lucy's clearly been using her sex appeal somewhere: there is a small piece in the *Evening Standard* asking if Shane is the meanest radio host in town. Encouragingly, they have used a large photo of the boys looking handsome and a very small shot of Shane looking gnarled. I am flicking through the TV pages when my phone goes.

'OK, it's not quite what we wanted, but we have made a story,' says a voice.

'I'm sorry, who's this?'

'Richard – who d'you think?' says Richard. 'Anyway, so we've got a bit of a buzz, let's capitalize on it. I've got some local radio in the Midlands. Shall we do it?'

'Great,' I say. 'Why not?'

'Call you back.'

I hang up, and then my mobile goes.

'Hi, it's Lucy. The *Sun* want to follow the *Standard* and start a bit of a campaign with their readers asking them to bet on how long Band of Five will last.'

'Oh right?' I'm not really sure how to take this brilliant brainwave. I now appear to be managing a national joke. 'Are we sure we want to do this?'

'They'll pay for downloads, because they can't judge without hearing the song, can they?'

'I suppose not.'

'So that's a yes?'

The next day the boys are all over the *Sun* and we're sitting in the back of an Espace on the way up the M40 to Birmingham, with Richard at the wheel.

'You all right in the back?' he asks, looking in his mirror over the top of his reflector wrap-around shades.

'It's very roomy,' says Mike.

'Plush,' adds Billy.

'It's new,' says Richard. 'You need a big car in this job.'

He goes on to tell a story about a mate of his who had to pick up Gwen Guthrie at Heathrow to drive her to the record company. She had a song out at the time called 'Ain't Nothing Going On But the Rent', which was riding high in the charts. This mate of Richard's had a tiny sports car, and Gwen was a large lady. 'All he could think was, I hope she's not going to be too fat for the car, I hope she's not too fat. Sure enough, when he got to the car park and put her in the passenger seat her arse spilled over so much my mate drove all the way to Polydor in the slow lane on the M4 in second gear!'

The boys laugh.

'That's some arse,' says Mike.

'Huge,' adds Billy.

For someone apparently so psychopathically dysfunctional, Richard is rather entertaining. He's been in the business a long time and seems to enjoy the fresh ears in the car.

'And her cab bill was something else,' he continues. 'We did a video shoot with her for her follow-up single over here, just in case it was a hit, so we didn't have to fly her back again, and when she left there was two grand filed in expenses. Apparently she'd fallen for one of the backing dancers in the video and was taking a cab up to Manchester every night. She'd shag him while the meter was running and take the cab back down again in the morning.'

'That's some shag,' says Nick, sounding impressed.

'Yup,' agrees Richard. 'But she was a confident girl. She wouldn't get out of the car for less than ten thousand dollars in cash.'

'What?' asks Josh.

'Don't give them ideas,' I say. 'That's an old Little Richard trick, only to be paid in cash.'

'There are plenty of them at it,' says Richard. 'One of my worst moments was with R Kelly. We'd collected him from the Kensington Hilton and driven him to Elstree to do *Top of the Pops* when he refused to get out of the car for anything less than twenty thousand dollars in cash. I mean, why would you do that when you are plugging your own record?'

'So what did you do?' asks Ashley, perking up. The subject of money is dear to his heart.

'We had to get it. We compromised on fifteen and the record company had to send a bike with the cash. Four and a half hours later he got out of the car.'

'That's stubborn,' Ashley remarks.

'You want stubborn?' asks Richard. 'I went to Heathrow to pick up James Brown who'd flown in for some awards ceremony. We had already been given his list of riders: he must be referred to as Mr Brown; he always travels first class, as does his hairdresser and stylist; he must be picked up from the airport in a Rolls; the band must stay in one hotel and he must stay in a different one; and all money paid to Mr Brown must be in cash. That word was written in huge letters.'

'I've seen that a few times on riders,' I say.

'I know,' says Richard, smiling across at me. 'So there we were, at the airport; the Rolls was ready, the list was under my arm. Two security guys came through first. We're there. The car's outside. I show it to the security guy who looks at me and says, "There's a problem." I go, "On page five of the riders it says Rolls-Royce." He shakes his head and replies, "Mr Brown doesn't travel in a black Rolls-Royce, Mr Brown only travels in a white Rolls-Royce." I say, "Oh dear, I am very sorry, but shall we just get going in this, and I'll organize another one for later?" He says no. Six hours later we leave the airport. Mr Brown sat in the lounge for six hours waiting for the right colour car. He'd travelled all the way from the States only to wait another six hours for the right car.'

'You'd have thought he wanted a shower, a shit and a shave,' I suggest.

'Exactly,' says Richard. 'Ten years later his riders were exactly the same except this time there had to be an oxygen cylinder at the side of the stage.'

'Is it true that the Stones have a whole resus kit next to the stage when they perform in case Keith keels over?' I ask.

'I wouldn't put it past them. Their backstage area's like a gentlemen's club, with crustless sandwiches, copies of *Country Life*, *The Economist* and *The Lady*, plus more herbal teas than a hippy café. They travel with their own furniture, too. It goes ahead of them so they have all the little comforts of home with them.'

When we pull up outside the radio station in some arse end of Birmingham we are greeted by three fans who squeal with delight as the boys get stiffly out of the car.

'You're in the papers!' says one plump little girl brandishing a pink pen and a pad.

'And you came to our school!' giggles another girl with railway tracks on her teeth.

I nod and smile. Paul's been using our email contact list to alert the 'fans' as to where our boys are going to be.

I watch the boys excitedly sign their first ever autographs and pose for photos on mobile phones. 'One, two, three,' the plump girl says, pointing her phone. The boys smile and strike poses, pointing their thumbs and index fingers. 'Oh,' says the girl, checking her phone, 'that didn't work, can we do it again?' The boys happily oblige, striking the same poses as before. 'Thanks,' says the girl. Josh leans over and gives her a kiss. Her cheeks flush scarlet underneath her orange make-up. The other boys quickly realize that this is the way to play it and do the same. It takes us about ten minutes to get inside.

Mark, the presenter of the morning show, is a nice-looking chap in his early twenties who is clearly destined for a shiny future in kids TV. His fixed white grin is blinding and his enthusiasm never appears to pall. He is all handshakes and jokes and large laughs – the antithesis of the addled Shane. And the boys respond well. When the station plays the song, Josh and Ashley hum along and sing the chorus live on air, while the other three click their fingers and do the 'ch ch' bit. The female producer can't stop laughing and flicking her hair, and Mark's so delighted with the amount of airtime he's managed to fill before the news that he asks the boys to hang around into the next half-hour to introduce a few songs. They get a couple of calls from Selly Oak, Redditch and Edgbaston in support of the boys, all of them saying they will buy the record.

'Great job,' says Richard, patting each of them on the back as they come out of the studio. 'You did well.' He winks at me – or at least I think he does, as he's still wearing his sunglasses. 'Next stop, Nottingham.'

Paul's all overexcited. Apparently our MySpace page is getting plenty of hits as is the website and people are beginning to download the songs, especially 'Jeans On'. We've got lots of traffic and a healthy number of girls who want to be added as 'friends'. Debbie's been listening less to her iPod and has spent the last few weeks channelling her inner teenage boy, blogging in the name of Josh, Ashley, Mike, Billy and Nick. Sometimes she bothers to call them up to get some genuine stories, but most of the time she looks at their schedule and just fills in the blanks.

Richard and Lucy have been trailing the boys all over the country, but still the record doesn't seem to be getting much radio play. Gavin's beginning to get a little bit twitchy. He's scheduled the single for release in ten days and he thinks there is more all of us could do to try to get the buzz going.

Paul and I are sitting in the office waiting by the speakerphone for Gavin's conference call to come in. Finally, the phone rings.

'Hello, this is Belinda here from Gavin's office,' says a surprisingly posh-sounding bird. 'I have Gavin, Lucy and Danny on the line. Are you ready?'

'Yes,' I say. 'I am here in the office with Paul and you're on speakerphone.'

'Hi there,' says Paul.

'Hello,' three voices reply.

'Right, I think I should start,' says Gavin.

'Go ahead,' I say.

'Well, the thing is, we're just not getting enough radio play,' he says.

'We've been plugging the arse off it,' says Danny, immediately defensive. 'There just aren't that many takers.'

'Why not?' says Gavin. 'It left this office a hit.'

As Danny witters on for the next few minutes about all the hard work Spin It have put in to plug the record, I kind of feel sorry for him. Whenever a record doesn't get much airtime it is always the fault of the pluggers, not the record company. The number of times I've heard the phrase 'it left here a hit' when the record patently isn't . . .

'Everyone likes it,' says Danny, 'it's just trying to get them to play it. It's a boy band problem.'

'Tell that to the six-time platinum Take That,' barks Gavin. 'We need more publicity.'

'OK,' says Lucy. 'I could try tipping the press off, if you want?'

'What, like Posh bloody Spice? Get these boys photographed out shopping?' says Gavin.

'Well, outside a nice restaurant? Get them to a few premieres?' she counters.

'Can't one of them fuck someone?' asks Danny. 'Or at least pretend to. We could do a whole Geri Halliwell/Chris Evans thing.'

'What? Two people who shared the same PR company went out for the sake of her record,' says Gavin, 'and I think all she ever said on the subject was "Yes, we are together", which was about as convincing as Elton John's miraculous hair growth.'

'Well, it did get her some badly needed press,' says Lucy. 'Can't we get one of them to go out with someone else on the label?'

'Which one?' asks Gavin.

'Josh is obviously the most handsome one,' I say.

'That's true,' agrees Paul.

So a plan is hatched to try to get Josh photographed out and about with some sort of lush lovely while the others are toured up and down the country doing as many radio gigs, or PAs, as possible. They include singing for free in the Bluewater shopping centre, the Arndale and the Bull Ring, plus numerous trips to Brighton where they are going down well with the gay community. Over the next few days I keep in constant touch with Lucy who tells me she is in negotiation with an agent of one of the recent evictees from the *Big Brother* house. It's not quite what I had in mind for Josh, or indeed any of the boys, but they appear to be open to some sort of contract.

In the meantime, Paul and I get the boys out and about to a couple of premieres. Esther manages to call in a favour from a mate at Burberry and the boys all look completely fantastic as they pose together down the red carpet at the latest Keira Knightley film. They are papped left and right. Paul keeps pushing them forward, trying to get them snapped standing next to Keira, but her PR is having none of it.

At the after-show party at 50 St James, the boys really let their hair down and no amount of telling them to play it cool makes any difference. Maybe it's the glitzy decor and chandeliers or the idea of frotting next to so many famous people that sends them into a tailspin, or perhaps they've been working too hard. Mike, Billy and Ashley storm the place like a bunch of locusts, shovelling down the free snacks and booze in frenzied panic. Nick is like a dog on heat, sniffing out women, mumbling over and over that he's in a band. And Josh is swigging back the vodka martinis, swatting the girls away like flies.

At 10.30, Paul and I are having a line in the lavs when he gets a call from a mate saying that someone's dropped out of going on *Lorraine* tomorrow and would we like to fill their slot. Would we ever! For the next half-hour we search high and low through the party for any sign of the lads. We find Billy and Mike surrounded by drinks at a corner table, trying to see how many shots they can knock back in one. Nick is on the dance floor, throwing shapes amid a small entourage of girls. We ask him if he's seen Ashley or Josh. He tells us that Josh left a while ago, and that he hasn't seen Ashley since he started dancing.

We all split up to search and return five minutes later empty-handed. I send a couple of texts and call his phone, but he doesn't respond. I am beginning to get a little worried. He is underage, after all, and shouldn't be drinking. There's no telling where he might be, or what he might be doing.

Eventually I take myself back to one of the lavatories for a piss. Standing at the urinal, I hear some grunting and groaning behind me. As I turn round with an amused grin on my face, the stall door slowly opens to reveal Ashley with his trousers down by his ankles and his plump bare arse pumping away like his life depended on it. I can't see who he's shagging, but pointing towards me are a pair of red high heels on the end of a pair of limp legs that are bobbing up and down. The shoes are not expensive: the £69.99 price tag is still stuck to the bottom of the sole.

'Ash!' I say.

'What?' he replies. His sweaty puce-pink face turns towards me, but he doesn't break his rhythm. Over his shoulder I can see the girl's face. Her eyes are closed in pleasure and her mouth hangs slack, her tongue loose. He clearly knows what he is doing. 'Give me a minute,' he says.

'Make it five,' shouts the girl.

I shrug my shoulders, zip up my trousers and leave the room.

Billy pukes twice before he sits down on Lorraine Kelly's sofa at five past nine in the morning. Somehow the others are managing to be bright and perky despite how hungover they all feel. Josh has been up all night as far as I can work out, although he is not really telling me where he's been. Ashley is looking rather pleased with himself and the others are all fired up on adrenalin. Lorraine is sweet and asks them how long they've been together and what sort of music they like, the answers to which they have more or less off pat by now. They are then asked to play out the show. This is the first time they have mimed to a backing track, and all but Mike are convincing. Perhaps it's his hangover, or the fact that he can't remember his words under pressure. He buggers three or four lines, and steps the wrong way in the chorus.

'They were great,' says Craig down the phone as I'm on my way to the office in the back of a cab.

'Are you sure?' I ask. 'Mike fucked up and they weren't very sharp.'

'They were great,' he repeats. 'Just don't put them on

Jonathan Ross. You've got to remember to manage what you have. Shakin' Stevens wasn't the sharpest tool so Sony never put him up for anything. He was OK to do *Swap Shop* or whatever, but they didn't put him on Parky. Don't hang your guys out to dry. You don't need to put them on the *Today* programme.'

'I see what you mean.'

'When's your record coming out?' he asks.

'Next week.'

'Have you got them down to do G-A-Y?'

'Um . . .'

'Call yourself a manager?' he laughs. 'Fuckin' 'ell, it's not rocket science. You've got a hot boy band. They've got a room full of hot boys. I can't believe you're going to try to launch a new boy band without doing G-A-Y.'

'I thought they only took established acts like Kylie or Madonna.'

'They're a nice bunch of blokes,' says Craig. 'Call Jeremy Joseph, I'm sure he'll give you a slot. They love discovering acts before anyone else.'

'And you think they're hot?' I ask.

'Stop being a needy old queen! You know they are. Call Jeremy, tell him Craig told you to call him. He owes me a favour. I'm sure he'll put them on for a song. I am business-carding you over the number. Speak later.'

I sit in the cab, waiting for the number to come through. I stare out of the window, looking at the stacks of semi-naked girls in Hyde Park. It's going to be another hot old day and they are picking their spots, laying out their towels, ready for a day roasting in the sun.

The cabbie has the radio on. Suddenly I hear the opening few bars of 'Jeans On'. 'Here's something new, by a band called Band of Five, and this is "Jeans On",' announces the DJ. Sitting totally still in my seat, I scan the cabbie's face for any signs. Is he smiling? Are his lips curling at all? Is he tapping his toe? Moving his fingers on the steering wheel? Will he turn it up? Or down? We're about halfway through. The second chorus comes in and his finger starts to tap on the steering wheel. On one 'ch ch' his head nods. As we drive along the Bayswater Road, he appears to be enjoying it. At least he hasn't turned it off or down.

The song finishes. I lean forward in the cab and poke my head through the partition window.

'Excuse me,' I say. 'Did you enjoy that?'

'What?' he asks.

'The song.'

'Oh,' he says, looking at his radio, slightly surprised to see it on. 'I wasn't listening.'

It takes an hour or so for Jeremy Joseph to return my call. The man behind the highly successful G-A-Y brand, he is upbeat and up for it. He says he's heard the song, that it's a good cover, and he's happy to have the boys sing it on Saturday night. He tells me it would be better all round if we stick to just the one, short and sweet. No one wants to dance to three songs they've never heard of sung by a band they've never seen. He says he'll put them on as a support act for whoever else they have on – maybe Pete Burns or the guys from *The X Factor*, he's not sure yet. He also suggests we think of something a little special to do if we want to make the press the next day, which is kind of the point of appearing at G-A-Y. The timing of the show is specifically late to miss the Sunday papers, so any photos or stories will hit Monday's at the same time as the single or the album is released.

And the bands play up to this. The Feeling recently performed dragged up as the Spice Girls. McFly stripped on stage. Charlotte Church chose a bottle of vodka over a bunch of flowers. In fact, some of the most iconic performances by some of pop's biggest stars have taken place on that tiny stage at the London Astoria. For a gay night in a small theatre with a capacity of two thousand, G-A-Y punches very much above its weight. I'm not sure if it's the fact that the performers don't get on stage until 1.30 a.m., which leaves them time to do a TV show or even Wembley before it, or that it's been going for fifteen years, so there's a bit of a history to it and some long relationships; all I know is they've had some amazing people there and they have got them to produce some of their most exciting work. Madonna launched her *Confessions* album there; post-cancer Kylie's first singing outing was accompanying her sister at G-A-Y. Mariah Carey's sipped Cristal there, Pink's done an hour and a half, Enrique Iglesias flirted brilliantly with the audience. He sang 'Hero' to a young bloke plucked from the crowd. The Spice Girls, Boyzone, Westlife and the Pussycat Dolls all started their UK careers there.

I call Craig back to thank him for helping me out and tell

him he can have half the fee. Sadly for me, he tells me that if there is a fee it's not even going to pay for the cabs there and back. Some acts get a bit, he says, some acts don't. Some acts are financed by the record company, some acts have so many dancers that the club can't begin to cover the costs. But it's not the sort of night designed to make huge amounts of money, he reminds me. G-A-Y hire the Astoria. The Astoria get the coat check and the bar, and Jeremy takes the door to help pay for the act and anything else. They did give Madonna the door, apparently, but she had such a great night that she offered to give it back. Eventually, after much to-ing and fro-ing, she kept the door, and bought Jeremy a sofa instead.

Paul, Esther and the boys are over the moon when I tell them, as are the Spin It boys. I think Lucy's retroussé nose is a little out of joint, but she recovers well and suggests that the record company send a photographer down to get some good shots. All we need to think about now is what the boys should wear. Esther tells me she is on the case. Nick and Billy come to me separately to beg for it not to be leather.

It's midnight and we are all backstage at the Astoria crammed into one dressing room knocking back the beer and the vodka and Red Bull. Paul, Esther, Lucy, Richard and I have come down to support the boys who are pacing around waiting for their costumes to arrive. Two doors away, Pete Burns is holed up in his dressing room. We occasionally hear him laugh, or his deep Scouse voice boom up the corridor. Jeremy and his business partner Michael are rushing around making sure everyone is having fun, got enough to drink, isn't running low on crisps. There are two small dogs, Gizmo and Hailey, rattling around too, along with various other technicians and Burns fans. Ashley's looking particularly edgy.

'This is going to be hell,' he says, pacing and exhaling, shaking out his arms. 'What happens if they hate us?'

'They won't,' says Paul, who is already quite pissed and wired on cocaine and excitement. This is one of his old haunts, but he hasn't been back for a while. He looks like he's itching to get out there and shake his middle-aged tush around, in the hope of pulling. 'You'll be fine, they'll love you. They've only ever booed Darius and Hear'say, and Jodie Marsh had a glass of wine chucked at her. And that's it. They're a nice audience.'

'So, do we flirt?' asks Mike, grinning.

'Your arses off,' says Paul, screwing up his nose.

'But we've only really sung to teenage girls,' says Billy.

'They're the same,' says Paul, 'only filthier.'

'Great,' grins Nick. 'This should be a right laugh.'

'Just be yourselves,' I say. 'This is the same as Loving It in Birmingham, only much better. Just relax and enjoy it.'

At half past midnight the cheering starts. The strains of 'Better the Devil You Know' come through the walls and Jeremy's out on stage geeing up the crowd, announcing tonight's acts and telling everyone it's only one hour till showtime! We all stand still backstage and listen to the applause.

'They sound excited,' says Josh.

'They've just released the balloons,' says Paul. 'They release a net of balloons every half-hour until the act comes on. Sometimes they're colour coordinated.'

'What do you mean?' asks Ashley.

'You know, green for Westlife, pink for Pink,' explains Paul.

'And black for the Darkness,' laughs Mike.

'I don't think they've played here,' Paul responds.

Esther's phone goes and she rushes off to the stage door to collect the costumes. Everyone looks across nervously at her. She returns a few minutes later with a large leather bag over her shoulder.

'OK,' she says, dropping the bag on the floor and starting to unpack it. 'These are all I could get my hands on at short notice and they aren't totally right but they'll have to do.' She starts to hand round white vest tops. 'These are optional really. I mean, if you want to go on bare-chested, you know, Josh and Nick, then you should. Here's a vest for you, Ash.'

Ashley bites the side of his cheek in irritation.

'I think they should all wear the tops,' I say, quickly. Having always been the fat boy not picked for football, I kind of know how Ashley feels, and I can do without one of my lead singers being demotivated right now.

'We are a band,' says Nick helpfully, 'and bands always dress the same.'

'OK then,' agrees Esther. 'These are the jeans, OK, and these are the jockstraps I want you to wear underneath.' She holds up a red satin pouch.

'Jesus,' says Billy. 'You want us to wear those?'

'It's only a bit of fun,' says Esther. 'These trousers have

Velcro down the sides and at the end of the song you just pull them off in one tug and you'll be left in the red thongs.'

'Do we have to?' asks Mike, suddenly a little less amused by the situation.

'Actually they're quite comfortable,' says Nick, already dressed in his, turning around and admiring his taut toned backside in the mirror. 'How do the trousers work again?'

'You just give them a tug at the waistband,' says Esther.

'Like this!' says Josh, whipping them off to reveal his long slim legs and red jockstrap.

Everyone laughs. Paul just stares.

'That's it,' says Esther.

'I think it's great,' I say.

'I hope the photographer gets the shot,' says Lucy, reaching for her phone.

'It'll bring the house down,' says Paul.

The boys get kitted up. More vodka and Red Bull slides down their necks.

'Are you all happy about where you're standing?' I say. 'We're singing live to track tonight.' Some of them more live than others, obviously. 'You remember from the sound check this afternoon?'

We go through the routine once again, more to kill time than anything.

After what seems like an age there's a knock on the door. 'Five minutes,' comes a voice. The boys start to pace the room in panic.

'Calm down, everyone,' I say. 'You'll be fine.'

'Ready?' asks Jeremy, poking his head round the door. 'You all look great.'

'Go get 'em!' says Esther.

'Good luck, boys,' I say. 'Let's go.'

I follow them out on to the side of the stage and look out into the crowd. The place is packed, heaving with hot sweaty bodies. Rows of expectant faces look towards the stage. The air hangs heavy with the stench of perspiration. There's a palpable buzz. The boys stand in the shadows, shaking out their legs. Mike turns and smiles at me. His eyes are glowing with energy. He can't wait to get out there. Josh is grinning, Nick and Billy are bouncing up and down on the spot. Ashley is rubbing his sweaty palms down the sides of his trousers.

Jeremy goes out on stage. The crowd wolf-whistle and applaud. He tells them that these boys are new and that they should be nice.

'Virgins!' someone shouts.

A cheer goes out.

'Ladies and gents, put your hands together for Band of Five!' yells Jeremy before clapping and leaving the stage.

The music starts and the band bounce out on stage, clapping above their heads. Thankfully, the lyrics and the music sound familiar to some of the audience and there's a whoop of approval. The boys line up at the front of the stage and belt out the song with a huge amount of energy and enthusiasm. And the crowd respond. Mike's shaking his hips like he's loving it, Billy's grinning away, they're all really going for it. Even Ashley seems to have shaken off his nerves. A sea of entertained faces looks back at them. By the time we've got to the 'ch ch' for the third or fourth time, everyone's joining in. When at the end the boys pull off their trousers to reveal the red satin jockstraps, the crowd roar, flash bulbs go off and mobile phones come out and are pointed towards the stage. I spot Paul's beaming face over the other side of the stage, and I can see Lucy nodding away at the photographer, telling him to keep snapping. I clench my fist with delight. They've done it. They've brought the house down.

Jeremy looks delighted. He comes over and shouts in my ear, 'You lot can come again!' Then he walks out on stage, clapping his hands above his head. 'Band of Five, everyone! Let's hear it one more time!' There's more clapping and whistling and cheering. The boys clap back and bow, lapping it all up. 'The single is, as ever, out on Monday!' announces Jeremy.

The boys all want to hang around, to drink more vodka, get a bit more attention, and watch Pete Burns perform. But I tell them to shift their backsides home as I want them fresh and fragrant for Monday – the biggest day of their lives. For once most of them listen to me. Josh tells me he'll only stay for one more drink with Nick, while the other three take the free lift on offer, which when you're still on £100 a week is probably the wisest choice.

It's early on Monday morning, and I can't sleep. I am skimming through all the commercial channels trying to catch 'Jeans On' being played somewhere. There's a small photo of the boys with their red thongs on in the *Mirror* and one of them ripping their trousers off in the *Sun* underneath the head-line 'Jeans Off!' Lucy and Jeremy should be happy, I think as I try to drink my hot water and lemon. I don't know who I'm kidding with this detox diet thing in the morning. What I wouldn't give for a proper cup of coffee.

My phone goes. It's Holly.

'Dad!' she squeals. 'They're playing your record on Heart!'

'Shit, where?' I spin the dial on the radio. 'Where? Where?'

'Heart!' she yells. 'Too late, it's finished.'

'What are they saying?'

'It's Jamie and Harriet and they're arguing about it.'

'Why? What?'

'Shut up, I'm trying to listen.'

I stand still, straining to hear the verdict. I am always tense when any of my artists releases an album or a single, but some-how with Band it is more personal. Not only did I put the band together, there is also a lot riding on their success. I need a hit, and I need it now.

It makes me hanker after the old days when charts were a little easier to fix. All you needed was a budget and a buying team. Your buying team was dispatched around the country to snap up singles in the chart return shops, and they'd get paid 50p per record they bought. Chart return shops were always easy to spot as they were the ones with new posters, bigger dis-plays and promotions such as a free box set (worth £6.99) of some huge star's back catalogue that was on the same label as the new star the label was trying to promote. In the olden days you'd buy a record in the chart return shop, someone would note it down, and then the figures were collated for a mid-week chart by Gallup, and then later again for Sunday. You needed to buy between five and ten thousand records to get yours to chart. But it did require a little bit of skill. There were plenty of stories of execs being caught buying their own records in stacks of six or seven at a time, and asking for receipts. I have a very old mate who got his record label boss fired as chairman of the BPI after he went round buying records in Brighton wearing his promotional jacket and T-shirt – the single, the seven-inch, the twelve-inch, the lot – and asking for receipts. One shopkeeper got suspicious and phoned another chart shop close by, telling them to be on the lookout. My mate was caught red-handed. But he wasn't the only one. We were all at it. Ask any manager working in the eighties and nineties and they'll tell you it was a given. You'd get £50K out of the record company and bill them later for 'promotional services'.

These days, of course, you can just keep downloading, although you have to be a little bit smart and use lots of different email addresses. Everyone is always sending out round-robin emails saying that if you download this song we'll send you £2, or £1, or whatever. The same sort of thing goes on on MySpace all the time. The record company sends out the call and suddenly Sandi Thom is very popular. The only problem is there aren't the great slush piles of cash available to do it these days.

In the States, of course, the practice is the same, it's just that the figures are so much higher and they have to buy up whole cities at a time. So, for example, if a management company and a record company decide to collude to break a new artist they might buy between 200,000 and 500,000 albums at a time. But the stakes are high across the pond, and the money is huge. If you have an album that is going to go on to make $20m nationwide, what's an initial layout of a million between friends?

All I have managed to do with 'Jeans On' is get Holly to ask all her friends to download the song and pass it on to their friends. I am also paying them a couple of quid to do so, but it doesn't exactly amount to much.

'Harriet is saying she loves it and fancies Josh,' says Holly.

'Josh?'

'She says she caught them last week when she was ill watching Lorraine Kelly. Jamie says he's with Shane-what's-his-chops and that they won't last a week.'

'Right,' I say. 'At least they're talking about them.'

'That's true,' she agrees. 'And anyway, Dad?'

'Yes?'

'All my mates love it.'

And hers are not the only ones. Lucy, Danny and Richard have been dragging the boys up and down the country. No letter-opening is too banal, no village fête too small, no radio station too far away. They now have to sing and dance and flirt like never before.

The next day at 10.30 a.m. we are all holding our breath for the position in the mid-week charts, waiting for Gavin to call. My mobile rings.

'Forty-four,' he says simply.

'Chart or downloads?'

'Both.'

He hangs up.

Right, I think we need to do something. We need to get everyone downloading and we need to get some hype going. Any old hype will do. Though preferably not like when Boyzone had a bit of a rough landing in New Zealand and a 'near death plane crash' story was leaked to the press without their parents being told first. Or indeed the Brian Harvey 'E's are good' story when he opined to the nation's teenagers about the benefits of drug taking. Something sexy is what we need, something fun. It is silly season after all. The papers are desperate to fill their pages and Lucy's still working on a *Big Brother* romance for one of the boys, but they keep asking for too much money. There must be some TV shows that need pretty-boy guests.

'Great news,' says Richard. 'We've got them an interview slot on *This Morning* and they're playing the video.'

'That's brilliant. We've spent so much money on that video it'll be nice to get an airing.'

'I agree. I am of the Simon Cowell school of thought that you shouldn't have your band singing live on TV if you can help it. You've spent a quarter of a million getting the sound as perfect as possible and another half a million making them look fabulous in the video. Why let them sing live on TV and bugger the whole thing up?'

'My thoughts exactly,' I laugh.

'But for future reference, they are members of the Musicians' Union?' he asks.

'They don't play any instruments,' I say.

'It doesn't matter,' he says. 'They might.'

The MU have so many bloody rules and regulations. Half the pluggers in London used to be members just in case they had to fill in for someone on *Top of the Pops*. I have a mate who mimed playing keyboards for the Spice Girls on *TOTP* and another who played with Echo and the Bunnymen even though he failed his Grade 2 recorder exam. The other thing that used to drive everyone mad was that any record that was broadcast over here to which a US artist mimed along, the backing track had to be played by members of the British Musicians' Union. So for Jon Bon Jovi to sing on *TOTP* the record company would have to book a studio in London and re-record the track with British musicians. Not that anyone would. They'd book the studio, pay the musicians not to come, then load up the original music in the machine and sit there all day waiting for the bloke from the union to turn up. He'd come through the door and you'd put on the track and say something like, 'It's coming along nicely – it just needs a bit more layering.' He'd ask where the musicians were, and you'd say, 'They're round the corner having a cup of tea.' Everyone would tick their respective boxes and piss off home. If no one went through this charade and the boxes were not ticked the TV show, the record company and the band would all be fined.

This Morning goes well. Fern and Phil like the boys. Mike tells a couple of gags, they get Nick to do a back flip for a laugh, and Billy does a break-dance spin on his head. The hits on MySpace and the website increase, as do the downloads. That night Lucy gets them to go to the Girls Aloud showcase in Covent Garden. It's a double bubble for the label and the boys go down a treat. The girls take them out on the town after the show and they are all chased down the street to China White. Josh is papped leaving the club at four a.m. with Sarah Harding and gets his face on page three of all the tabloids. Come Friday we've got photographers outside the office who follow us to the record signing at HMV on Oxford Street. Paul's emailed all the girls on our fan base about it as it's bang in the middle of the school holidays when no one has anything to do.

Four hundred girls turn up. Josh is mobbed by mobile phones, and the others also get their fair share of attention. 'One, two, three!' I see them smile and pose over and over again. It's an extraordinary feeling watching the tide turn, the moment when a band reaches a critical mass, when their faces are frequently in the papers and their record is being played more and more on the radio. People know their names. 'Josh – over here!' 'Mikey – to me!' As I stand and watch the boys going through the motions, smiling and signing, I sense that this is it. They've dipped their toes into the pool of fame and their lives will never be the same again. Even if this is all there is to it, and they return to civilian life afterwards, something will have changed. They've had a sniff of it. They know what it's like. It's got right under their skin. Little do the girls know as they push and shove their way forwards that these stars they are lusting over are still only earning £100 a week.

Saturday is tense. Richard's got the boys travelling all over town, from one radio station to the next. Ashley is the colour of putty, Mikey's lost all his humour, and Nick's lost his voice. Not that we've ever really used it, but it would be useful for him to answer the odd question during an interview rather than leaving Josh to carry the can. Debbie, Paul and I spend the whole day at the office calling up everyone we know and asking them to download 'Jeans On'. I even give one of my ex-wives a call. Needless to say, she tells me where to get off and starts moaning about my lack of maintenance, adding that if I don't cough up some more soon she'll have my flat as well. I am so annoyed I crack open the bottle of cheap red wine I've had hanging around the office for months.

Come Sunday, Paul and I are already quite drunk by the time people start turning up at the office. We have decided to have a little bit of a piss-up while listening to Reggie and Fearne count down the chart on Radio One. Paul is so over-excited he's knocked back half a bottle of champagne already, and it's only a quarter past four. We know we are definitely in the Top 40, it's just a matter of where. Reggie is already on number thirty-five and we haven't featured yet so things are looking good. The longer we sit and drink and wait the better. All the band are here except Josh, who is not answering his phone. He knows to come to the office so I'm not that worried. Danny and Richard are standing in the corner nursing a beer apiece.

Debbie's serving crisps, and Holly is sitting on the arm of my leather sofa chatting up Ashley, who I now realize after the other night is quite an accomplished ladies' man. So accomplished, in fact, that I am not that sure I want him anywhere near my fourteen-year-old daughter. Gavin's promised to turn up a little later, and Lucy's on her way. It's a strange, unrelaxed type of party, partly celebratory, partly loaded with tension. Everyone shushes each other between each of the tracks, straining to hear what the next record is.

Lucy and Gavin arrive at the same time with four bottles of champagne just as we all cheer as the programme moves into the Top 20 without a mention of Band of Five.

'Fu-uu-uck!' shouts Mike, beating his chest. 'We're in the top twenty!' He and Billy jump up and down hugging each other, while everyone chinks glasses.

'That's amazing news,' says Gavin, popping a bottle of rosé champagne. He hands me some of the pink bubbles in a plastic cup. 'You must be very pleased with yourself.'

'I am quite pleased,' I smile, taking a swig. 'D'you think we might make the top ten?'

'Could do, could do,' he sniffs, running his hands through his thin hair. 'There are some strong releases this week, but you never know. All the signs are good.'

'Really?'

'We've got strong sales and a late surge towards the end of the week. All that Josh/Sarah Harding stuff worked in our favour.'

'Good, good,' I nod.

'Where is he, by the way?' asks Gavin, looking round the room.

'I'm not sure, but he'll be here.'

'And at number fifteen,' says Fearne – the whole room falls silent – 'it's Adele's new single—'

I don't hear what it is because the whole room cheers again.

'We're higher than Adele!' says Mikey, running around high-fiving everyone.

Billy and Nick run at each other, pulling up their shirts, leap into the air and bounce bellies. I can't believe it either. This record is hot!

'Lucian was right to go with a cover,' I say to Gavin.

'He's always right,' slurs Paul, filling his glass with some pink fizz. 'He's got a nose for things, hasn't he?'

'Yes,' nods Gavin, moving away. He's just come from a Sunday lunch with his family so he needs a few glasses to catch up.

'I love that Adele track,' says Reggie.

'It's very summer,' agrees Fearne.

Everyone sits silently holding their breath.

'And now, at number fourteen, it's a lovely group of boys.'

Everyone looks at each other.

'Westlife!'

'Whaaaay!' scream Billy and Mike.

This time it's Ashley who leaps into the air. His mobile rings. It's his mum.

'I know, I know,' he says. 'Are you listening? Above Westlife! Fucking amazing!'

'I can't cope with this,' says Danny. 'Anyone got a fag?'

'Here,' says Paul, before turning to announce to the

room, 'And anyone who wants to smoke in the office can!'

There's a murmur of appreciation, and half the room lights up.

'Can you believe it, boss?' asks Billy, squeezing past me with a cigarette in his mouth and one eye closed.

'I think you've all done really well,' I say, patting him on the back. 'Amazing.'

'Hats off,' says Richard. 'We could be top ten.'

The Westlife cover trails off and the room goes quiet again. Everyone's shoulders are slightly hunched, their ears straining.

'So, let's recap so far,' says Fearne.

'Ahh,' huffs Mike, 'get on with it!'

'So that's the chart so far,' says Reggie eventually. 'And at number thirteen, going down—'

'Shiiiiiit!' Mike is now bouncing up and down on my sofa like a child high on additives.

'Mike! Mike! Get off that!' I shout.

'We're in the top ten, we're in the top ten!' Nick, Billy and Ashley scream as they start a Mexican wave in front of the gold disc wall.

'This is great!' says Paul, shaking my hand and jumping from one foot to the other. 'So-o-o exciting!'

'Ex-cel-ent track that,' says Fearne. 'And so is this one. New in at number twelve, "Jeans On" by Band of Five.'

The room erupts. The boys leap into the air, and someone's pink bubbles splash me in the face. Everyone starts to slap everyone else's backs. Debbie kisses everyone. So does Paul. Holly hugs Ashley and he squeezes her arse. I am about to march over and break up their little moment when Danny and Richard grab my hand.

'Number twelve, number twelve, that's a great result, great result,' says Richard, patting the top of my arm as well. 'We can improve on that easily.'

'Good stuff!' says Danny. 'My man!'

Over Danny's shoulder I see Josh finally arrive with another bloke. He looks ecstatic. He is beaming and shaking hands with the rest of the group; soon they're all jumping up and down together like a cup-winning football team. I weave my way to him through the crowd, smiling, my arms slightly open.

'There you are!' I say, giving him a huge hug and a slap on the back. 'I thought you'd miss the party! We've been waiting for you. Number twelve! Isn't that great?'

'It's fantastic,' agrees Josh. 'So exciting. By the way,' he says, turning sideways, 'this is Steve, my new boyfriend.'

That stops me in my tracks. 'You're gay?' I say it so loudly the rest of the room grinds to a halt, turns and stares.

'Not gay,' corrects Josh. 'I just love Steve.'

The room inhales a collective breath. Paul promptly bursts into tears. Jesus, I think as my head falls into my hands. This is all I need.

8

No one said managing a boy band was going to be easy. 'Jeans On' has been number one for three weeks now. It's been called the sound of the summer. I've had interview requests coming out of my ears; TV shows want to put the boys on. The critics have slagged us off everywhere, of course. We've had between one- and two-star reviews for the album in the *NME*, the *Observer*, the *Sunday Times* – in short, everyone who has bothered to review it hates it. Except for the public, who are buying it in droves. The single, if you include downloads, is already gold, having sold over 400,000, although we're not sure it will make the 600,000 required for platinum status. The boys are loving all the attention and seem to be liked by the public. Each of them is beginning to get fan clubs and web-sites and letters sent to the office. The only problem is, the most popular by far is Josh.

I know I am not the first person to be managing a gay stud-muffin who is adored by the girls, but I am not sure what to do about it. Firstly, Josh is denying he is actually gay. He keeps saying he isn't gay but that he loves Steve. I could understand that a bit more if I could see the appeal of Steve. So far he's just proved to be a smug, arrogant, annoying little shit who works behind the counter at a bank in Piccadilly. They met on that Keira Knightley film premiere night. Somehow Steve managed to blag a ticket to the party and was all over Josh like a cheap suit. He followed him to the night out at G-A-Y, and the rest, as they say, is a pain in the neck for all of us. I have tried to talk to Paul about it but he is inconsolable. Little did I know that he's been in love with Josh ever since he walked into the auditions in Shepherd's Bush. He'd only not made a pass at him out of respect for what he perceived to be the man's sexuality.

'I mean, if I knew the bar had been set that low,' he says to me over a large drink one night, 'I'd have had a crack myself. Have you seen him? Have you seen him? What's Steve got that I haven't?'

It's true. Steve appears to be utterly unremarkable, other than his ability to stick to Josh like glue and dispense evil looks at anyone who comes anywhere near him. I swear, when some bloke talked to Josh the other day I actually heard Steve growl. However, he does seem to make Josh happy. In fact the boy is giddy with delight. I'm not sure if it's the fame, the rising success, or the love affair, but Josh is flying high. The others are, of course, less delighted with the situation, for not only is

Josh getting more attention than the rest of them, but Steve is also always hanging around.

I have decided to keep the whole thing quiet for the moment. It is partly my fault after all. Much like you kind of knew George Michael was gay, particularly when he was spotted dancing like a nutter at the back of the stage during a Frankie Goes to Hollywood gig in Birmingham, I should have seen the signs. No straight boy likes Mariah Carey for a start. My alarm bells should have rung right there and then. When Will Young said he wanted to have tea with the Queen, I think a whole nation's gaydar whirled into action. His outing was hardly the greatest surprise. Louis Walsh always expresses profound shock at the fact that Steven Gately was gay, although he seemed to be the only one who was. The same goes for Westlife's Mark Feehily.

'You'll be amazed how many male stars' sexuality depends on the quality of the gak they've been snorting,' says Craig when I call him for advice.

'I've never fancied another bloke when I've been wired.'

'You've got a good dealer then.' He laughs. 'I've seen so many famously heterosexual boy band members with their tongues down other lads' throats. Or, you know, it's you managers, slipping those innocent boys a line and some amyl nitrite to get your wicked away.'

'What should I do?'

'You're in a bit of a quandary,' he says, 'because he's the sexiest member of the band. And the band is new. I mean, when George Michael came out he was well established and the builders whose girlfriends liked him still came to the concerts. Girls like queens, but they only like good queens. Like Will Young. Bad queens like Boy George who are in court for tying up male hookers are not so popular with the ladies.'

'Right. Queens they can take home to Mum, as it were?'

'That's it. So if he's a good queen, sit on the story. I'm going through a tunnel now so you might lose me.'

I do, but I also take his advice. Lucy is instructed to keep Josh's romance out of the papers and everyone is given the three-line whip to keep it quiet. I take Josh to one side and tell him for the sake of the band and record sales he must keep schtum. He is not best pleased but he is an ambitious man so he gets it. I just hope he manages to keep that little shit Steve in line.

The single is going so well that Gavin and I have a conversation about delaying the follow-up. We are a long way off from deleting yet, when a label purposely stops producing a song because it's becoming detrimental to an artist's career. Bryan Adams' 'Everything I Do' is a famous example of a song that just would not go away. It spent sixteen consecutive weeks at number one and sold 1.53 million copies. It drove half the country mad, yet the other half continued to buy it, so in order to save Bryan's career they simply stopped producing it. The same thing happened to 'You're Beautiful' but for a slightly different reason: its continued success was delaying the release of the follow-up single and the album. Although there is no exact science to it, the label does try to come up with a co-ordinated plan. The idea is to get enough traction on a single to garner interest in the album. Very few artists make money out of singles; it's the album we all want to shift. But if a single hangs around too long, the effect can be negative. You can't release the follow-up if the first single is still high in the charts. In the old days bands like the Beatles could have three hits in the Top 10, but now things are a little more coordinated and organized so press campaigns you have worked on for weeks get delayed and whole schedules get put back. Equally, if you're doing well, why stop it?

Band of Five's album, despite the critical mauling it received, has already turned gold, selling over 100,000 copies, but Gavin thinks it needs a boost. We had planned to follow on quite quickly with the second single; if we delay it, we could find ourselves head to head with Cowell and *The X Factor* for the Christmas number one. Which is not a battle my brain would relish, although I can already hear my ego shifting around in its big boots thinking it's a great idea.

Gavin also tells me that the *Now* series have asked to include 'Jeans On' on their latest compilation, which is a nice £50K to split between us, although it will take a long time before the boys see any of that. I remember hearing someone say that being a pop act is like being allowed into a bank with a shovel, the only problem being you have no idea how long you are allowed in there to shovel up the cash before someone kicks you out. That's half the reason why pop acts are worked so hard, because by the time the next *Now* series is being put together there's no guarantee they'll have a single on it. We've been allowed into the bank, we've crossed the threshold; it's time to shovel like fuck. It's also time things shifted up another gear.

I walk across the hall to Paul's office. He is sitting behind his desk on the phone.

'Right,' I say, rubbing my hands together, 'I think it's time the boys went on a tour.'

'Hello, is that Hakkasan?' Paul says down the receiver. 'I'm afraid I'm going to have to call you back.'

'I said I've been thinking,' I repeat. 'I think we should tour.'

Paul sits up and scratches his bleached crop. 'Really?' he asks. 'Are they up to it?'

Ever since Josh came out as Steve's lover, or indeed a lover of Steve, Paul's been quite down on Band of Five. He was critical of the photo shoot they did for *Heat*, saying I should have gone for a more upmarket magazine, which, bearing in mind he devours it religiously every week, is a little rich. He has also ceased to come to any TV stuff or radio interviews. In fact I don't think he's seen them since he burst into tears. Maybe he's too embarrassed? Maybe he can't stand the sight of Josh? Maybe he doesn't like them a whole lot any more?

'I don't see why not,' I say. 'They did a Radio One roadshow last week in Torquay and they went down a storm.'

'Were they lip-synching?' he sniffs.

'Not all of them,' I smile. 'Why don't you give Simon a call and see if he can get a promoter?'

Simon is an old friend of The One Management family and has agented all my acts in the past. It's his job to negotiate any payment and any live performances for my acts; it is also his job to see that they get paid. And seeing as Band of Five are not signed up to a 360 deal (I was careful not to give away our touring for a paltry £100,000) Simon is about to become the band's best friend. For a mere 10 per cent of their earnings he is the bloke who can line their pockets and keep them in shoes and ready meals while they wait for a few years for any album money to filter through the record label's accounting system.

Paul puts a call in and apparently Simon seems confident that he can find a promoter.

Tour promoting is one of the odder aspects of the music business. A tour promoter effectively takes a punt on a band or act and guarantees the artist a certain amount of money a night for the joy of promoting them, which entails booking the hall, insuring the gig, sorting the advertising and the crew. The money the promoter makes is entirely dependent on the cut he has with the band and the amount of ticket sales. So, if the band is new, like Band of Five, the promoter is likely to ask for an eighty-twenty split of the pot, which is what is left over after the expenses have been taken care of. If the artist is established and well known then the split can be more like 97.5 to the artist and the rest to the promoter. In that scenario, of a potential £1m profit from a tour the artist will get £975,000 and the promoter will make £25,000, provided that all the tickets are sold. The twist is that a nightly fee is guaranteed by the promoter to the artist, however many tickets are sold. So there is a lot of risk for very little reward, especially if you are talking figures like the £5m AEG Live have been quoted as offering Michael Jackson for ten nights at the O$_2$ Arena in London, rising to £15m for a maximum of thirty nights.

Of course, when selling Michael Jackson tickets the promoter can more or less name his price. But part of his usual equation when calculating how much he can make is how much to charge for the tickets. Small bands like mine are probably in the region of £30 a ticket; large ones are about £45; special gigs like the Spice Girls go for £95 a pop. Get this wrong, price the gig too highly, and the promoter can end up in deep trouble. The guys who did Barbra Streisand's recent tour over-egged their tickets to the tune of £300 each and ended up losing about £1m. The promoter of Billy Joel did the same. Joel has very loyal fans, but not enough of them were able to part with the asked-for £150. The losses were rumoured to run up to £3m.

Even then, there are so many people taking a slice of the pie it's amazing anyone makes any money at all. Take Hammersmith Apollo, for example, which has a capacity of 3,400 seated and 4,800 standing. They would be standing for us, so we'd have 4,800 tickets at £30 each. When all the advertising, hall and crew costs are deducted there's £12 per ticket left. The promoter takes £2. The agent takes £1 or ten per cent of what's left. I, as the manager, take my 20 per cent of the rest, which is £1.80. The band are then left with £7.20 per ticket, out of which they have to pay their roadies, their tour manager, their food, hotel and transport costs, as well as their musicians, dancers and anyone else they have on their books. And then at the end whatever is left over must be split the usual five ways.

Since record sales no longer finance the life of a band as

much as they used to, the gloves have come off with regard to ticket prices and bands are trying to charge as much as they can without losing bums on seats. eBay has demonstrated that punters are prepared to pay higher prices than previously thought – hence the Stones getting away with their £150 tickets. But it remains a difficult call to make. Simon always says it's like betting on the horses, only you have to go with your bet. But then he also says it's an insane promoter who bets on a band that hasn't had a hit.

Some fans, though, are more loyal than others. There used to be 300,000 heavy metal fans in the entire country, but if you put on a heavy metal gig somewhere you could more or less guarantee they'd all turn up. Pop groups, on the other hand, have a very fickle fan base. Loyal fans of boy bands can switch allegiance as soon as they reach puberty, and when they do they are almost to a girl/woman mortified by what they were in to before. Which gives us another reason to shovel: by the very nature of the fans we have, the maximum we've got them for is four years.

But it is also the relationship with the promoter that is changing, as more bands sign 360-degree deals with companies like Live Nation, with venues all over the world, buying up acts like Madonna for $120 million; life for the small promoter has become more difficult. More subtle aspects have also changed. A few years ago it was the promoter's gig and they invited the band, so they would be in charge of the passes and the band would have to ask for laminates for themselves and their friends. Now it's the promoters who have to ask to go backstage to the gig they've actually paid for.

More people are going to see live music events than ever before. The Mums on Chardonnay crowd are packing out the O_2 to relive their youth with their children, dancing along to the Spice Girls and Take That. Weirdly, there's also a well-off thirtysomething generation who are refusing to grow up and are happy to ditch their suits for the weekend, stack up on Es and coke, and go to a music festival with a tent in the back of their saloon. Live outdoor music events are booming. There were 220 open-air events last year and music festivals sold out in hours, not days. Tickets for the V Festival went in five and a half hours; Glastonbury was even quicker, selling out in three. Although this year with Jay-Z headlining and then not, it is proving a little more problematic. However, there are so many people wanting to be entertained and to indulge in a bit of nostalgia, and it's not just the punters who are happy. For promoters, putting on a festival in a field means they get to cut out the venue – so they do get a cut of the bar, and the merchandising, and the food. The band enjoy it because all they have to do is turn up and play the gig; there are no touring costs, no hotel and no catering, just a few roadies and a bus. So if you are getting £1m to headline the V Festival about £900,000 of that is profit. Vince Power, who runs the Mean Fiddler organization and does the Reading Festival, is reported as saying that bands are mainly an excuse for him to get a hundred thousand people into a field and sell them burgers and beer.

Sadly, Band of Five are not festival headline material yet, and being a pop act they are unlikely ever to make it into a field surrounded by beer and tents and hip middle-youthers pretending to be fifteen. Most of their fans are under fifteen and are unlikely to be allowed out without parental supervision. But Paul says Simon thinks he can get us a promoter. Obviously we won't be touring beyond the UK – you need a lot of money to get over the water. Europe isn't too bad – you can still put your rig on a truck rather than a boat or a plane, like you'd have to with a world tour or the US – but I think at the moment Dover is where we'll stop.

A couple of days later Simon calls, suggesting we meet up with Stuart, an old pro who's been in the business for years and with whom I've had a few dealings in the past. He says he thinks he might be able to secure us a few dates.

'He's talking theatres,' says Simon. 'You know, five hundred to a thousand a night – Norwich, Nottingham, that sort of thing. And possibly, when we see how sales do, he might slip in a night at the Shepherd's Bush Empire at the end.'

'How many's that?'

'Two thousand,' he says.

'We should be able to fill that,' I reply. 'The album's on the way to going platinum.'

'And Josh is Torso of the Week in *Heat* magazine,' Simon laughs. 'Let's see how the figures add up.'

'OK,' I say. 'I think I might get Tony to tour manage, give us a quote.'

'What, cokey Tony?' he asks. 'Always one in the back pocket?'

'That's him.'

'Are you sure?' He's laughing again.

'Well, he did the schools tour very nicely. I think he deserves a go. Plus he's cheap.'

Two days later, Paul and I are sitting in a bar in Soho with Simon having a swift beer waiting for Stuart to arrive. Simon is joking and laughing at Josh's sex symbol status. But then Simon is always laughing. He has the easy smile of a man who makes easy money sitting at his desk taking calls.

'I can't believe the photo,' he says, waving *Heat* in my face. 'Is that chest waxed or what? I mean, the bloke looks gay. If I didn't know better . . .'

'I know, isn't it funny?' I laugh a little too loudly. Paul simply stares into his beer.

'But I suppose all publicity is good publicity.'

'Well, you say that. That's what Gareth Gates thought when he shagged the pregnant Jordan. If ever there was a case of one and one never becoming two, that was it. Ah, there we are.' He gets out of his chair and walks towards Stuart, taking him firmly by the hand. 'Stuart, great to see you. This is Paul.' Paul shakes Stuart's hand. 'And of course you two know each other.'

'You haven't changed,' Stuart says to me. And indeed neither has he. He is still a smooth old bastard with eyes like a gimlet who can read a balance sheet at forty paces, noting profit and loss with a glance. 'How's the marriage?'

'Over,' I say. 'How's the business?'

'Doing well,' he says, parking his slightly chunky arse down in my warm seat.

'Now that the pleasantries are over,' says Simon, 'would you like a drink?'

Stuart orders a ludicrously expensive bottle of wine, then proceeds to talk numbers. He's willing to back the boys, he's happy with the idea of a three-week mini tour, and he thinks we should charge £35 a ticket. 'I think that's what we'll get away with,' he says.

'And you'll do the publicity and promotion?' asks Paul.

'I'm over fly-posting,' he says. 'And ever since several music biz heads of marketing got served with ASBOs by Camden Council, I think so is everyone else.'

'They were never very cost effective,' says Simon. 'Half would go in the bin, half would be sold down the market, the rest would be defaced by rival music companies, and about four of them would paper the route from the airport to the gig.'

'That's true,' says Paul. 'I remember a band I know who used to tour ahead of someone else on their label, who they hated; they'd always write "is a cock" by his name. For years the bloke couldn't understand why his posters were always being defaced.'

'I've got my local teams for publicity,' confirms Stuart. 'They're all quite professional – a couple of university entertainment officers, but mostly they're all tour managers waiting for their band to tour.'

'Good, good,' I say. 'What do you think you'll guarantee?'

Stuart looks down and starts to punch away at a mini calculator he's taken out of his pocket. 'An eighty-twenty split,' he says, rather than asks.

'Sure.'

'And a guarantee of ten grand a night.'

'Sounds OK to me,' I say.

Stuart puts out his hand to shake on it, then takes a large sip from his glass of red wine. The rest of the afternoon is spent listening to Stuart and Simon gossiping. Stuart is currently promoting an enormous gig at Wembley.

'It's a nightmare,' he says. 'It's sixty-five thousand tickets and I've got touts coming out of my ears. I tried to move one on the other day and he threatened me; he had me up against the wall with a blowtorch to my face. He had a gas canister under his arm, like the fucking bloke in that film *No Country for Old Men*.'

'Jesus,' says Simon. 'What did he want?'

'Money,' says Stuart. 'It's what they all want. And they make a fortune. They're buying and selling outside, making a hundred quid on my tickets when I'm only making fifty pence. I have to sell two hundred tickets to make the same as him. It drives me mad.'

'They can make a good living,' says Simon. 'It's all cash in bloody hand.'

'I see them all over the world. Some of them follow the big bands everywhere. They do a couple of months' "work" and then they live it up.'

'They're not the sort to save, are they?' Simon remarks.

'God no. They spend it, drink it, fuck it, snort it,' Stuart replies.

'Rather like the bands they follow,' I say.

'That's true,' he agrees. 'Half the time I look at them and I think, why didn't I just become a ticket agent? You put a fiver on top of the price of the ticket and that's it.'

'It's the smell of the grease paint,' laughs Simon.

'It's a mug's game,' says Stuart. 'D'you know who really buggered up touring for us?'

'No,' says Simon.

'The bloody professional tennis players. Years ago you could make a stash of cash, put it in a suitcase and head for the border. But those days are long gone. Ever since Boris Becker and that girl – Steffi? That's the one. Ever since they got investigated for tax evasion they've been down on us lot like a ton of bricks. Everything has to have a receipt these days. There's no cash around. Much less fun. Stories like Led Zeppelin's manager getting a gun in the face after a promoter refused to pay him are over.'

'I remember that,' I say. 'They used to go around saying their manager was so great he got them paid even when he had a gun pulled on him.'

'Yeah, well,' smiles Stuart. 'Let's have another bottle of wine.'

'Good idea,' says Paul, waving his hand at the barman. I smile and nod, hoping that I'm not paying.

'So, who's doing your merchandising?' asks Stuart. 'And what sort of shit have you got?'

Half the joy of touring is the swag, or merchandising. Once you have your fans captive in the arena or theatre, the idea is to try to get them to part with as much money as possible. Although it's in the venue's interest to shift as many drinks and burgers and store as many coats as they can, for the band it's all about the tat. How profligate your audience is depends on what they have come to see. Measured in pounds per head, it's heavy metal fans, at £10 per head, and, bizarrely, World Wrestling Federation followers, at £15 per head, who are the highest spenders of all. The figure is more or less inversely proportional to the age of the people attending the concert: the older your audience, the less they spend. Only super groups like U2 and big solo stars like Bruce Springsteen can persuade the older fan to dig into his pocket, getting about £4 to £5 each. Coldplay is more or less at the bottom with £2 to £3 per head, with McFly, Justin Timberlake and Kylie making about £5 to £6 per head. One-offs or specials like the Take That reunion tour can really coin it in at £7 per head.

The great thing about merchandising is that once the government has taken 17.5 per cent, the venue's got their 25 per cent and the merchandiser, the producer and the copyright have been paid, the rest goes to the band – after I've creamed off my 20 per cent, that is. The record company, thankfully, gets nix – unless, of course, you've sold that along with your touring as part of your 360 deal.

The bad thing about merchandising is that it attracts bootleggers outside the venue, and all the rough crime that goes with that. Plus, if the tour is cancelled or the group splits then you can be sued. S Club 7 landed themselves in deep water when three members of the band were caught smoking weed. They were hit with an £800,000 lawsuit after their merchandising company said their drugs scandal had ruined sales of the lunchboxes, make-up bags, mugs and stationery they had coughed up £630,000 for the right to produce.

I think merchandising is one of the few things that might make Band of Five a bit of money. It might help pay off my ever-increasing overdraft, contribute to Holly's school fees, and give the boys a little more than their current £100 a week. Fortunately, Paul has been on the case for a while. He's employed a graphics company to come up with a logo, along the lines of the Stones' tongue or the Take That upside-down and right-way-up letter Ts, to go on everything from mugs and key rings to knickers and pillows. There's been talk of dolls, although I'm not sure if there's the demand for a group of small plastic boy toys that look nothing like Band of Five. But Britney's doll did well, with millions sold; I hear there's a rehab doll doing the rounds at the moment. You should never under-estimate the strange power and money-earning alchemy of celebrity tat. Ozzy Osbourne merchandising was worth upwards of £27 million at the height of his fame.

The boys spend the next ten days in rehearsals back at Pineapple Studios, working out their set. Seeing as they only have one album to tour, I've had a chat with Esther, Paul and Gavin and we have added a couple more covers to pad out the show. So now, as well as the album tracks, they sing 'Let Me

Entertain You', 'Relight My Fire' and 'Valerie' – just to mix it up a bit and to make it look like they're worth £35 a ticket.

As well as rehearsing they've had their photos taken, both as a group and individually, and I've signed off on T-shirts, jackets, baseball caps, socks, bras, pants, a calendar, notebooks and a whole load of pens on which are images of the boys in their underwear; when you press the top, their pants fall off. Not that it's their real arses. The company had pages of stunt bums on file for us to choose from.

We are all so busy in the office that when Leanne calls to say that she's nearly finished her album after all this time, it takes me two days to call her back. She's pissed off, but by way of placating her I ask if she wants to play a couple of nights with the boys. After all, one of her songs is on the album. Maybe she could sing it with them? She's none too keen to start off with, but then I mention she could perhaps do 'Valerie' on her own with Josh as well. She practically bites my hand off.

Backstage at the Royal Norwich Theatre, everyone's feeling tense. The boys are pacing around in the dressing room like caged leopards on speed, muttering lyrics and marking out their dance routines. Three dancers who look like they've just been pulled off poles at Stringfellow's are limbering up, stretching, doing the splits and generally showing everyone their bum-cracks.

'Where the hell did you get those girls?' I hiss at Esther, taking her to one side.

'Who? Cindy, Ann and Lesley?' she asks.

'The dancers,' I say.

'They've done loads of boy bands,' she replies.

'That's what worries me,' I say as I watch one of them tweak her tits into her bikini top.

Dancer shagging is a given on any tour. So much so that many of the bigger boy bands who are now married with wives and babies back home no longer allow themselves the luxury. Not only does it cause friction with her indoors, but the inevitability of someone falling out with someone else after a post-coital tiff is enough to make it not worthwhile having them around. There is the attitude of what goes on tour, stays on tour, but walls have ears, people gossip, and there's always the possibility of some twat with a camera phone. Or I suppose you could combine the two, as Gary Barlow did: marry a dancer and bring her on tour.

Talking of taking your squeeze on tour, I can see Steve in the corner of the room, staring out everyone, his lips wrapped around the neck of a Beck's beer. The beers were part of the boys' rider, as well as crisps and a whole load of Haribo sweets that are sitting around in bowls all over the place. As riders go, it doesn't exactly rank up there with 'Cristal, one box of bendy straws, one special attendant to dispose of used chewing gum, tea service for eight, a Honey Bear pack of honey, two air puri-fiers, bunny rabbits, puppy and kittens', which was requested by Mariah Carey. Or indeed 'air conditioning always on full, Haribo gummy bears, Doritos, Kool-Aid, Hansen's cherry vanilla, microwave popcorn, bottle of absinthe and a bald hooker with no teeth', which was Marilyn Manson's demand. Or 'Kraft mayonnaise, Grey Poupon Dijon mustard, Skippy creamy peanut butter, twelve-foot boa constrictor, a sub-machine gun and local AA meeting schedules', which was Mötley Crüe's rider of choice. Some are aesthetic, like Barbra Streisand wanting rose petals in the loo. Some are religious: Prince asks for all alcohol to be removed, as he is a Jehovah's Witness. Others, like Van Halen's request to get rid of all brown M&Ms, are just to see if the management is paying attention. The Red Hot Chili Peppers have a fully equipped gym by the stage so that they can work themselves up into a sweat before they go on. James Brown used to order up two girls 'under the age of twenty-one'. Duran Duran insisted on Blue Smirnoff. Others, quite frankly, just don't bear thinking about, like liver on the radiator – the reason being that liver doesn't answer back, get pregnant, want your number or give you a dose.

'OK, guys!' shouts Tony from the middle of the mêlée, running his hand over the top of his shiny bald head. 'You need to warm up your voices.'

'You what?' asks Mike.

'Look after those cords and they'll look after you,' he says. 'There's some hot ginger tea there for you, laced with Manuka honey.' He indicates five steaming mugs on the table. 'Drink it or gargle with it.'

'Do we have to?' asks Billy, frowning.

'Do what Amy Winehouse did the other day and warm up with a fag and some Jack Daniel's if you want.'

'She's got so much talent she can afford to lose some,' snarls Steve from the corner.

Get back in your box you little shit, I think looking over at him.

'Ten minutes,' says a bloke dressed in black who's poked his head round the door. 'Yup, yup,' he agrees down the mike of his headset.

There's a knock on the door and Stuart walks in, giving it the camel-coat-holding-cigar thing. He is looking a little over-dressed for a night out in Norwich in October and the cigar is unlit due to smoking regulations, so the effect is somewhat diminished.

'I just wanted to say good luck,' he says. 'You've very nearly sold out, and this is a big venue – thirteen hundred seats. So I am very proud of you.'

'Thanks,' says Josh, shaking his hand.

'There are banners out there for you, my lad,' he says, winking at Josh. 'Who's Mister Popular?'

'They're all very popular,' I laugh, patting Nick and Ashley on the back. 'Number one for five weeks – very popular in my book.'

The boys stand around in their jeans and matching tight white T-shirts gargling and drinking and jumping up in the air and exhaling loudly. 'We Will Rock You' is blaring out front of house; we can hear the audience stamping their feet in time to the music.

'Three minutes, everyone!' shouts Tony down the walkie-talkie that is strapped to the top of his right shoulder.

'Gather round, boys, let's have a group hug and a chant.'

'What?' asks Mike.

'Trust me,' sniffs Tony. 'Robbie does this every time before he goes on stage. It's the AA mantra. "Grant me the serenity to change what—"'

'Look at that,' I say, walking over to the beers and helping myself.

'It's marginally better than Russell Brand, who has to sit in a toilet shivering like the old junkie he used to be to get himself in the mood,' says Paul while shovelling in an unlikely mix of cheese and onion crisps and jelly babies. He looks at me. 'What? I can't help it. I eat when I'm nervous.'

Two minutes later the dressing room empties. The boys, the dancers and the small token band we've hired to bash out the music, along with the backing tape, are all just about to go on stage.

'Ladies and gentlemen,' says the announcer, 'put your hands together and give a warm Norwich welcome to – Band of Five!'

The boys run on, arms above their heads, and take up their positions while the dancers shimmy up and down the stage. The crowd goes mad. I poke my head out and see row upon row of ten- and eleven-year-old girls with their parents. There are a few who are a little bit older, but mostly it's children. Some are waving photos of the boys, others are waving banners and placards that say things like 'I love you Josh', 'Kiss me Ash', 'I want your babies Mike'. And some are more explicit. 'Josh – you make me wet' is one of the more unpleasant signs being frantically waved by a pre-teen at the front. I look at her screaming face and I am reminded of a piece of advice a tour manager once gave me: 'Stay away from the front row. That's for roadies only. That's where the scary girls are.' I can see that he's right.

God, the noise! What is it with girls and screaming? The boys can't hear themselves sing; come to that, neither can anyone else in the theatre. I can't even hear myself think. I watch the boys for a few more minutes from the wings. Esther is next to me, singing the song, linking the words and the moves. She is like the sixth member of the band. I swear, if any of the boys ever got ill or too hungover to perform we could put some shades on her and send her out there. No one would know the difference. It's happened plenty of times before, when a musician has overdone the whisky and the coke and can't play the next day. Many's the time a roadie's donned a hat or US footballer's helmet and played the set.

That's one of the odd things about roadies that people tend to overlook: some of them are as talented as, or better than, the musicians they look after. Obviously there are the ones who are there because they get the drugs in, pull the birds in over the mosh pit, and can crack a joke or two. But some are employed full-time by a band member simply to look after his guitars. Much like a tennis player has a bag full of fresh rackets during a match, so the roadie will hand over the correctly tuned guitar for a specific song or solo. Keith Richards has got hundreds of guitars and he can get through up to forty every night. They have new strings that are changed after every show and they're tuned for 'Brown Sugar' and 'Jumpin' Jack Flash'. He's handed a specific guitar for a specific song. It's quite a high-pressure job and the roadie gets paid properly for it. Good roadies can earn up to £1,500 a week.

You can still hear the screams backstage, but at least you can hear the actual singing a tiny bit better through the sound system. The boys sound OK, but I think the sound check was better earlier this afternoon.

I have to say that despite everyone's negative reaction to Tony, and given that this is only the first night of three weeks, I think he's running a nice tight tour. This is a small ship with an efficient crew and a decent catering truck. Some of the stuff I've eaten when out with bands has been rank. Sometimes they don't even bother with food. Famously, the early E17 tours were known as the Golden Arches tours as they spent all their £5 per diem money in McDonald's. Tony's coughed up for a van. Well, the band have, although they don't realize it yet. And the food is good. Not quite the four cordon bleu chefs that some bands travel with, of course. There are no Japanese sushi chefs such as the more health-conscious or elderly stars insist on. But they're pleasant, and the chilli con carne's nice.

It's hard work catering for a big touring band. They must cook breakfast for maybe two hundred people who have travelled overnight from one venue to another. The rig has come down at two a.m. and they've arrived somewhere else at six a.m. Everyone's had four hours' sleep, and the first truck to set up is catering. They're up and running immediately, doling out a full English. It can also be hard to get ingredients in some parts of the world. It's difficult to cater for vegetarians in Germany and Eastern Europe, for instance; they're always putting bits of bacon in the tomato soup. Although, famously, if you're searching for the roadies on a Paul McCartney tour, the best place to look is McDonald's. They all have to sign up saying that they're vegetarian, but when you're hauling ten tons of shit around all day, somehow a salad sandwich isn't going to touch the sides.

The boys come off stage just before nine p.m. Their set is only an hour and fifteen minutes and they started a little bit earlier due to the average age of their audience. Both Stuart and I baulked at the idea of matinées, so this 7.30 start without a support band was a good compromise. They come through the door in their sweat-drenched blue satin catsuits, which they wear for their last few songs. Slashed to the waist with bouffed sleeves, I thought they were hideous when Esther first showed them to me, but she assured me that the girls would like them, and there was a little nod towards *Dancing on Ice* about them. She told me people expect a show when they come to see a band, and satin and sequins are all part of it. Personally, I think they look extremely gay. Although no one else appears to think so.

'Oh my Go-o-o-d!' screams Nick as he stands in the doorway. His face is pouring with sweat, and his satin trousers are dark with stains. 'That was fucking amazing!'

'They loved it!' agrees Mike, bouncing around, hugging me, hugging Paul, and hugging Ann and Cindy.

'That was awesome!' says Josh, shaking his head, quivering

with adrenalin and running his hand through his dark hair. 'The best night of my life!'

Ashley is already knocking back a beer. 'I fucking love it! They fucking loved us! Boss, boss, did you see? We were fucking brilliant!'

Billy is exhausted and speechless. He just sucks on his beer and walks around the dressing room with his hand in the air waiting for everyone to slap it.

First backstage is Stuart, and with him he brings seven young girls who've won some sort of competition in the local newspapers.

'Excuse me, Glynn,' he says, moving aside the six-foot-four-inch bit of Welsh beefcake he's hired as our personal security man. 'Boys, boys, boys – that was fantastic. Well done. You brought the house down. Great stuff. Now, these here ladies are your greatest fans. Treat them well.' He smiles, tapping the side of his short nose.

'All right, girls?' says Josh, coming over. 'Did you enjoy the show?'

'Yes,' says one, and the other six giggle. They must be all of eleven, if they are a day.

'Do you want me to sign anything? Photos?' he asks.

'Yes please,' replies the same girl. All the others giggle again.

One of them hands over a pink Miffy autograph book and a sparkling pen. 'To Claire,' she says.

'OK, Claire,' smiles Josh. 'Are you a fan?'

'Oh yes,' she says. 'I've loved you for years.'

'Years?' sniffs Mike as he walks over. 'We've only been going for a few months. D'you want me to sign?'

'Um, OK,' says another girl. 'It's Geri – like the pop star.'

'Great,' says Mike. 'Here?' He points to the front of the ticket.

'No, no, that's for Josh. On the back is fine.'

While Mike swallows his pride and signs his name in a way I am sure he must have been practising for months, there is shouting and screaming from the corridor outside.

'Of course I can come in!' comes a bellowing voice. 'I'm related!'

'It's the band only,' I can hear Glynn reply.

I poke my head out of the door to see Dionne and a couple of her mates doing battle with Glynn. For a group of large thirtysomething ladies there is a lot of pink flesh on show. Dionne's enormous cleavage is pouring over the top of her T-shirt, which seems to be fighting to stay in place.

'Oi, there you are!' she says, spotting me and pointing a square-tipped nail. 'Tell 'im! Tell 'im who I am!'

I am tempted to tell her to piss off. After all, Ashley is sixteen in a couple of weeks and we don't need her hanging around any more after that. But I remember someone telling me that Nigel Martin-Smith upset Robbie's mother once when she tried to get backstage at *Top of the Pops*. Robbie apparently never forgave him and for that matter, apparently neither did she.

'Let her through, Glynn,' I say. 'She's Ashley's mother.'

'That's right,' she shouts, pushing herself right up against poor old Glynn. 'I'm his muvver! Without me there'd be no

Ash! And without Ash there'd be no band! And where would you be, eh? Un-fucking-employed! So excuse *me*.' She squeezes past and beckons her mates. 'Come on, girls,' she says.

When she reaches me she pats me on the shoulder and says, 'That man wants firing.'

'I'll see to it, Dionne,' I lie.

'You do that.' She pats me on the shoulder again. 'Oh,' she adds, 'before I forget, I've got this tape here. Ash's Uncle Charlie. He can't half sing. You should have a listen. There are plenty more stars in this family!' She slips the tape into my top pocket. 'Is the bar that way?'

'Yup,' I say as I flatten myself against the wall of the corridor to let Dionne and her mates pass.

A whole hour passes before I manage to get Dionne to go home and the fans to piss off so that we can go back to the Travelodge and wind down. The boys have got an early-morning interview with BBC Radio Norwich and I don't want them to be too hungover. The venue's only half sold for tomorrow night so they've got some serious promoting to do.

As I come through the revolving doors of the hotel I can see about eight or nine girls sitting at the bar. That's the amazing thing about rock and roll: put a guitar in the hands of the sweatiest, ugliest bloke in the class and suddenly girls who would never have given him the time of day before now fancy a shag.

'Yabba-dabba-do,' mutters Nick under his breath as we walk into reception.

'Guys, guys, gather round,' I say quickly.

'What?' says Nick, straining to get in there.

'OK, boys, I am not going to keep you on a tight leash.'

'Thanks, boss,' says Mike, rubbing his hands together and preparing to walk over.

'All I ask is that you don't drink too much and screw up the interview tomorrow, and you don't fuck anyone who's underage.'

'Underage?' asks Ashley.

'You included,' I say.

'But I'm the one who is underage,' he smiles.

'Well, make sure she's over, then. The press will forgive most things, but not underage sex. There are many pop stars who've had near misses, been taken to court or been threatened by a national newspaper.'

'What happens if she's up for it?' Ashley persists.

'She is still underage,' I say.

'Can we go now?' asks Nick, itching to get in there.

'Yes. And have a good evening. You deserve it.'

At midnight the bar's still packed. Nick is dancing with two girls at once. Josh, Billy, Mike and Steve are trying Malibu with all the different mixers behind the bar. Ashley is running in and out its front door smoking fags and chatting up a gaggle of giggling girls. Esther's dancing with whoever asks her. And Paul, Tony and I have the best part of three grams and are talking about our days in the music business.

'OK, what's the worst thing you've seen?' asks Paul.

'Easy!' says Tony. 'Lee Ryan from Blue standing in a

Japanese hotel ordering a drink while pissing against the bar.'

'Oh,' says Paul, sounding a little disappointed. 'I remember when I was in Japan managing this dance act.'

'When was that?' I ask.

'Before our time,' he smiles. 'We were getting twenty grand a night in cash for PAs all over Japan and I said to the bloke who was the DJ, I said, "I've got loads of cash in my room for you." He said, "Keep it, and pay me in hookers. Send me a different Japanese girl every hour." So I went to the concierge and said, "I want a girl every hour on the hour from midnight until seven a.m." They said, "Who for?" And I went, "For him." He looked like Mike Tyson's dad. He was enormous. Then one after another they came and left and he stayed in his room all night. They're very compliant, Japanese girls.'

'So are all prostitutes,' I sniff. 'My favourite story concerns a rock legend who's still touring.'

'Who's that?' asks Paul.

I tap the side of my nose. 'Anyway, he'd bend ten hookers over a couch and would go in and out of them, one at a time, as he went down the line, and then he'd come inside the last one. He had a big bag of coke and some ludes. That was his thing.'

'So he didn't have an orgy with them all eating each other?' asks Tony, trying to get the image straight in his head.

'No, it was more like parking your bike,' I say. 'Over the sofa, one at a time.'

'Jesus.' Tony sounds very impressed. 'That makes the thirty-four-gram six-foot line of coke I chopped out for a boy band backstage at Wembley seem rather tame.'

'Talking of which,' Paul says, 'where's it gone?'

'What?' asks Tony.

'The blow.'

'Oh,' shrugs Tony. 'I think I gave it to Ashley about half an hour ago.'

9

I haven't seen the boys for three weeks now. They've been travelling all over the country playing every night and doing publicity most days. It's amazing how quickly they've turned into a slick, well-oiled machine who no longer need a full-time babysitter. Although I've spoken to them all on the phone every day and they seem to be having the time of their lives. Tony keeps telling me how well it's all going, and the ticket sales have been amazing. They've almost sold out every gig and we've thrown in a couple of matinées to keep them on their toes. The feedback has been excellent. We've had a couple of sniping reviews in the press, but Paul thinks he can fix those second time round by giving them special access to the band.

'It's quite easy to buy press when you've got a bit more money,' he assures me as we walk through the swing doors of a Travelodge, this time in Reading. 'We can take them to New

LIMERICK
COUNTY LIBRARY

York for a week, fill them full of coke and give them a free bar and access to the band. Now that they're more established it should be much easier. Record companies are always fixing reviews with tame reviewers, or getting them "in place", as they say. I'm sure we can get the boys even more positive stuff by lining a few stomachs and powdering a few noses.'

We walk across the lobby towards reception. The place smells of cigarette smoke and old alcohol. There are two cleaning staff hoovering and someone else going around straightening up chairs.

'I do apologize about our appearance,' says a pale blonde girl behind reception. 'We had a bit of a party here last night.' She smiles. 'So, how can I help?'

'We're here to see Band of Five,' I say, taking a Fox's glacier mint off the front desk and shoving it in my mouth.

'I'm afraid we have no one staying here of that name,' she says.

'But you must have,' I say.

'Um, maybe they're booked under a different name?' she suggests, helpfully.

'Oh, right,' says Paul. 'Like Connie Lingus!' He laughs.

'Um . . .' The girl taps away and then looks up. 'No, she's not here.'

'Oh God.' I yawn. I can really do without this. Paul and I left town relatively early to get here and we need to leave as soon as possible. 'What are the other names Tony uses?' I ask Paul.

'Hang on,' he says, closing his eyes. 'Chris P. Duck?'

'No,' says the girl.

'Mike Hunt?' I say, getting increasingly annoyed.

'Nope.'

'Lord Elpus?' says Paul.

'That's the one,' she nods. 'He's got almost all of the top floor.'

Paul and I walk up the three flights of stairs to the top floor, towards a fugging stench of booze and fags. The first door on the right is slightly ajar so we walk in. Through the weak sunlight streaming through the thin orange curtains we can see Nick and Mike asleep, naked, on the beds. In there with them appear to be three girls who are just as bare. There are bras and panties strewn over the floor, used condoms and torn packets thrown around the room, half-drunk bottles of beer and champagne, ashtrays full of cigarettes, and smears of cocaine streaked across various flat surfaces. There are also ripped-up packets of fags that have been used to make roaches for joints. The place stinks of sex, alcohol, sweat and flatulence. If I had more of a hangover I think I might actually be sick.

'Lord Elpus,' says Paul. 'This is disgusting.'

Mike rolls over and stretches, grabs his naked tackle, gives himself a scratch and farts so loudly he wakes himself up.

'Oh, hello, boss,' he says, rubbing his eyes. 'What time is it?'

'Midday,' I say, ostentatiously looking at my watch.

'Oh, right.' He smiles. 'We had a bit of a late one.'

'I can see,' says Paul.

'Where's everyone else?' I ask.

'I'm not sure,' he says. 'Josh is in the honeymoon suite.'

'The honeymoon suite?' I'm not sure which is more bizarre, that there is such a thing in a Travelodge in Reading, or the fact that Josh is in it.

'Yeah,' says Mike, finally covering his midday lob-on with a sheet. 'He was being a bit arsey, saying that as he was the lead singer he needed the best room, and seeing as he was travelling with his partner they needed privacy.'

'What, Steve's still with you?' asks Paul. 'Doesn't he have a job to go to?'

'Sticks to Josh like a limpet,' he says.

Just then there's a rustling under the sheets and a fourth girl appears from nowhere.

'Oh, hello,' says Mike, sounding surprised. 'Who are you?'

'Denise,' she replies.

'Hello, Denise. While you're down there . . .'

Paul and I leave the room. Quite frankly I've seen enough to know what sort of stuff's been going on in our absence. Carnage. I also can't believe Josh is arguing over his room. I know half the bands in the world have to stay in different hotels simply because you can't divide one presidential suite by four or five egos, but this is a bit soon for him to start playing Charlie Big Potatoes. Maybe the *Heat* covers and *Now* interviews are going to his head.

Halfway down the corridor I see Tony slipping into another room.

'Tony!'

He doesn't hear, so Paul and I follow him. Inside the room Billy and Ashley are fast asleep in their pants, spread out on their beds like starfish. Tony has his back to us and is picking up their jeans, T-shirts, socks and shoes – effectively packing their suitcases. The door of the mini bar hangs open. Its shelves have been drunk dry, there are dry-roasted peanuts all over the floor, and a large plastic water bottle that has been cut and punched and made into a homemade bong stands in the corner. The room stinks again, but this time it's marijuana and socks.

'Morning, Mum,' Billy yawns from his bed.

'Morning,' says Tony.

'All right?' I say from the doorway.

'Oh, hello,' says Billy, looking towards me and scratching his crotch. 'How are you? Fuck, you missed a good one last night. Even Glynn got laid.'

'How was the gig?' I ask.

'Good, man,' he sniffs. 'I got three pairs of panties chucked at me and Josh's stalker came again.'

Tony fills me in. Josh's stalker checks herself in at all the hotels they stay in under the name Mrs Penrose, which is Josh's surname, then proceeds to act like she's married to him, turning up at the concerts every night and then hanging around in the lobby afterwards. I am a little taken aback, but you have to admire her dedication. This sort of behaviour is unusual in a boy band fan; it's more the sort of thing you get with groups or singer-songwriters with slightly more profound lyrics. 'I put my jeans on and I feel all right' is not the sort of thing that usually inspires a stalker. Other bands like U2 who write emotive and evocative songs like 'Stuck in a Moment You Can't Get Out Of' – which was supposedly about Michael

Hutchence – are much more likely to speak to people who are depressed, or who have been abused, or who are unbalanced in some way. Talk to singer-songwriters and they will tell you that when they're performing there are some people in the audience who think they are actually singing directly to them. They'll get a moment of eye contact and think it significant. Some guys, like Robbie Williams, are so stalked by their fans that they have SAS security who put mirrors on floors and doors to see who is coming up the corridor. I know of one pop star whose security team actually handcuffed a fan to a chair to control her. But you can hardly blame them, when some girls just won't take no for an answer. They knock on your hotel room door at three a.m.; they bribe people left and right. Christ, someone was willing to sleep with Glynn last night just to get close to Band of Five, and they've only been going a few months.

'Are you all right there?' asks Tony, looking at Billy and nodding towards his crotch. 'Because I can give Dr Roberts another call?'

'Dr Roberts?' I ask. 'Who's been signed off sick?'

Dr Roberts is Tony's tame doc on Harley Street. For £100 a pop he'll sign anyone off sick. Which is crucial when you've got a gig to cancel and your insurance only covers you when your act has laryngitis or is suffering from 'exhaustion'. Although there are plenty of ways and means to get them out there when they're simply hungover, when a cup of coffee and an Anadin have failed. I remember hearing a story about a singer who'd taken so much coke he couldn't get his throat muscles relaxed enough to sing. The tour manager rang around and eventually got his hands on a steroid injection which he administered to the side of his neck. The singer got through his concert. The show went on. I'm sure it wasn't his finest performance, but let's hope the dancers more than made up for it.

'No, not sick exactly,' says Tony. 'He's just got himself an itch, haven't you, son?'

'An itch?' asks Paul.

'A dose. The clap. An occupational hazard if you're in a boy band. The last lot I toured with travelled with a clap doctor because they just couldn't help themselves. They were constantly on strong antibiotics.'

'Deary me,' says Paul.

'Well, I always say to them, never go through a hooker without a bag on,' declares Tony, nodding his bald head, like a man who knows. He puts his fists out in front of him and gently moves his pelvis back and forth. '*Never* go through a hooker without a bag on,' he repeats.

'I always thought you went through doors,' says Paul. 'But then I don't bat for your team.'

'But you're OK?' Tony asks Billy.

'Yes thanks, Mum,' he smiles back.

Paul and I watch as Tony busies himself packing the boys' suitcases while they lie around in bed. Tour managers are often called 'Mum' by the band, mainly because they behave like a mum, sorting everything out, making sure that the band have their pants and socks, that they turn up on time, are sitting in the bus when they are supposed to be, doing the sound check, eating their lunch/supper. Some band members become so institutionalized they end up relying on their tour managers for everything. I heard Robbie Williams once left his bag on the train because he was so used to someone else dealing with that for him. Tampons, condoms, money for hookers – all needs are catered for. Luke Goss once asked his tour manager to buy him a Porsche. The bloke was given £20K and told to drop the car at the house at midday the following day. He arrived with the 911 but was half an hour late, so was bollocked rather than thanked.

Forty minutes later all the boys are standing in the foyer of the hotel, and to a man they look terrible. None of them looks like he's had a wash or a good night's sleep for weeks, which they haven't. And Ashley has piled on the pounds. There are some pop stars who befriend the catering truck while they are on tour, and Ashley is clearly one of them. Esther's got her work cut out when we get back to town.

You can practically see the Travelodge heave a sigh of relief as we all walk slowly towards the minibus. The crew left Reading twelve hours ago to reconvene tonight at the Shepherd's Bush Empire. It's the last night of the tour, a special one-off concert at which Leanne will be making a guest appearance. The place is sold out and expectations are high. The record company is really putting up the bunting, and killing the fatted calf. They've hired a club for an end-of-tour party and the guest list is packed with showbiz press and various celebrities who have come out of the closet as Band lovers. Girls Aloud have always been nice about the boys wherever they've gone, but now Mark Owen and Jason Orange have gone on record to say that they like us. We have become one of the nation's guilty pleasures. All we need is for Kate Moss or Agyness Deyn to come to the after-show party tonight and our new-found hip status will be sealed.

The boys file into the bus, their hungover silence preceding them. Josh and Steve stand back, and I can see that Steve is caging for a lift. A couple of the boys are muttering, telling him to piss off, so I decide to intervene before the situation comes to a head.

'I'm sorry, Steve mate, this is for the band only,' I say.

'But I'm with Josh,' he says.

'That's as may be,' I say, 'but today, I'm afraid, no partners are allowed on the bus. No one else has anyone with them.'

'Josh!' he says, turning to his boyfriend, looking all injured and hurt.

'Look,' says Josh to me, 'Steve's—'

'Not a member of the band,' I say. 'When you've got your own limo driving you around then you can do what you want.'

'Not long now,' huffs Josh. Steve doesn't look like he's moving that quickly so to speed things up I dig out a fifty for a taxi to the station. That seems to get his feet moving along and Josh says his goodbyes before getting on the bus.

I let the boys sleep for half an hour or so, dribbling on their shoulders, before handing around cold Cokes to pump them full of sugar and revive them. Today is a big day. Before the Empire date we're off to meet the marketing director of the Zing Fruit Juice Company who is considering sponsoring the next tour and parting with three quarters of a million quid for the boys to endorse their drinks. This is a good deal for us and I don't want their hangovers or 'exhaustion' to ruin it. As Kylie, Robbie, the Spice Girls and Take That will tell you, endorsements are the cherry on the cake of your career.

The Spice Girls would have made more money from the Victoria's Secret gig they did to launch their last piss-poor single 'Headlines' than from the record itself. The same is true of their Christmas ad for Tesco, or Take That's modelling for Marks and Spencer. I know that Robbie makes more out of T-Mobile and Sony Ericsson than he did out of selling records. But you have to be so careful who you get into bed with, as it were. The Post Office, with its track record of countrywide closures, can't have done Westlife's image much good; Iceland must be less than impressed with Kerry Katona as their role model. Still, more often than not these things, when handled the right way, can work a treat. E17's Pepsi Cola ad, in which a woman pushed Brian Harvey around in a pram, was not only seminal, it also earned the band a million pounds.

The Spice Girls, however, got a little greedy at the height of their fame when they seemed to be endorsing everything from soft drinks to sports cars. They came unstuck when they were sued by Aprilla, who had signed the girls for £500,000 to promote the Spice Sonic scooter, complete with a silhouette of the girls. Aprilla had also agreed to sponsor their forthcoming tour – only for Geri to leave the band some weeks later. The band had to cough up a million in damages and court expenses.

Signing yourself up to a brand has its responsibilities. Not only are you supposed to promote the product, you are also required not to slag it off. When James Blunt said that he hadn't agreed to the selling of his music he inadvertently caused the collapse of music download site Q Track after being paid £400,000 to promote it at a big party in Cannes. At least he turned up, which is more than the Spice Girls did when they were supposed to visit a car factory in Coventry. The entire staff had been given the day off for the visit and their friends and family had also been invited to join in the fun; after all, the Spices had enjoyed their free cars, and the company had sponsored their tour. Everyone was waiting and the bunting was out when the organizer got a call saying there was a problem and the girls weren't coming. There was no explanation. The day was cancelled.

'That sort of diva behaviour is par for the course,' says Paul when I finish my Spice Girls rant. 'A mate of mine was looking after Jay-Z in Paris when he did a deal with Reebok for his own brand of shoe called the Steven Carter.'

'Steven Carter?' asks Billy.

'That's his real name,' says Paul.

'No wonder he changed it,' says Billy. 'It makes him sound like an accountant.'

'Anyway, Reebok wanted him to do some PAs – London, Madrid, Paris. He said he wanted a PJ, so they hired the jet to fly him to these three airports. He stuffed it with twenty people, it sat on the tarmac in Paris and they wouldn't let the press on. Jay-Z's people kept on saying, "We aren't ready yet.

We'll tell you when we are." And all the press just sat there for three and a half hours waiting for him to be ready to let them on.'

'Way to go,' says Mike, clicking his fingers and then immediately regretting it. 'Jesus, my head hurts.'

'Thing is, you just have to get on with it,' says Tony from the back of the bus. 'I remember George Michael flipping out and being really pissed off because *Top of the Pops* used their entire balloon budget on his song.'

'What, there weren't enough?' asks Josh.

'No, there was one song that got the balloons each show and he didn't want the balloons. He kept on saying that it wasn't a balloon song, and he wasn't a balloon bloke. We had to spend bloody ages talking about bloody balloons. In the end they just released them over his head and there was nothing he could do.'

We all sit back in the heavy orange velour chairs and gaze out of the window at the dark clouds and the driving rain. November is always so goddamn grey and depressing, particularly if you haven't had a holiday in nearly a year.

'I can't believe this is our last night,' sighs Ashley, his face squashed against the window. 'I love touring.'

'You just love the groupies,' giggles Mike.

'Not as much as you do,' says Nick.

'I love the way they always say the same thing,' says Mike. 'You've got them in the hotel room and you're warming them up and they start saying things like "I'm not a groupie, it's just because I like you". Or, "It's got nothing to do with the fact that you're famous".'

'Yeah, right,' laughs Josh. 'That's so a lie.'

'I know,' Mike says.

'I remember reading that James Blunt said he wouldn't mind if they just said, "You're famous, let's fuck",' says Paul.

'Well, he certainly knows what he's doing,' I say. 'Isn't he the bloke who ended up with a swimming-pool-load of girls in LA?'

'That's fame for you,' pipes up Tony from the back of the minibus.

'Do blokes like him have girls all over the world?' asks Ashley.

'Pretty much,' I say. 'There are groupies you do in each city you go to. When you go back to Japan, say, there's your Japanese groupie. She'll think you're her boyfriend and tell everyone as much. You can repeat-shag your way round the world if you do the same tour over and over.'

'There are certain pop star bikes everyone does,' says Tony. 'There's some girl called Candy, or something like that, who does all the rappers when they come over.'

'What?' asks Ashley, turning round.

'Well, you can see how it happens, can't you? The rapper comes over here from the States and he gets told, "When you're in London you've got to do Buckingham Palace, Harrods and this hot bitch Candy." I've met her, and she's cute. She's done 50 Cent, Puffy, The Game – they've all had her. And she's fine about it. She's the rap bike.'

'I suppose that's better than being the pop star baby mother,' says Paul. 'Like that Lisa Moorish. How many children has she got by different pop stars?'

261

'Two – Liam Gallagher and Pete Doherty,' says Tony.

'And Finley Quaye,' says Paul.

'Really?' I ask.

'Well, I'm not sure,' he says. 'But she does have a lovely selection.'

'Anyway, can we all behave tonight?' I say. 'We've got press in and half the record company turning up, so you've got to press the flesh and walk the talk.'

'Yes, boss,' smiles Mike. 'Anything you say, boss.'

The bus falls silent as the traffic slows around Heathrow. Someone behind me yawns, and someone else sighs. Then I suddenly hear 'When You Find the One' – the next single – on the radio.

'Turn it up,' I ask the driver.

'Oh my God!' says Josh. 'It's on!'

The band join in, singing their song at full volume. Next to us a car starts to hoot its horn; two young girls in a VW Beetle start waving. One of them suddenly undoes her seat belt, lifts up her top and bra, and shoves her breasts against the window of the car, snogging the glass at the same time. The boys roar their approval, giving her the thumbs up. Then Billy gets out of his seat and drops his trousers, squashing his white mooning arse against the glass. Both the girls get out their camera phones and snap away.

'Pull your fucking pants up, Billy,' I shout. 'Don't be an arse all your life.' With all this money at stake and so many egos and reputations riding on this it's sometimes hard to remember that I'm managing a bunch of teenage boys.

'There you go,' says the radio presenter, 'Band of Five with "When You Find the One". Such a nice bunch of lads. That's being released next week and they're hoping for the Christmas number one with this, and let's hope they make it.'

Eventually, after dropping Tony off in Shepherd's Bush, we pull up outside Zing's offices in some groovy modern warehouse conversion in Kensal Rise. The reception is orange, the sofas are chrome and apple green, and there's an expansive leather tasselled rug on the poured-concrete floor. Water coolers seem to be everywhere, along with piles of fresh fruit in large chrome bowls on various plastic white tables, ready to munch at your comfort and convenience. The effect is very bright, light, healthy and, indeed, Zingy. The antithesis of what the boys are feeling. Their puffy toxic faces glow pink in the unforgiving light. Ashley's got red spots clustered all down both sides of his neck. They look positively raw.

'Hi,' I say as the boys loaf in behind me. 'We're here to see Victoria and, um, Hugh.'

'Right,' says the girl, looking the boys, Paul and me up and down. 'Hugh and Victoria?'

'That's right – Band of Five?'

'Oh my God!' she squeals, her face flushing as she tries to stifle a small giggle of excitement. 'They're expecting you.'

'Good.'

She stares at the boys with a wide-eyed smile on her face.

'Do you want to call up and say we're here?'

'Of course!' she says, picking up the phone.

Upstairs and over a glass walkway lined with pots of

echinacea flowers, Hugh and Victoria's office is large and airy with huge glass windows and views of a canal. At opposite ends of the room stand large glass desks with anglepoise lamps and fat black leather chairs; in the centre is a cluster of brightly coloured beanbags and a low table.

'Hi, hi, hi,' says Hugh. He is wearing jeans, trainers and a fun T-shirt, the epitome of the modern trendy businessman who regards Richard Branson as an icon and who's all for dressing down on Fridays. 'Welcome to our humble little empire.' His hand is soft and manicured, and his handsome face glows with macrobiotic health.

'Great to meet you,' says Victoria as she wafts towards us, sporting expensive layers with low-key hair. She shakes my hand with clear eye contact and works the room like one of those professional brunettes who brightly engage millionaires about their stocks and shares. 'We're so glad you are thinking of joining the Zing team. Zing is all about youthful optimism, and through our organic juices in recyclable cartons we want to spread our message of wellbeing around the nation.'

'And we at Zing think that Band of Five, with their clean-cut image, are perfect for our market,' Hugh adds. 'You're young, healthy boys with countrywide appeal.'

I look across at my motley crew of hungover teenagers, shifting and scratching uneasily. I can practically hear their livers screaming to be let out for a bit of air.

'We've been on tour,' I explain with a smile, 'so none of us is quite looking his best at the moment.'

'Don't worry,' laughs Victoria, 'there's always airbrushing.'

'And stretching,' jokes Hugh, glancing at Ashley. 'The Spices have had inches added and taken away with photo-shopping.'

'And there's always surgery,' smiles Paul. 'Kylie has a little nip-tuck every year when she goes back to Oz just to keep the showgirl on the road. And have you seen Madonna recently?' He lifts his eyes with his fingers. 'Next step, the Bride of Wildenstein.'

'It's so unnatural, isn't it?' says Victoria. 'I find these women amazing. They won't drink water if it comes in a plastic bottle because it's so bad for them yet they happily inject botulism into their faces and silicone into their breasts. It's one of those unfathomable modern dichotomies.'

'Yeah,' agrees Nick, nodding away. 'And they look shit.'

'Absolutely,' she agrees. 'So, shall we all sit?'

She looks across at the beanbags, and my heart sinks. How is a man supposed to be able to negotiate with his gut hanging over his jeans, his legs straining to cross themselves and his bollocks spliced in half by the seam in his trousers? The boys, of course, being young and relatively fit, rush over and hurl themselves on the floor. They roll around on top of each other laughing and play-fighting. Paul squats down, with his legs apart, and tries to look relaxed. His trousers scream at the gusset, gathering so tightly I can tell which way he dresses. Hugh pops himself down like a man who says 'Ohm Shanty' twice a week. I gingerly place myself on a yellow bag, trying not to do myself an injury.

'OK,' says Victoria, moving across to a whiteboard, 'this is what we thought.'

She talks us through the ideas for their fruit juice campaign. It involves television advertising, posters, and local and national radio. The colours are bright and the message is upbeat, appealing to the six- to fourteen-year-old market; they're launching a special lunchbox drink as one of the five fruit and veg we are all supposed to have every day. The boys start off vaguely interested, but by the time Victoria reaches the pie charts about market share and expansion of product range most of them are taking fluff off their trousers or fiddling with mobile phones.

Just as everyone is about to lose the will to live two girls arrive with trays of sandwiches that Hugh informs us are freshly made from organic ingredients locally sourced from the deli around the corner. Josh peels himself off his beanbag and takes a sniff.

'Um,' he says, curling up his nose, 'I'm off carbs at the moment. Any chance of some sushi?'

'Actually,' agrees Mike, 'that would be nice.'

I have to say that Victoria is not the only person who is a little bit stunned. It was less than a year ago that Mike was ordering tomato ketchup and chips in a bloody Chinese; now he's turning down sandwiches and asking for raw fish.

'Oh, right,' says Victoria, her voice rising with surprise. 'I'm sure that won't be a problem. Just so long as you don't mind waiting.'

'Not too long, I hope,' says Josh, patting his stomach.

I remember a mate of mine once telling me that it took just two weeks to become a cunt in the music business. He was looking after some rappers from Birmingham – an oxymoron in itself. He said they looked shit; it was just a crappy club record that started to do well. And then, amazingly, they went to number one. They did *Top of the Pops* and were naive and sweet and grateful. A fortnight later they were booked to go to Elstree and they arrived four hours late in two stretch limos. My mate went mad, telling them they were about to be thrown off the show. They got out and told him to piss off. Their personalities had totally changed; suddenly they were rock stars. As he said, from no one to cunt in two weeks. I suppose I should be grateful that we're only at the sushi stage after eight months.

Half an hour later the sushi arrives, by which time Josh and Mike have already eaten three sandwiches apiece out of hunger and boredom. So when the huge plate of salmon and tuna is placed before them there aren't that many takers.

Another hour later, with the deal agreed, we are on our way to the venue to sound check, via the office. We have so much fan mail for the boys to deal with I thought a quick hour of them signing autographs might help out Debbie, who has been signing for all of them for the past few months.

As we pull up outside the office in the minibus, the boys are hosed down by a couple of paps. 'Oi, boys, over here!' shouts one, pointing his enormous camera right up close into Josh's face. 'Josh! Josh! Give us a smile, mate!' Josh pulls his cap down low over his face. 'Go on, ma-a-ate, smile,' says the other taller guy, blocking the door to the office. 'A smile won't hurt – give us a smile.'

'Excuse me,' I say, pushing towards the door, 'can you let us pass?'

The two paps start to jostle the boys between them.

'Calm down, calm down. We're just trying to get into the office.'

'Come on, guys,' says the one with the enormous camera.

I manage to press the bell. 'Debbie, it's us, let us in!' The buzzer goes and I fall through the door, rapidly followed by Mike and Ashley. Nick and Billy are not far behind. It's only Josh and Paul who have been corralled off by the paps.

'For fuck's sake, smile!' yells the taller pap as Paul finally manages to grab Josh's arm and haul him through the door. 'Fuck you, you big fat poof!' the pap shouts after him as we slam the door. 'Bender!' yells the other through the letterbox before Paul manages to spring it shut. One of them kicks the door.

'You all right?' I ask them.

'Jesus,' says Billy.

Ashley is wiping sweat off his face.

'I can't believe it,' says Nick. 'How did they know where we'd be?'

'It is our office,' says Debbie, getting up from behind the desk. 'Anyone want a coffee? Josh? Are you OK?'

The boy hasn't said a word and looks white and a little shaken.

'They called me a poof,' he says, very quietly. 'D'you think they know?'

'No,' says Paul. 'They were shouting that at me.' He puts his arm around Josh. 'Don't worry about them – they're scum and they know it. They don't know anything.'

'Not wishing to be rude or anything,' says Josh, taking Paul's arm off his shoulder, 'but no one knows who you are, let alone if you're gay.'

'Are you kidding?' says Paul, genuinely taken aback. 'I regularly score top ten in the list of London's leading homosexuals, right behind David Furnish.'

By the time Debbie returns with a tray of skimmed, double-shot caramel or framboise lattes, the paps are long gone, as is any thought of them. The boys are far too immersed in the two sacks of fan mail in the middle of my office. And the stuff they are coming across is shocking.

'Jesus,' says Billy, waving a photo in the air, 'here's another one.'

We all gather round to have a look at a close-up shot of a young girl's beaver that she's snapped herself, printed off on her home computer and popped in the post to the boys.

'What's wrong with these girls?' asks Billy. 'What do they think they're doing?'

'They're desperate,' says Mike, turning the photo around and taking a closer look. 'I suppose this is what it must be like being a gynaecologist. You see so much pussy it stops being interesting.'

'More pants,' announces Josh, holding up a pair of flowered knickers.

'Worn?' asks Ashley.

'I don't really care,' says Josh, chucking them on to the pile.

'How are we supposed to respond to this?' he asks me. 'Dear Emma, thanks for the underwear, I wear it every day?'

'No, no,' I say, 'don't mention anything, just sign your name on the headshot here with the big black pen and that's it. Put her name on too if you can be bothered, but quite frankly you've a couple of hundred to get through in the next hour or so, so I think you'd better get cracking.'

'I can't believe I've got to do all this,' moans Nick, yawning and lying back on my sofa. 'I've had enough.'

'You should try working for a living,' I say.

'Yeah right!' he laughs, like he does.

'This is just the start, mate,' I say. 'If you want to make it outside of here you need to be endlessly promoting, endlessly travelling, endlessly doing TV shows from Stockholm to Sydney.'

'I'd rather be Victoria Beckham,' pouts Mike from the sofa. 'Endlessly photographed, endlessly shopping.'

'That's not a career,' says Josh, adding another pair of teen pants to the pile.

'It's a lot less tiring,' Mike yawns.

'Thank your lucky stars you're not Kylie,' says Paul. 'She's been working her arse off ever since she slipped on those dungarees in *Neighbours*. D'you think she'll still be trussed up like a trannie when she's fifty like Madonna?'

'Ouch,' says Mike. 'The gay backlash starts here!'

'Get a move on, you lot,' I say. 'We've got a sound check in an hour, then some food, and then you're on stage. How long can it take to sign your bloody name?'

*

It's one hour before the show and the band, Paul, Esther and I are all milling around backstage. One of the dancers, Cindy, has spent the last ten minutes in a corner with Tony having a heated discussion. There's been lots of arm waving and dramatic walking away, pivoting and marching back. Finally, Tony nods something in agreement and begins to walk towards me.

'OK,' he says, clearing his throat. 'Cindy won't dance with Nick.'

'Right.'

'She says she shagged him in Salford and he hasn't spoken to her since and now she's refusing to do the "When You Find the One" routine with him,' he says, pulling his bottom lip. 'I've tried, but there's no changing her mind.'

'OK. Can anyone else do it?'

'There's a bit of solidarity between them but I think maybe I can get Ann to fill in.'

'Tell her I'll pay her double for tonight, and get her a job on the Zing commercial.'

'Done,' he says, tapping the side of his nose.

'I told you,' I say to Paul, 'dancers are more trouble than they're worth.'

My phone goes. I look down.

'Talking of trouble – it's my ex-wife.'

'Which one?'

'Monique.' I sigh, then answer. 'Hello there, darling—'

'Don't darling me,' come the highly strung tones of ex-wife

number two. 'Finally you have a band I want to see. Finally you have a band I would like to take my friends to see rather than that indie rubbish you were doing for bloody years. So I call your office. They tell me they have no tickets, but that I should call some man called Stuart, which I do – and he is bloody rude by the way – and he tells me the guest list is full, I can't come and my friends can't come. Then I remind myself why I divorced you in the first place: you were always such a selfish fucking bastard!'

'How many do you want?' It's the only way to shut her up.

'Five – and in good seats.'

'They're on the door.'

'Thanks, darling.' She blows me a kiss down the receiver and hangs up.

'You gave her *five* tickets?' asks Paul. 'A woman who made your life hell and stripped you of your final assets?'

'Yup,' I nod. 'She always did manage to wrap me round her finger.'

'As far as I remember you were more interested in the wrap than in her fingers,' he laughs. 'And anyway, haven't you forgotten something?'

'What?'

'Linda and Holly are coming down.'

'Oh shit,' I say.

'Double shit,' he adds, smiling and rubbing his hands together.

'Is it too early for a drink?'

I walk into the boys' dressing room to lighten their bar of a

272

few beers. I am greeted by the sight of all five of them bent over a sofa with their pants down.

'What's going on in here?' I ask. 'It's supposed to be the hookers bent over the sofa, not the talent!'

'Jabs,' says Tony, coming into view holding a syringe.

'B12?'

'Yup,' he nods, his hand on Josh's buttocks. 'They all kept complaining about being tired and I thought short of giving them all a line, this might work.'

'Good idea,' I nod.

'Ready?' he asks Josh.

'Go for it,' says Josh, clenching his whole body.

Vitamin B12 jabs are pop's great placebo. No one is quite sure whether or not they actually work, but everyone uses them. As soon as a star becomes cranky or tired or hungover or jaded or non-compliant, out they come. A quick jab in the bum and humour and harmony are soon restored. There are numerous stories of them being used to calm down irate and overtired lady pop stars, and many managers and record label execs swear by them. But I've also been told that some tour managers have injected water into their stars when they were tired or bad-tempered and the effect was more or less the same: they'd be bouncing around on the sofa half an hour later declaring themselves fully restored. I have to say that at this late stage in the proceedings any means is fine by me. We've got one last gig to get through before we can give the boys a week off, then we start the blitz of publicity to see if we can get 'When You Find the One' to number one for Christmas.

I pick up my couple of beers and I'm just about to leave the room when I spot an enormous tattoo all the way down the length of Mike's right arm.

'What the fuck is that?' I ask, staring at it.

'A tattoo,' says Mike.

'When did you get that done?'

'In Reading,' he replies.

'What the fuck do you think you're doing?'

'You don't own me.'

'What?'

'You own twenty per cent of me,' he says, his jaw coming out as he steps forward, 'so let's say this bit of me is mine.'

'It looks shit.'

'Fuck you. I can do what I want with my body.'

'It's all red and scabby. Are you planning to have it out tonight?'

'I don't see why not,' he says.

'Well, all the press are here, and as I said, it looks shit. Like you've got eczema down your arm.'

'I don't care.'

'I do. Anyway, what does it say?'

'It's Hindi, and it says "Band of Five".'

'Right,' I say, taking a swig of my beer. 'It's still shit. Oh, by the way, boys, don't run over tonight otherwise we'll have to pay a fine.'

'A fine?' says Josh, rubbing his backside.

'To the council. I'm not sure how much it is but Brent charge a grand a minute over the curfew for Wembley.'

'Really?' says Ashley.

'There's a great story about that,' says Tony, flicking the syringe with his finger. 'When the Cure came off stage at Wembley once the crowd were going mad and they wanted to carry on. Some bloke stood there with a clipboard saying, "It's a grand a minute." So Robert Smith yelled at his manager, "Go and get him forty grand – we're going back out there!"'

'Well, don't do that tonight,' I laugh, shooting Tony a look. 'Anyway, we've got a party to get to.'

In the end the gig goes brilliantly. Josh and Ashley sing their hearts out and the others mime along brilliantly. The band and the backing singers belt the numbers out and the dancers bury the hatchet enough to make the show run smoothly. Leanne comes on at the end and sings 'Valerie' with Josh and Ashley while the others dance and click along. It's the highlight of the night, and everyone is thrilled. A delighted Gavin slaps my back at the after-show party. Holly comes bouncing across to me in the nightclub – though quite what her mother is doing letting her out this late I don't know. I am about to have words with her when I see Monique coming towards me. It's a clash of Lewis–Tyson proportions, I think. Time to duck out and find the VIP area.

I spot Glynn in the corner standing in front of some roped-off area and head towards him. On my way there I bump into Craig.

'Mate!' he says, slapping me on the back. 'You did it! They're great!'

'You like?'

'I *love*,' he says, rolling his eyes in mock ecstasy. 'They're slick, they're handsome, and two of them can sing – what's not to love?'

'Thanks, mate – that means a lot to me.'

'Meet my mate Jim,' he says, indicating a good-looking party boy standing next to him. 'He's in the business. Once had Pink hurl herself off a wardrobe on to his cock.' Craig roars with laughter. 'She nearly lopped it off. He almost woke up a woman.'

'That sounds painful,' I say.

'It was,' Jim acknowledges.

'She enjoyed it so much, she wanted to do it again,' grins Craig.

'Oh I just couldn't,' says Jim, cringing slightly at the remembered pain.

'Anyway, top show,' says Craig, raising his glass of cranberry. 'See you later. I'm off to see if there's a lonely old page three girl who needs a lift home.'

'He loves a page three stunner,' says Jim. 'Was it your mate from Blue who got the boy band hat-trick?'

'Who, Anthony?' asks Craig.

'That's the one – Jordan, Jodie and Linsey Dawn McKenzie.'

'The lucky bastard!' declares Craig. 'Come on.'

What is it about celebs shagging other celebs? I remember one rock star mate saying that it's all about collecting scalps. You're shagging Paris Hilton and you can't believe it, and they can't believe they're shagging you. He told me there's a celeb code that helps you seek each other out in a crowd. It's like you're all part of the same club, and you can invariably trust each other not to sell stories. Also, when you're in a room where everyone is staring at you and treating you differently, there aren't that many people who understand what that feels like. No wonder, then, that they end up in bed together. It's a private party no one else can join.

Much like the VIP area at this party. In fact it is so VIP that Glynn barely allows me in. However, judging by what is going on in the dimly lit room I am kind of glad he's being so burly.

'Welcome to my cocaine buffet,' sniffs Mike as I walk in. 'Here we have Bolivian, Colombian, and a cheeky little one straight from the streets of Peru!'

He laughs and steps back to reveal about forty lines chopped out on the table. Nick and Billy are hunched over the top of it with £20 notes up their noses in a head-to-head race.

'Aaaaaaahhhhh!' say the crowd of about eight people gathered around the table as the boys snort their way along its length.

'It's touch and go, it's anyone's race,' says Mike, commentating above the loud music. 'Who's it going to be? Who's it going to be?'

'Go on!' yells a very pretty girl who I've seen on the TV, or in a magazine.

'Move it, Billy!' encourages another blonde with breasts so underwired she could practically lick her cleavage. 'Snort!'

'And Billy's the winner!' shouts Mike, clapping his hands and congratulating both the boys. Billy holds his hands and his rolled-up twenty above his head, cheering himself and his marvellous hoovering talent. His nostrils are frosted white like a margarita glass. 'Hooray, hooray!' he cheers. Everyone else joins in. Nick coughs and wipes his nose with the back of his hand. His eyes are watering.

'Right, who's next?' asks Mike, holding out two rolled-up notes.

'Me,' says Ashley.

'And me,' says Josh.

Steve pushes his boyfriend forward, clenching a fist to wish him luck. Ashley high-fives Mike and Nick, geeing himself up for the battle.

'It's nose to nose – nostril to nostril,' laughs Mike. 'It's the two singers head to head – let's see who's got the better lungs!'

I walk over to take Ashley by the arm and walk him out of the VIP room. He's only just turned sixteen. Not that there is a right age for drugs, it's just he's still supposed to be in my care. He shouldn't even be in a nightclub in the first place. What would Dionne say? I am about to grab his arm when he spots me.

'Fuck off, old man,' he snarls, putting the rolled note up his nose. 'Leave us kids alone.'

10

I am sitting at my desk nursing one hell of a hangover and hoping I didn't make too much of an arse of myself last night when my phone goes.

'Hello, it's Kate here from the *Sun*.'

'Hello?' My heart is beginning to race already. This is not going to be good.

'Now,' she starts, 'I won't mention the coke problem—'

'What coke problem?'

'Josh Penrose's coke problem.'

'I've never seen him do any.'

'So he does have a problem?'

'I never said that.'

'But you didn't deny it, now did you?'

'I don't need to, because he doesn't have one.' My mouth is dry, my palms are sweating. Is this the hangover, or just plain fear?

'Really? Well, why was he trying to check himself in to the toilets of a nightclub last night using his credit card?'

'Maybe he was just drunk,' I try.

'Anyway, as I said,' continues Kate, 'I am not interested in the drugs – everyone's at it these days. They're hardly glamorous any more, are they? I mean, when Kerry Katona's cocaine's poster girl, it's got an image problem. Even men your age are at it!'

She laughs.

I laugh right back. 'I know!'

'So you do?'

'What?'

'Take cocaine?'

'What? Who? Me? No! Stop twisting everything I say.'

'Anyway, it's not the drugs – which, now that you've confirmed them, we will overlook. It's the fact that Josh is gay.'

'He's not gay,' I say, remembering Josh's line that he just loves Steve.

'Oh, right?' she says, in a way that means she has something up her sleeve. 'We have evidence to the contrary. We have footage of him snogging a man that was filmed last night at your after-show party.'

'How did you get that?'

'Well, put it this way, your security guard has handed in his notice and is currently having a nice little mini break in Grand Canaria courtesy of readers of the *Sun*.'

'I'm sorry?'

'Glynn,' she says. 'Ring any bells?'

'Glynn?'

'Yes. Tall bloke, Welsh? He confiscated the film off a fan last night who managed to get into your VIP area and then very sweetly handed it on to us.'

'Glynn did that?'

'Afraid so.'

'But he's been touring with the boys for a month!'

'Some people, eh?'

'I'm gob-smacked,' I say, sitting back in my chair, genuinely puzzled and affronted. How could Glynn have behaved in such a way? He was part of the family. He had fun with the boys; they treated him as part of the gang. Hell, they even passed him over a couple of groupies when there was a glut.

'So you don't deny the tape?'

'Sorry? Oh, I'm sorry,' I say. My mind is fogging over; I can't really think. Glynn – the bastard. The man's a total shit. 'I think I'm going to have to call you back.'

'I'll give you an hour,' she says, 'or we are running as is.'

I sit at my desk, shaking my head. It's amazing what a bit of celebrity does to people. I remember Esther saying that when she worked on *The X Factor* and *Pop Idol* it was only a matter of weeks before all the next-door neighbours came crawling out of the woodwork to sell whatever tittle-tattle they had. I suppose we've been lucky. All the fun and games the boys have had, and so far nothing has reached the papers.

I call Paul. It takes me two attempts to rouse him. When he finally picks up he doesn't sound good.

'Hello?' he croaks.

'What happened to you?' I ask.

'Don't ask,' he says. 'Safe to say I am never doing it again. I feel shit. My head is fit to explode and I think I might have to be sick.'

'Great, well, this should sober you up. I have had the *Sun* on the phone and they know about Josh.'

'Oh.'

'Is that all you have to say?'

'I thought they were on to him after those paps the other day,' he sniffs. 'It wasn't exactly the best-kept secret in town.'

'Thanks for the heads up,' I say sarcastically.

'Does it matter?'

'I don't know if it matters. Will it matter to the legions of girl fans who send him their knickers? Will it matter to the readers of *Heat* who voted him Torso of the Year? Will it matter to the Zing bloody Fruit Juice Company who want to give us three quarters of a million quid in exchange for some clean-cut healthy living? How the hell should I know!'

'You're sounding hysterical,' he says. And he's right. I am hysterical. This is a year-long project about to go out the bloody window before we've even started to make any money. Of course I'm hysterical. 'No one cares if you're gay or straight these days.'

'That's easy for you to say. And anyway, we know that's not true, otherwise why is half of Hollywood still in the closet with sham marriages and girlfriends who have beards?'

'Because they have to act as leading men,' he yawns. 'Trust me, it'll be fine. "When You Find the One" is released this week, it'll be great for publicity.'

'It may be fine,' I snap, 'but what should we do now?'

'Phone the PR.'

'What, that child? She couldn't organize a piss-up in a night-club. Her press contacts don't extend beyond music reviewers and Biz bits.'

'No,' says Paul. 'Call *the* PR – Max Clifford. He's great in a crisis.'

I get through to Esther, who is calm and positive. She says that Max is the man to call and that they all used him when she was doing *The X Factor* and *Pop Idol*. Apparently, that was one of Simon Cowell's first questions to anyone involved with the show: do you have a PR? The second question was, how much shit is there on you? And the third was, do you want Max Clifford's number? He was there to keep them out of the papers. After all, no one who's worked in the record business for any length of time is squeaky clean. The parties Cowell gave at the Savoy when he was at Fanfare records are legendary. So you can understand why Clifford is so gainfully employed.

Anyway, Esther passes his number on to me and I give him a call. And the man is amazing. I tell him what is going on and within an hour he's managed to broker some sort of deal where Josh pours his heart out to the *Sun* and tells them all about his love for Steve and they promise to paint the whole thing in a very positive light. They say they'll run some nice photos of the two of them together. They say they'll let Josh talk about what it was like to grow up gay in Manchester, and all in all every-one will be delighted. All I need to do now is break the news to the boys and persuade Josh that this is his only option.

Josh is stunned when I tell him what has happened, and shit scared. I can hear the panic rising in his voice. He can't believe that Glynn sold the footage, and he can't believe that anyone is that interested in his sexuality or his love life. He is stammering and stuttering down the phone, and soon he starts to cry. It takes me a good while to calm him down and convince him he won't be strung up, that the best way to deal with this is to confront the issue head on. Which is something I kind of wish we had done in the first place. Maybe if we had been honest about Josh's romance with Steve from the outset and promoted one of the other boys as the band beefcake we wouldn't be in this position. Josh agrees to do the piece, if Steve doesn't mind. Amazingly, Steve thinks it's a great idea and promises to be on hand for photos and questions or anything the press want. He is really only too happy to oblige.

When I finally manage to track down the other boys, they are only really worried about how this might affect the single release, the future of the band and their finances. I assure them that all will be absolutely fine. After all, there are lots of successful boy bands with gay members who are out and proud. Why should they be any different?

Two days later, Josh is front-page news. The headline is huge: 'My Gay Love – by Josh Penrose of Band of Five'. And it's everywhere. They're discussing it on the BBC news in the morning when I wake up; it's the hot topic on Radio Five Live's phone-in as I make my way to work in the car. Although it's a *Sun* exclusive, all the other papers have carried the story somewhere in their second editions. When I pull up outside the office there are some eight or so photographers waiting outside, plus a local news cameraman and two radio guys. They're not really waiting for me, although quite why they think Josh is going to turn up at the office on a day like today is beyond me. Still, you have to admire them for trying. Josh is, in fact, in a suite in the Charlotte Street Hotel with Gavin, Lucy and anyone else the record company thinks might be useful in a crisis.

'Do you have any comment to make?' asks the radio reporter as I walk up to the door and buzz the bell.

'Only that Josh is a charming, lovely guy with immense talent and I hope that he and Steve are very happy together,' I say.

'So, will Band of Five be splitting?'

'No.' I give a gentle laugh. 'The lads are fully behind Josh; they are all very happy together. And they're going to be number one this Christmas.'

Inside the office, Paul greets me, beaming from ear to ear.

'Oh my God!' he declares. 'Things are going so, so well. Messages of support are flooding into the website – thousands of them, and they're all positive! They are mostly saying that he is so brave to come out, that they all love him. They've been interviewed by some bloke from *Heat* who also said how brave Josh is and how honest he is and how the band will definitely grow from here. It's amazing.' He grins. 'Outrage have said they support him. Oh, and everyone's saying they're going to buy the new single. We couldn't have planned it better if we'd tried! Is there another member of the band we can out? All we need now is a message of support from Elton and we've got a clean sweep!'

'It is amazing,' I say.

'I know,' he agrees. 'Oh, and a researcher's called from the Jonathan Ross show to ask if the boys want to come on.'

'Really?'

'Well, I suppose they've got something to talk about now,' says Paul.

'Tell them yes,' I say. 'But only if the Four Poofs put Josh on their T-shirts. We may as well chase that pink pound.'

The reaction to Josh has been so overwhelmingly positive over the last ten days that it is beginning to piss the others off. The Four Poofs did put his face on their T-shirts, and the conversation about his relationship with Steve dominated the show. Steve came along, sat in the green room and waved like a nutter every time his face was shown. Mike tried to bring the subject back to 'When You Find the One' (out on Monday), and Ashley tried to talk about the tour, but it was Josh's show. And now I've started to get phone calls from the boys asking me to have a word. Two days ago the friction was so bad that when they had to go on *Richard and Judy* they asked for two cars. So Josh is coming in this morning for a bit of a chat. I can hear him pulling up outside the office because the small group of hardcore fans who now gather regularly outside the office release a high-pitched scream. It takes about seven minutes of photos and autographs before Debbie starts simpering downstairs.

'Hi, Josh; hi, Steve.'

My heart sinks. I was hoping to have a proper chat with Josh about the band and what's going on without Mrs Penrose in tow.

'Hi guys,' I say, hiding my irritation as they come up the stairs and into my office. 'Nice to see you both. How are you?'

'I'm exhausted,' declares Josh, sticking his cowboy boots up on my desk. 'If I have another fan pointing a phone at me and saying "one, two, three" I am going to put my fist in their face. Why can't they just take the photo already? Why do they always have to count? Why is it always one bloody two bloody three! And then the fucker doesn't work and they have to do it again. I tell you, I now know how to use almost every mobile phone ever made. I'm always the one who ends up taking the photo. It's driving me mad!'

'He's stressed,' says Steve, pointing out the obvious. 'Which is why we're glad that you've called this meeting.'

'Yes?' Already I don't like the use of the word 'we'.

'Well, we've been thinking. Seeing as Josh does all the singing and is now doing all the publicity and he's the face of the group, he should be getting more money.'

'Right.'

'I mean, it stands to reason, doesn't it?' Steve continues. 'He does all the work so he should get more of the money. He's worth it.'

'I didn't know you'd taken on a new manager,' I say to Josh.

'I'm not his manager,' says Steve. 'I'm his partner.'

'And what do you think, Josh?' I persist.

Josh just shrugs. 'Dunno,' he says.

'He's too close to it all,' says Steve. 'It's obvious to me that he's being taken for a ride. He does all the work and only gets a fifth of the money.'

'Well, there isn't any money at the moment,' I say.

'When's the Zing payment due? Because Josh is fronting that campaign and he's not getting any money, are you, Josh?'

'No,' says Josh. He's removed his feet from my desk and is now staring uncomfortably at the floor.

'OK,' I say, nodding, 'let's see what I can do to keep you happy.'

Sitting here looking at these surly barely-twentysomethings who are about to piss on my parade, I am rather annoyed with myself that I didn't see this coming. There are plenty of stories about girlfriends getting involved in a band and stirring things up – it's called the Yoko Effect, after the most famous spanner in a band's works. The new girl becomes the bee in the boy's bonnet and keeps asking annoying little questions like, why are you not singing as much as you should? Why aren't you at the front? Where's your picture? Shouldn't you be earning more? You're the only one with talent, the others are losers, so why are you supporting everyone? The girlfriends who were attached before the band became famous are usually OK. They are so busy trying to see off passes made by groupies, and other more glamorous girls, that they tend not to get involved in the day-to-day running of the operation. The only friction an old girlfriend usually causes comes as a result of jealousy on the part of the boyfriend, who rather wishes he could dump the minger from home and go out with someone a whole lot more bootylicious, like his mates.

Craig had warned me that it's nights out on the town with glamorous girls and other celebs that rot a boy band. They hang out with other bands and start to feel embarrassed that their fans are ten years old. Especially when the R&B rapper from the US plays to and gets respect from his contemporaries. I suppose I've been so busy worrying about what the boys were doing, where they were hanging out, and how to break the Josh-is-gay story that I didn't see the Steve Ono thing coming. Also, I suppose in my mind, because he's a bloke, I've never really thought of him as a girlfriend-about-to-cause-trouble. Silly me. Not a mistake I shall make twice.

I spend about an hour listening to Josh and Steve grumble on about how unfair their lives are while making placatory noises and promising them that I'll try to sort something out.

After they've gone, while I'm pondering what to do to keep my band together, Simon calls and offers Band a private gig.

'I'm not sure who it is yet,' he says. 'It's some Russian's daughter's birthday party. They're offering a quarter of a million for the night if we can get you back in time for all the "When You Find the One" PR – are you interested?'

Are we hell! The private gig market is something I've been dreaming about. There is so much money to be made out of spoilt children's parties, or profligate magnates showing off to their friends, it's ridiculous. The Sultan of Brunei was always the best one. He had endless parties. He lavished millions on his daughter's eighteenth, hiring Janet Jackson and All Saints. Janet apparently got a million dollars for her set and the girls got half that, but they all left the party with diamond-encrusted watches, so everyone was happy. Now, with the explosion of cash coming out of Russia, the type of person wanting pop-star talent at their parties has changed. Although blokes like Philip Green still cough up fortunes for the likes of George Michael, for his son's bar mitzvah, it is much more likely these days to be some nameless aluminium dealer on his yacht in the South of France. Recently, the Sugababes got £250,000 for seven songs and half an hour's work at some Russian boy's twenty-first. They performed in a villa by the end of a pier near Cannes to some fifty kids who were much more interested in driving the Bugatti Veyron the boy got as a present.

Interestingly, girl groups are more popular than the boys. Girls Aloud make about £200,000 for twenty minutes at a party, and Amy Winehouse made £500,000 during Paris fashion week playing for Louis Vuitton. But the big boys still pull in the big money. Rod Stewart and Robbie are a million quid each. And the size of the audience doesn't matter. Last summer the Pussycat Dolls played to an audience of eight in a yacht in the Med for £500,000, and Sting played to a room of twenty for forty minutes for the same amount.

However, with so much dodgy money flying about you have to be careful to look after your talent. Jamiroquai sat on the tarmac at Biggin Hill waiting for the cash to arrive in an account before anyone would let him take off. Simon's told me numerous stories of sending bikes to Heathrow to collect Jiffy bags of cash from prospective party throwers. He says it's important to have the wad on the table before you release the talent.

Some talent won't get out of bed and on to a plane no matter how much you pay them, or their favourite charity. I heard Coldplay were offered a half-a-million-pound cheque to Oxfam if they sang at a businessman's private gig forty minutes down the road, but even the lure of a chopper, let alone the money, wasn't enough to get them out of the studio. Annie Lennox was the same. Not even a million-dollar donation to her charity of choice was enough to get her on the plane over from New York. Simon was furious. 'I know jetlag is terrible, but really,' he ranted on the phone at the time, 'is it that much to ask? They didn't want to insult her by offering her money, so they offered to pay a charity instead. There are plenty of rich people who privately donate to charity who find the music business and charity a load of nonsense. D'you know how they could make money very quickly for charity if they wanted to? By giving us a bit of their time! But they're just very loud about the rest of us doing it. You've got some celebrity do-gooders shouting, "Give us your money!" Why don't they give some of theirs? Instead they give us twenty of their precious minutes on the telly and we're supposed to jump for joy and get out our chequebooks!'

Fortunately, the idea of making a bit of cash in hand before Christmas goes a long way towards restoring harmony in the band – as does the idea of an adventure to a dacha in the deep snow just outside Moscow. The Russian has let it be known that a private plane full of champagne and caviar will be at our disposal, and any other riders will be honoured. The only thing they wish to warn against is diverting the plane off its course.

It seems the last pop star they hired, for a gig in Kazakhstan, diverted the plane via Amsterdam. He and his pals had tucked into so much Charlie on the flight back that they fancied picking up some hookers on the way home. Apparently, the pop star in question had initially wanted to go to Warsaw or Prague for a lap dancer and some how's-yer-father, but there was only enough fuel for Holland.

'What shall we ask for?' quizzes Mike as he sits around in the office signing headshots for fans.

'Barbra Streisand once demanded a patch of real grass for her dogs,' says Paul.

'A bidet?' I suggest.

'You what?' Mike says.

'I remember Shirley Bassey having a bidet put in her dressing room when we were doing *The Tube* with some band or other. Do you remember, Paul?'

'I remember *The Tube*,' he says. 'It was bloody mad. It was Friday night, live at five p.m. from Newcastle. You had to arrive on the Thursday for sound checks and it was a cokefest. It was insane. You never slept on the Thursday night. You'd be in the Railway Hotel with all the TV producers, the band, the pluggers, everyone, and then at eight a.m. you'd ring for breakfast and there'd be full ashtrays and lines everywhere. You had the whole day to arse about until the show, after which there was a mad dash for the seven thirty p.m. flight back to London. If you didn't make it you had to spend another night in the Railway Hotel, returning to the scene of the crime.'

'Everyone was on that flight,' I say.

'God, yeah. There were forty cars lined up outside the studio and a mad dash for the plane. The presenters, producers, bands, everyone was on there, and the party continued all the way back to London. Mad. Lines were left in the loo for people. Those were the days.' Paul looks wistfully out of the window.

'Fuck it,' says Mike. 'Put down a bidet.'

'But you're a boy band,' I say. 'Bidets are for girls.'

'Says who?' shrugs Mike. 'I like to wash my feet.'

Three days later I meet up with Tony outside the office early on a Saturday morning. He looks like he hasn't slept and he's got a huge selection of jeans thrown over his shoulder.

'What are those for?' I ask.

'I'm covering all eventualities,' he replies.

'I don't understand.'

'Get in.'

On our way to collect the boys before heading off to Biggin Hill, Tony explains that the last time he did a private gig with a boy band he got his fingers burnt. They were due to fly to Romania to do some sort of beauty contest. The jet was at the airport, standing by. He had four boys to get to the airport in four different cars from four different parts of London. The jet was costing £14K, the band were going to make about £25K on the trip, but one of them didn't turn up because he didn't have a pair of jeans to wear. Tony told him to get into the car and that he'd go and buy him a pair. But the singer said, "Stick your gig," and that was it. The band had to pay for the flight and everyone lost money.

'So this time,' he says, 'I'm not taking any chances.'

In fact, he need not have worried. All the boys turn up on time and the atmosphere on the plane is great. It's like old times – just the band, Tony and me. Steve was firmly told his presence was not required, as was Mikey's new girlfriend, who's some WAG turned soap star – or is it the other way round? Anyway, we have no liggers or hangers-on. It's just the band, and it feels good. There's much joking and delight as each of the boys knocks back the champagne, tucks into the caviar and washes his feet in the bidet.

We're whisked through Moscow airport and collected by a long stretch limo that takes us miles and miles along wide, straight roads lined by a snow-filled silver birch forest. It is quite surreal, and a little bit disconcerting. We have no idea where we are going and no idea how to get back. After about two hours in the car we eventually arrive at a floodlit mansion that looks like something out of MTV's *Cribs*. There are dogs and men with guns patrolling the grounds, and huge flames flickering at the entrance. A large bloke with a flat nose and a torch checks the car over before we are allowed through the gate.

Inside, the party is a humourless affair. Fifty people dressed in their garish finest chomp jadedly off ice sculptures groaning with oysters, salmon and caviar. There are magnums of Veuve Clicquot everywhere, and endless waiters endlessly circulating with trays of ice-cold vodka. But no one seems to be having much fun. The men are huddled together drinking shots and the women, poured into their floor-length Versace dresses, stare at each other, waiting to be entertained. There doesn't seem to be much communication between them. The boys look a little overawed, but we're not going to be here for long. We have a forty-minute set to play to a backing track and then we'll be straight out of here, back in the car and on to the plane. We have publicity to do for 'When You Find the One' on Sunday afternoon, so this is almost as in and out as it gets.

The gig goes well. The boys do their routine mostly miming to the track, but no one seems to notice. In fact, not many people are paying them much attention at all. Despite the enthusiasm of Katya, the host's eighteen-year-old daughter who is apparently being educated in the UK and therefore knows all the songs and the actions and the names of the boys, everyone seems to be rather nonplussed. Most of the men carry on talking through the set. Only a few very bored, thin women come to the front during 'Jeans On' and give their hips a work-out. But you can't help feeling their moves are not directed towards the band but are for the benefit of their billionaire husbands, who occasionally proffer a glance in their direction. To the sound of weak applause we are straight off stage and back into the limo – to find that the bar has been restocked and there are gold watches for everyone on the seats. They go some way towards assuaging the boys' disappointment with their dreary reception. As does the vodka.

The journey to the airport is amicable enough, but it all kicks off on the plane. The boys are drunk and tired and have been in a confined space for several hours, so I suppose it's inevitable that something has to give. Oddly, it's Mike who starts it.

'I've been talking to my girlfriend,' he says to me, 'and I think you don't take me seriously enough as an artist and I want to sing more. I'm fed up with miming songs that I haven't written to a dead mike.'

'But you're making lots of money doing it,' I say.

'Am I fuck,' he says. 'We've been working twenty-four-seven for nothing. I'm still on a hundred a week and I've had a number one single and an album in the top ten for six weeks.'

'The money will come through, Mike,' I say. 'You'll get the money from this gig.'

'When?' chips in Billy. 'Because I've had enough of being the only poor bloke in town.'

'OK, when it's gone through our bank and accountants,' I say cheerfully.

'But you don't need money at the moment,' Tony points out. 'Everything's taken care of for you.'

'I want some dough right now,' says Billy.

'Yeah,' says Ashley. 'And why has Jerry got some cash?'

'Because he wrote some of the songs,' says Tony.

'We want to write our own songs,' says Ashley.

My heart sinks. Here we go. Why is it always about the money? There is nothing that pisses a band off more than when one person appears to be doing better than the others. In Band's case it's Jerry, but Robbie left Take That because Gary was writing the songs and he was getting the money and

Robbie was in Gary's band. Even Keith and Mick make the money on Stones songs while Charlie and Bill have to rely on touring. Smart bands like U2 and Radiohead split royalties. Their credits simply say 'U2' or 'Radiohead'.

I start to explain to them how the money will be rolling in soon in the form of royalties, the Zing deal and all the touring money also coming their way, plus their cut of the merchandising, which is ticking over nicely. And if we all keep cool heads there's plenty more where that came from.

'But we're bored of singing other people's songs,' says Ashley. 'We want some sort of credibility as artists.'

'But you *are* credible,' I counter. 'You've had a number one hit. There's nothing more credible than that.'

'We just want to sing,' slurs Nick.

'But you can't!' laughs Josh.

'What d'you mean?' His eyes narrow.

'You're the dancer, Nick.'

By the time the plane lands at Biggin Hill at four in the morning, it's trashed. Quite how the boys managed a fistfight in a Learjet at 40,000 feet is anyone's guess, or indeed who started it, and quite how I managed to persuade the pilot not to sling us all out over Germany I don't know. By the time we touch down I appreciate that he never wants to see or hear from us again. The plane will have to go through a new refit. There's vodka and broken glass everywhere, there's caviar on the ceiling, some of the cream leather upholstery has been ripped, and one of the walnut desks has been uprooted. The boys look battered and drunk and tired and bloodied and sheepish. To say *I'm* embarrassed is an understatement. Mortification doesn't even come close. We are obviously going to be billed a fortune for repairs.

At the airport, things don't improve. There's a stand-off of such epic proportions that Tony ends up ordering separate cabs for everyone and we all have to wait until five a.m. before they arrive.

The next day it's the same. Come the midday show on Capital Radio that we're supposed to be doing to promote the single, they all arrive in separate cars and you can cut the atmosphere with a knife. Lucy tries to smooth things over before they go on air, but in the end the only person who talks during the interview is Billy, which is quite hard considering his swollen top lip and that at least a quarter of the questions were directed at Josh about his coming out. After the excruciating interview, the boys are asked to do some idents to advertise the station and big up the band and the single. They all, less than politely, refuse.

'The problem,' Craig tells me a few hours later when I meet him for a late lunch and a large glass of wine, 'is that if you peak too early you've got nowhere to go. You're now just managing the decline.'

'Thanks for that,' I say, feeling overwhelmed with depression and exhaustion.

'Well, it's the truth, mate,' he says, momentarily distracted by the passing arse of a waitress. 'I mean, the album is now huge, right?'

'It's over six hundred thousand and double platinum.'

'So what do you do now? You've got no career to build. It's now all about maintenance and crisis management.'

His words are ringing in my ears two days later when I get a call from a newspaper saying that Mikey's been caught in a hotel room with three grams of coke and two strippers. Apparently he's tried to deny it but they've got the credit card receipt from the hotel and mobile phone snaps from the room-service girl Mike forgot to tip at five in the morning to prove it. Needless to say, his soap star girlfriend is wearing large sunglasses this morning telling anyone who wants to know that it's over.

'It's that four a.m. rule, I'm afraid,' says the journalist on the phone. 'However nice they appear, the mask goes at four a.m. and they dial in hookers and coke. I mean, if he wanted not to get discovered he should have thought about things a little more. Footballers always use cash when they go to a hotel and book in under different names. They call ahead and say they've lost their house keys and don't want to wake the wife – you know, because most classy hotels won't let you book in at four a.m. And they've all got five or six pay-as-you-go mobiles so you can't trace what's going on.'

'I'll be sure to tell him for next time,' I say dejectedly.

'Yeah,' agrees the hack. 'Think it through a little more, because we're watching – as are all the waiters, hotel employees and nightclub staff around town. You'd be amazed how vigilant people are when there's money to be made.'

'But they're only in a boy band,' I say. 'They're hardly representing their country at anything. They're young boys having fun; they're not doing anyone any harm. They aren't married, they don't have children. Why do you care?'

'They're famous, mate,' he sniffs. 'That's all we care about. They lost their anonymity the day they signed that record deal. They wanted to be famous. They got their thirty pieces of silver.'

It's a lot less than thirty, I think after I hang up. I wonder if they even knew the day they signed their record deal, or walked into that hall off the Shepherd's Bush Road, that they were giving away their anonymity that cheaply, their every move, their every transgression, their every relationship, thought, weight issue, haircut, sweat stain and broken nail papped and reported for our delight and delectation.

Some, like Victoria Beckham, thrive on such attention, becoming ever thinner and ever browner with an ever-increasing bust in the hope of titillating or eliciting more interest. Others, like Britney, self-destruct under the weight of our persistent and prurient curiosity. Some self-harm, like Amy Winehouse; others self-improve, like Kylie. And some, like Beyoncé, turn up day after day at the recording studio because there is nothing else for them to do. They have long ceased to have real friends, because they are rarely if ever home, and they have long ceased to have real lives because shopping, even window shopping in the mall, or indeed just walking around, is not something they are able to do any more without a crowd gathering and a gang of photographers in pursuit. Michael Jackson's existence has now been reduced to that of a permanently globetrotting house guest, flitting from one millionaire's gaff to another in his attempts to flee press attention. He wears odd disguises, including burkhas and women's clothes, in an attempt to fool them. He has to book two hotels in every city he stays in so that he can retreat to one once he's been discovered in the other. He never stays anywhere more than a week and he changes his telephone numbers just as often. It is a sad and lonely existence.

But even with his faded fortunes you sense that a comeback of sorts is possible. What happens to others after the limelight has completely faded? There is nowhere for an old pop star to go. If you're clever you can develop another skill, like Kim Wilde who became a gardener, or do a Toyah Willcox and write about your facelift; but who wants to employ an ex-member of a boy band? They can hardly answer the phones in an office or work in a shop. What do they do? There's panto and corporate gigs, there's Russian yacht parties and reality TV. *Hell's Kitchen*, *I'm a Celebrity* and *Strictly Come Dancing* are the saving grace for the faded pop star. Some make enough money to make their future bulletproof, but most do not. What happens when you have the flash lifestyle but no real money? You take a leaf out of the Spice Girls book: you re-employ your old manager because you are contractually obliged to, and you tour again. You go from stadiums to arenas and then eventually back to the theatres where you originally made your name.

This industry eats you up and spits you out again, and only the really strong survive. The normal music biz story is to go from nothing to something in the blink of an eye; you drink too much, assault someone, take coke, inject something else and choke on your own vomit. So for someone like Elton to come back from a coke overdose, be without a cigarette, a drink and a line and still be in the industry some fifteen years later, with a sense of humour, is quite something.

Others just can't cope with the girls. You end up like one lead singer who has been stung by one too many lawsuits in the past. He now has a piece of paper you have to sign if you are going to have sex with him, stating that you go willingly, and that you have no legal claim over him. None of the rape claims or paternity suits have ever been substantiated and the girls always settle for a quick $40K before it goes to court. Hey, girls, what could be more romantic – sign here and get it! Or you could be talked about like a piece of meat, which is what another singer did. Having been introduced to a girl by his friend, he ended up shagging the bird, and the next day he rang his mate to tell him what a night he'd had. He went on to reveal in great detail quite how filthy the girl had been. She did this and that; I bent her this way and that way; she wouldn't leave me alone. 'I can't thank you enough, I owe you one,' he said. To which his friend replied, 'What time did she leave?' 'She's still here,' said the singer. 'I'll put her on.' She was sitting right next to him . . .

But that sort of behaviour is totally fine. As is Prince's demanding that no one looks at him when he comes into a meeting, despite being dressed in purple with stunning identical twins on either arm. In fact, the only thing that really gets you talked about in an industry of excess is being tight. The manager of Led Zeppelin used to say that if you wanted to kill Jimmy Page, the best way would be to throw two pennies in front of a London bus, but if Robert Plant were there as well it would be touch and go who would go under the wheels first.

I can't help thinking as I check the front-page story of Mike's hooker-and-coke shame the next day that the ones who have got it right are the songwriters. They have all the respect, all the royalties, and none of the fame.

Lucy calls and tells me that they're going to say Mike's not well for a few days. 'The next few weeks are crucial,' she insists. 'We're head to head with Cowell for the Christmas number one.'

We take Mike off the publicity tour. Max Clifford puts the word out that he is seeking counselling. There is talk of putting him in rehab for a couple of days, but there's a debate over who will pay. If you go in for 'depression', apparently the record company foots the bill, but if it's for 'drug dependency' then the performer does. Since no one can decide who's going to shell out the idea is shelved and Mike goes to spend some 'time with his family' while we send the others out in separate cars. The transport bill for the next couple of weeks is going to be stupid, but I have a feeling it's the only way to keep the band happy. And Lucy, Danny and Richard at Spin It have their work cut out for them if we stand a chance against the PR might that is *The X Factor*. They've had twelve or so weeks of prime-time TV to launch their act, and they have the weight of a whole station behind them. It's going to take more than a few interviews with Fern Britton to see off that sort of competition.

It's the week before Christmas, and Lucy has the boys doing back-to-back radio and as much TV as is possible. Nothing that involves plugging the record is too trivial. We managed to get the band to turn on Bond Street's lights; Oxford Street was sadly beyond even Lucy's pulchritudinous charms. But Chris Moyles is behind the record, which is a first for us. I think since Mike disgraced himself in such a public way he has somehow managed to tickle the fancy of a few blokey broadcasters who admire a lad who knows how to enjoy himself. Jamie Theakston's breakfast-time show on Heart is championing us over Cowell. I am crossing all appendages.

Gavin calls me with the mid-weeks on Tuesday and says we're a few thousand behind the X Factor winner – but then they're booked to bang out their boring ballad on every show going, so we need to keep at it. He also tells me that the boys are in the running to do next year's Comic Relief record.

I call Paul, who is travelling with Band to an appearance at HMV on Oxford Street, to share the excellent news.

'It's the holy grail,' I explain on speakerphone. 'It's what everyone wants.'

'How can that be,' asks Ashley, 'when you don't earn anything?'

'It's a kudos thing,' Paul tries to enthuse the occupants of the Espace. 'Think of all the bands that have done it and what big stars they've all been.'

'Yeah, but the Spice Girls' "Headlines" sold jack shit,' says Josh.

'Or "Headlice", which is what everyone else called it,' giggles Nick.

'That was Children in Need, and anyway, the point is you get the backing of the BBC,' I say. 'They put you on everything, they make it work for you. You can't buy that kind of support.'

'I dunno,' says Billy. 'It sounds like hard work to me.'

'It's *always* hard work,' I say.

'That's easy for you to say, sitting in the office with your feet up earning twenty per cent,' says Josh. 'You're not the one doing their fourth gig of the day and it's only eleven thirty.'

'We could do it for the fans,' suggests Mike.

'That's a good idea,' I say. 'Do it for the fans, they deserve it.'

I love it when pop groups start talking about 'the fans'. They all do eventually. It's like a disease. 'Giving something back to the fans', which effectively means that the band have re-formed or are currently involved in flogging a piss-poor live album. It's this delightful idea that the fans need to be fleeced once more. We didn't earn enough money first time round, so 'for the fans', here we are again – and it will cost them £75 a concert ticket, £45 a T-shirt and £20 for the live CD. Those poor fans, they're so tragic, let's give them another record to make them feel better.

There's some mumbling in the car which I can't make head nor tail of. Then I hear Josh's voice.

'OK, let's do it for the fans.'

'Great,' I say. 'They'll be thrilled.'

Which is more than I can say for the band when they turn up at the office on the Sunday before Christmas to hear the chart rundown. Unlike a few months ago when the execs turned up late and everyone, bar Josh, arrived at around four, four fifteen, anxious to hear the whole chart rundown, now the execs are early and the band dribble in at about six thirty, ready for the only position that counts – the number one spot. Mike and Ashley are the first two through the door and they both look terrible. Mike is white, spotty and thin, and Ashley's face is hollow – he's lost a lot of weight. They walk straight over to the booze table and knock back a beer each like they're dying of thirst.

'How are you both?' I ask.

'Fine,' says Ashley, rubbing his nose on the back of his hand. 'We haven't been to bed yet.'

'Oh,' I say.

'Been to some club in the East End,' says Mike. 'The music blew my brains out.'

Nick and Billy turn up a few minutes later, both a little pissed.

'We've been at the Wolseley,' Billy announces, slapping me a little too hard on the back. 'It was Terry's birthday lunch.'

'What, my Terry?' I ask, feeling my heart picking up a pace.

'Is he yours?' asks Nick. 'He's the manager of that band, Road to Reality.'

'My old band,' I say.

'Oh yeah,' nods Nick. 'They said to send their regards.'

Before I have a chance to react, Josh walks in with Steve on his arm, and the tension mounts. He goes over to the drinks table and pours himself and Steve a glass of champagne. They toast each other. I'm not sure whether they can't feel the atmosphere in the room or if they're choosing not to acknowledge it. Either way they don't react.

There's ten minutes to go before they announce who the Christmas number one is, and Gavin decides to make a speech. He turns the radio down and begins to tell everyone how pleased he is with what we've achieved this year. 'You've exceeded our expectations. We can't believe how well you've done. Lucian is pleased and impressed. He's asked you to come to drinks on his terrace this week.'

'Not the hits terrace!' teases Paul.

'At seven p.m. on Tuesday,' he smiles. 'So, congratulations, Band of Five!' he adds, raising his glass. 'All we need now is a Best Breakthrough Act nomination in the Brits.'

Everyone raises their glasses at him, but their hearts don't seem to be in it. Josh is in one corner, the boys who've been up all night are in another, and the boys who are pissed from lunch are swaying slightly on the spot, their faces gently crumpled with the confusion of trying to keep up.

'OK, so here's the moment you've all been waiting for,' says Fearne Cotton on the radio. 'Have Band of Five done enough to make it to the number one slot?'

I look round the room. Everyone is staring at the radio, mouths slightly open.

'Oh no!' exclaims Fearne. 'So near and yet so far – at number two with "When You Find the One"—'

Gavin turns the radio down.

'Number two, number two . . . number two's not bad, guys,' he insists.

'I can't believe it,' says Ashley, shaking his head.

'No one remembers who came second,' says Billy.

'That's not true,' says Paul. 'Some of the best songs never made it to number one. Wham's "Last Christmas"?'

'That was only because of bloody Band Aid,' says Mike.

'Still, you should be proud,' says Gavin.

'What? Of being beaten by *X Factor*?' says Josh.

'Of being number two,' insists Gavin. 'It's good!' He smiles and gives Josh a matey punch on the arm. 'Come on. Where were you this time last year?'

'Number nothing!' enthuses Paul, knocking back a glass of champagne.

'Absolutely,' I say. 'Happy Christmas, boys!'

I've kind of been expecting the phone call I got this morning. I'm just amazed that it has arrived so early. Ten in the morning is not the sort of time to learn that you've been chucked and that the band you spent nearly a year putting together and managing are splitting up.

It was Josh who called. Well, he's always been the one calling the shots. He says he wants to go solo, that he's been working on some songs and has a different idea about where he's headed, and that the rest of the boys don't really see much point in carrying on. I pointed out that the Zing deal would collapse as a result and he said none of them cared. They'd had enough of being treated like a product; they had their own plans and ideas. Ashley wants to write his own songs. Mike and Billy want to team up together as they've always wanted to, from the age of six. Nick is considering a part in *Hollyoaks*.

'*Hollyoaks*?' I say, sounding more than surprised.

'Yeah,' says Josh. 'He's been talking about auditions for some time.'

The only thing to do is to wish them well through gritted teeth and call Craig for a drink. Thankfully he's fallen off the wagon and is once again drinking for Britain.

'Well, good luck to them,' he slurs, 'because they're going to need it. I remember Duncan from Blue complaining that he didn't know what to do when it was all over. No one was booking his car and telling him what to sing or where to stand. I mean, what time are you supposed to wake up when you've got nothing to do?'

'I suppose so,' I say, finishing my fourth drink and looking along the bar, hoping to catch the barman's eye.

'You all right for cash?' asks Craig.

'I've covered my costs, paid Holly's school fees, my bar bills and my ex-wives.'

'Good,' he nods wisely. 'Any spare?'

'I'm waiting for the royalties,' I say. We look at each other and start to laugh. 'But how do you get it right these days?' I ask.

'I don't know,' he shrugs. 'Tina Turner. She's a grandmother one minute and then she whacks on the wig and the mini skirt and she's "Private Dancer". And you never read anything in between. Sade. What happened to her? She made a fortune and no one knows anything about her. Dido's the same.'

'Talking of which,' I say, 'Leanne delivered her album last week and it's really rather good. It's a bit teenager from Harpenden, but you know, what else would you expect?'

'That's the future,' nods Craig, belching slightly.

'What is?'

'Female singer-songwriters.'

'Really?'

'Pop's dead. Forget boy bands. They're more bloody trouble than they're worth. Girls. The future's female, mate, female. It's girls all the way.' He taps the side of his nose and sniffs. 'And there's no need to thank me for that.' He smiles. 'Got any coke?'

Female. Well, that's good – I've already got one of those. Maybe I should put all my eggs in Leanne's basket.

My phone rings.

'Hi, I'm one of the researchers from *Dancing on Ice*. I know this is a long shot and everything, but I was just wondering if, um, Josh – Josh Penrose – would be interested in taking part in the new series?'

'D'you know,' I say, 'I think it would be right up his street.'

LIMERICK COUNTY LIBRARY